PRAISE FOR
GET UP & FIGHT

"Rusty is proof that your dreams can come true if you fight for them and never give up."

–MAUREEN BRAZIEL, retired Director of Athletics at Polytechnic Institute of NYU & former international judo champion

"Rusty was a warrior with a heart of gold and a fierce sense of humor. She led the battle for equality in judo by immersing herself in the sport and inviting everyone else to participate. Rusty had a very clear vision of what inclusion looked like and the tenacity to make it happen."

–LYDIA MURPHY-STEPHANS, Former President, Pac-12 Networks & US Olympic Speed Skating Team Member

"Everyone has a purpose in life but not everyone is blessed to discover what that is. At an early age, Rusty Kanokogi's purpose was extremely clear. Rusty boldly lived her purpose by not only changing the world of Judo, but the sexist inequalities of the world. Rusty Kanokogi is the true meaning of GIRL POWER!!!"

–KYM HAMPTON, WNBA legend, global ambassador for women's basketball, model, singer & motivational Speaker

"It is rather easy to look back over time and see the trail left by dedicated individuals that have made the sport of judo more equitable for women worldwide, especially, the incredible contributions Rusty Kanokogi has made which are chronicled in this excellent volume… It is clear that without her amazing determination and perseverance change would have been more difficult and taken much longer… She changed the culture."

– JIM BREGMAN, 1964 Olympic Games Bronze Medalist

"This book is an inspiration, just like Rusty was. If you didn't get the chance to meet her or travel the world with her like I did, this memoir is the next best thing to being there. Reading it, I felt like I was with her all over again. This book shows you how complex—and at the same time, funny as hell—Rusty was. As you read you will ask yourself, did she really say that? From experience, yes, she did. I bought copies for my whole family. "

– EVE ARONOFF-TRIVELLA, member of the 1988 Olympic Judo Team

"What makes this book special is that it's not only about overcoming immense hardship and achieving monumental success for women in judo, but it shows how Rusty had enormous courage despite huge chances of failure. Her obsession with judo and its core values takes the reader on an emotional roller coaster through the obstacles, challenges and highlights of her life. She was a woman on a mission, and nothing would derail her. Her legacy lives on in "Project Rusty" and in all the girls and women who today can step on the mat without fear of having their medal removed because of their gender."

– DR LISA ALLAN, Executive Committee Member, International Judo Federation

"When you merge a trailblazer with a bulldozer, you get the Mother of Women's Judo, Rena 'Rusty' Kanokogi…Rusty's unrelenting fighting spirit makes her the true Wonder Woman of judo. She has inspired the underdog to strap on the hero's cape and pursue their right to compete in Olympic judo. This riveting book reminds us that our rights were not given, but earned through the dedication and determination of humanity's inspired champions like Rena "Rusty" Kanokogi…a true American icon, thanks to Rusty's legendary indomitable spirit, my daughter will be able to compete in judo without having to alter her appearance…This book is a must read for all who would appreciate reading about one of America's great pioneers, as well as the next generation of Judo champions."

–JON ADLER, former Director, Department of Justice's Bureau of Justice Assistance & President, Federal Law Enforcement Officers Association Foundation

GET UP & FIGHT

THE MEMOIR OF RENA "RUSTY" KANOKOGI, THE MOTHER OF WOMEN'S JUDO

RENA "RUSTY" KANOKOGI &
JEAN KANOKOGI, PHD

Copyright © 2025 by Rena "Rusty" Kanokogi & Jean Kanokogi, PhD
Get Up & Fight
The Memoir of Rena "Rusty" Kanokogi, The Mother of Women's Judo

SECOND EDITION

All rights reserved. No part of this publication may be reproduced, distributed, or transmitted in any form or by any means, including photocopying, recording, or other electronic or mechanical methods, without the prior written permission of the publisher, except in the case of brief quotations embodied in critical reviews and certain other noncommercial uses permitted by copyright law. For permission requests, contact: Jean@rustykanokogi.com.

This book is a work of memoir. Everything in this account is true and reflects the author's recollections of experiences over time, as remembered and retold by Rusty Kanokogi to her daughter, Jean, at the time it was written (primarily between 2004 and 2006). Additional historical details were added after Rusty's passing in 2009. Some names, identifying details and characteristics have been changed to protect the privacy of certain individuals, some events have been compressed, and some dialogue has been recreated.

All photos, unless otherwise credited, courtesy of the Kanokogi family. Credited photos reprinted with permission from original photographers.

ISBN:
978-1-7360890-8-8 Paperback
978-1-7360890-7-1 Hardcover
978-1-7360890-6-4 eBook

Library of Congress Control Number: xxxx

Project Rusty, LLC
Whitehouse Station, New Jersey

rustykanokogi.com

IN DEDICATION TO RENA "RUSTY" KANOKOGI

Mom, you have always been the wind beneath my wings—
especially when you barked all that hot air at me, inspiring
me to get up and fight. You always knew hot air rises.

– Jean Kanokogi, PhD

PHOTO CREDIT: PETER PERAZIO.

"In life, either you're the hammer or the nail. Be the hammer."

— Rena "Rusty" Kanokogi

CONTENTS

Foreword xi
Preface xv
Prologue xxv

PART 1: CONEY ISLAND KID

Chapter 1 1	Chapter 10 22
Chapter 2 3	Chapter 11 26
Chapter 3 6	Chapter 12 29
Chapter 4 8	Chapter 13 32
Chapter 5 9	Chapter 14 34
Chapter 6 11	Chapter 15 37
Chapter 7 13	Chapter 16 39
Chapter 8 15	Chapter 17 42
Chapter 9 19	Chapter 18 46

PART 2: THE FIGHT—ON AND OFF THE MAT

Chapter 19 50	Chapter 27 70
Chapter 20 52	Chapter 28 73
Chapter 21 54	Chapter 29 76
Chapter 22 57	Chapter 30 79
Chapter 23 60	Chapter 31 82
Chapter 24 62	Chapter 32 85
Chapter 25 64	Chapter 33 89
Chapter 26 66	Chapter 34 92

Chapter 35 94	Chapter 53 156
Chapter 36 97	Chapter 54 159
Chapter 37 101	Chapter 55 166
Chapter 38 105	Chapter 56 169
Chapter 39 109	Chapter 57 171
Chapter 40 112	Chapter 58 176
Chapter 41 114	Chapter 59 183
Chapter 42 117	Chapter 60 186
Chapter 43 121	Chapter 61 189
Chapter 44 124	Chapter 62 196
Chapter 45 128	Chapter 63 198
Chapter 46 134	Chapter 64 202
Chapter 47 137	Chapter 65 209
Chapter 48 140	Chapter 66 213
Chapter 49 142	Chapter 67 215
Chapter 50 146	Chapter 68 220
Chapter 51 149	Chapter 69 222
Chapter 52 152	

PART 3: THE LAST BATTLE

Chapter 70 226	Chapter 83 279
Chapter 71 230	Chapter 84 283
Chapter 72 233	Chapter 85 285
Chapter 73 235	Chapter 86 289
Chapter 74 239	Chapter 87 294
Chapter 75 241	Chapter 88 297
Chapter 76 244	Chapter 89 300
Chapter 77 246	Chapter 90 302
Chapter 78 251	Chapter 91 304
Chapter 79 258	Chapter 92 307
Chapter 80 261	Chapter 93 310
Chapter 81 271	Chapter 94 313
Chapter 82 274	Chapter 95 315

Chapter 96 317
Chapter 97 320
Chapter 98 323
Chapter 99 325
Chapter 100 329
Chapter 101 333

Chapter 102 336
Chapter 103 340
Chapter 104 343
Chapter 105 346
Chapter 106 351

Epilogue. 353
Acknowledgments 366
Notes 369
About Rusty 374
About Jean 376

FOREWORD

RUSTY WASN'T ONE OF US, SHE WAS US. I MET Rusty so many years ago when she attended a Women's Sports Foundation (WSF) function. She came right up to me, introduced herself and told me we have work to do and went right into telling me about the inequality and blatant discrimination in sports and especially in her sport of judo. I knew from that moment on, knowing Rusty would be a lifetime experience. She was one of those rare individuals who really epitomized the true heart and soul of what the WSF is about. Rusty led by example.

Aside from her own family, she inspired so many generations of men and women. When women do something exceptional or accomplish something great, they always talk about how we help other women, but if a man does something, they say he helped both genders—but Rusty influenced as many men as she did women. She influenced all of us.

Rusty kept her dreams of women's judo as an included sport in the Olympics in focus and maintained the highest level of honesty and integrity despite the uphill battles she was always fighting to break the gender barrier.

When I asked her what she was most proud of, she told me it was when she helped a child who thought he or she couldn't do something and then she showed them that they could! She was one of those people who believed that if you expect a lot, they will give a lot. Rusty had that special quality that made you feel like you could fly... that you could do anything, because she was right there with you. She was always in the solution. That's what sports teaches you, to size things up very quickly, and then you get in the solution. Rusty was relentless in this mindset to the very end.

We were lifelong friends, worked on many issues, including Title IX, and socialized often. Her immediate family is comprised of a samurai descendant, a military leader and a US federal agent with a PhD. The co-author of her memoir is one of these people. Reading her story, you will ride the adventure of Rusty. It will educate you, empower you and inspire you.

– Billie Jean King, August 15, 2020, New York, New York

FOREWORD XIII

Rusty & Billie Jean King at the Women's Sports Foundation Dinner in 1994.

Rusty & BJK at the WSF Athlete's summit.

Rusty & BJK embracing at one of many gatherings.

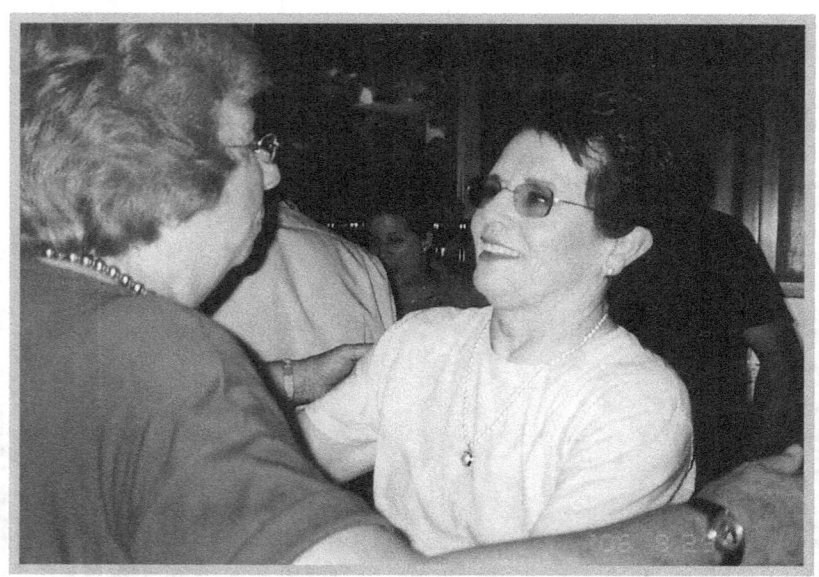

Rusty and Billie Jean King embrace at the US Open in August 2006.

Rusty, Billie Jean and Ryohei smile for a photo at the WSF Dinner in 1994.

PREFACE

AS RUSTY'S HEALTH WAS DETERIORATING FROM her battle with multiple myeloma; I would spend significant time with her where we would just talk. At this point, there were no barriers—no putting on airs and graces—it was just straight conversation about everything, from judo and family to her worldview. We talked about the memories we both had from my childhood, those years I was growing up and Rusty was growing up and out—in her mission, her accolades, and her accomplishments for women in judo. We discussed the difficult times: training in our small dojo in "the hood" in Brooklyn, our domestic and world travel (both personal and in the name of judo), and the inevitable antics that came along with every trip. We reminisced about each of the amazing people that we'd crossed paths with, or shared pivotal times within our lives, both on and off the mat.

"Mom, I know that I will be doing everything I can to continue what you have spent your life working on," I remember saying to her during one such conversation. "What do you want me to continue doing specifically, that is the most important to you?"

She looked at me with a deadpan stare indicative of her matter-of-fact personality and generous sense of humor, and answered with one word," Everything!"

We both just stared at each other in that moment; it felt like an eternity. When I soberly reminded her that I also had a day job fighting crime, we both broke down laughing, of course. But the seriousness of her words was not lost on me; I was reminded, yet again, by just a simple, certain look she gave that her expectations were set so far beyond what anyone could ever imagine—not just for me, but for everyone.

During this same conversation, she asked that I make her three promises and keep them. First, I was always to look out for and take care of my father. She expounded that he is a true saint, innocent to the core, and one of the best human beings she has ever had the privilege to spend time with. It was so evident, just in that very simple statement just how deep her love for him went; they were true soulmates. She infused her humor into the moment by reminding me how much he enjoys good food and exercise and to make sure he gets plenty of each for the rest of his life. It truly is my pleasure to keep this promise; not only is my father an amazing man full of humor, stories, and philosophies, but he is also my mentor, life guide, and sensei.

The second promise was to obtain my PhD in psychology, which I did in 2018. I had only just begun the journey a month before she passed away, so as with so many of my greatest accomplishments, Mom had been there to see me off.

The third and last promise was to make sure her story, *this* memoir, got out and into the world, because, in Rusty's eyes, there was so much work still left to do. By this I mean, not only the battles she'd had to get women's judo to where it was as an Olympic sport, not only the battles she endured shattering glass ceilings along the way, but the message she wanted every reader to know: no matter what odds are stacked against you, no matter how many people tell you that you can't do something, if your heart, desire, guts and commitment are in it, you can prevail. When Rusty uttered this last statement, I saw life breathing back into her body as she reminisced over all of her many wars and triumphs, and her greatest reward from a lifetime on the front lines: women's judo's inclusion in the 1988 Summer Olympics. It was this debut on the international stage toward which she had worked indefatigably for nearly forty years.

When I asked her what details in her memoir did she want me to take out, she sat quietly for a moment, thinking, and then looked at me straight and told me not to change a thing. "History should not be erased," she said. The true story must be told so that the same mistakes are not made again in the future. Living a good, clean life with transparency and accountability, she said, is what allows you to triumph.

I'll always remember this conversation because I knew I had my work cut out for me; the easy parts were the PhD and looking out for my father. The real challenge would be to get her memoir out and preserve her voice and her story as she tells it. She knew I could rise to each challenge and that's why she treated me no differently than anyone else and set the bar high.

Other things we reminisced about during this conversation was her love and respect for

Dr. Shigeyoshi Matsumae, because of his support and true genuine friendship toward her, our family and for the sport of judo. He came through for her in the eleventh hour in 1980 at the First Women's World Judo Championships in New York in 1980, and that was something Rusty—and my father and I—would never forget.

In other conversations we would joke and laugh about different times we'd had together through the years. One of our favorite pastimes was going to Nathan's for hot dogs; no matter where I was standing, whether it be in front of her, to her side, or behind her, every time I bit into a hot dog, Rusty got a squirt of hot dog juice in the eye, bypassing her glasses without fail.

One of our on the mat antics that we cherished most was the time that we were doing *uchikomi*, form practice, in our dojo and for a split-second Rusty turned her head, momentarily lapsing her attention. I hadn't noticed this, as I expected to attack to a strong resistance, as usual. I attacked with proper form and, unencumbered by a counter-attack, threw my mother through the wall of the dojo. We both laid there laughing hysterically as plaster and debris fell on our heads, the other students staring, not knowing whether to laugh, help us up, stay silent or ignore the commotion altogether. A moment later my father came over with a serious look on his face. "Now I must fix the wall," he said, before storming off, all but ensuring we would not stop laughing for several more weeks at least. As we spoke these stories induced Rusty's full belly laugh, despite the intense pain she was in. During these conversations, she sat there with broken bones, her body riddled with cancer, yet her mind and spirit were leaded with strength and determination to ensure her legacy continued after she was gone. It would live on in her stead, she told me, in each and every one of her students, people she'd helped and the lives she'd changed for the better. These people would carry on what she taught them and build from there, she explained.

"They each have their own character," she said, "I just helped strengthen it and, at times, give it a more robust purpose."

Rusty had a way of making anyone she met feel important and wanted to join her cause to fight for the equality of all, —not only in sports, but across the board. Aside from being a trailblazing pioneer and a woman who shattered glass ceilings, she was also my mother. It was an interesting dichotomy, mom versus coach, matriarch versus sensei. On one hand, as a nurturing Jewish mother, Rusty would often put a giant plate of food in front of me and encourage me to eat, then in the very next moment, realize what she had done and take the food away, telling me that I was nuts to even think about eating so much with judo practice in an hour.

Occasionally, during these times, we would stop in the moment, stare at each other, and just laugh because it was such a unique relationship.

As my mother, Rusty introduced me to all things Disney. She loved Mickey Mouse and anything that fell under the Disney umbrella. I think that was her escape, because our entire home growing up was a cross between the international judo headquarters, space for her anti-discrimination projects, and the Walt Disney World.

Rusty loved roller coasters and she convinced me to ride Space Mountain with her as a kid. Getting on the ride, I was tucked in some tubular shuttle and stacked nearly on top of Rusty. By the end of the ride, I was pale and green, but she was jubilant and enthused and insisted we ride it again. Bribery in the form of an ice cream cone afterward worked its magic, and I accompanied her.

Another roller coaster Rusty loved was the Cyclone in Coney Island, Brooklyn, where she'd grown up. After pre-bribing me with hot dogs from Nathan's and a few carnival games, she got me to ride it with her. Again, I sported the pale and green face from the ride, but she was euphoric again from the thrill. This ride is one of the few remaining wooden roller coasters, and even back then it was quite jittery. I wouldn't trade these times for the world—and the normal color did eventually return to my face.

Rusty toughened me up, but she always knew I was also very much like my father, an even combination of both of their personalities. For example, I easily, yet calmly, will tell someone off when needed. Rusty protected her family and students, on and off the mat. I was about ten when at the grocery store with my parents, I witnessed the full force of her capacity for confrontation. As Rusty was loading items from her cart onto the cashier's conveyor belt, she saw out of the corner of her eye that some woman had rammed my brother, who was a toddler at the time, with her cart, hard enough to knock him down. My father was at the far end of the conveyor belt bagging the items. Rusty, who had been holding an egg carton in her hand when she saw what happened, did not miss a step. Within seconds the egg carton that had been ready to be placed on the belt, landed smack dab in this woman's chest. Pandemonium ensued. If Rusty had not taken action, the woman would have actually run my brother over with her cart. While the eggs were flying and the woman was screaming, my father calmly continued bagging the groceries. This was a true display of mama bear being mama bear.

Early in my life Rusty introduced me to an understanding of what inequality meant, explaining it to me when I was a mere thirteen years old, in a very simplistic form. She told me then that you should be equal, but you will often get less than simply because you are a woman. Those cut and dry terms have continued to resonate with me throughout my life. I was part of everything she did to fight for equality—some even say I am the daughter of women's judo because I was there, in the trenches with her, from her tenth year in the judo world, up until her fiftieth.

I learned from my mother some of the little known, and ever important, nuances in life that have stayed with me to this day: it's not only what you know, it's what to do with what you know, including how to share it with others so they too can benefit from your knowledge, and how you can use that knowledge and power you possess to help build yourself and others up along the way. Success, she taught me, is based a lot on how others you touch prevail and overcome adversities with your guidance. Rusty was known to have an iron fist with a velvet lining, and she instilled judo philosophy and her own brand of Brooklyn philosophy into our home and our lives.

Throughout a lifetime with my mother, we developed Rusty-isms that perfectly encapsulated her unique attitude; phrases like, "what would Rusty do?"

In many instances, the answer to that question would be that Rusty would yell "cowabunga!" and charge headfirst into something, regardless of the terror of any of us witnessing it. Applying that Rusty standard to any obstacle before you, whether it be a haunted house or an obstruction in your mind, is unbelievably empowering, and is something I hope readers who never had the pleasure of meeting my mother, or training with her, will learn as they read her story. Rusty's relentless indomitable spirit and drive were contagious and capacitating. With Rusty, you were made to feel like you could do anything, no matter what it was. Though I went on to build a career in federal law enforcement, and Rusty was not in this field, she remained my mentor, and helped me forge my own way in the world through the work, I was passionate about, independent of her. She guided me every step of the way. When I debated if I should go to law school or obtain a PhD in psychology, without hesitation, Rusty insisted I pursue the PhD. She had foresight and told me I would have to work hard to do well in that field, and work hard I did.

In 2018, nearly nine years after she left us, I achieved the degree and fulfilled this second promise I'd made her almost a decade earlier. Today, as a result of this hard work, I am able to volunteer my time as the Director of Mental Health and Peer Support Services for the Federal Law Enforcement Officers Association, a position that allows me to have a positive effect on many lives.

Over the years, I shopped around Rusty's manuscript with various authors, publishers, and people in this industry, but it never quite felt like it was the right time to release the book. Or maybe it was never the right circumstances.

I don't know why, but now more than ever, I feel Rusty's story must be told; her story, of resilience and perseverance, tenacity, and hunger—of constant blows and never-ending fight—has to be shared because when times are tough and the outlook bleak, people need something they can wrap their entire self around. They need a story of empowerment and triumph, where the little guy can and does prevail; a story where the least heard individual in the room can raise their voice, be heard and make a difference to change his or her world—or the entire world, for that matter, depending on whatever goals they set. This story is needed in today's narrative because it is loaded with purpose.

As life guided Rusty, she had many purposes; whether it was to protect friends from bullies, encourage her mother and father to speak, support her brother, or to bring the Japanese culture to America and further judo to support equality, Rusty was always resolute in her determination to win at all costs, and never, ever give up or stand down from a fight worth having. She didn't just expect to be handed equal opportunity; it had to be earned. Rusty believed if you could do the job, then you should get the job, regardless of gender—as long as you were qualified; if you were good enough, it didn't matter who or what you were, you should have the same opportunity to prove yourself as anyone else.

For me, this memoir fulfills one of the numerous promises I made to my mother in one of our last conversations all those years ago. But it also means so much more. It is a vehicle to share her story and a tool that can be used as an illustration to inspire and empower anyone—woman or man, Brooklynite or Manhattanite, child or grandparent, businessman or bohemian, athlete or fan, whether watching with bated breath as history is made from the stands at an Olympic stadium, or on screens in homes around the world. Rusty made history with a life well-lived, in dedicated pursuit of equality, and inspired countless others to do the same. She was not the first woman with *chutzpah* to shake up the status quo and forge ahead in the name of a fairer and more equitable tomorrow, and she certainly will not be the last. Rusty never was alone in this work, and if she were here today, she'd be the first to tell you that, while she accomplished a great deal in her fifty-something years as a judoka, none of it would have been possible without the help and voluntary enlistment in the cause of all the supporters, friends and allies she met along the way.

Life has a funny way of balancing the scales of injustice, eventually, but as is often the case, timing is everything. In the epilogue, I will outline what happened in the years after Rusty and I finished compiling what would later become this memoir; after her passing left a giant, Rusty-sized space—in our family, in the international judo community, and in the hearts and minds of thousands; after accolades from a lifelong career brought her the kind of recognition so often denied to the living. In these pages, I will share some of my own personal stories, along with some of my most cherished life lessons from Rusty, my mother and forever my sensei.

In the years to come, Project Rusty will continue the work my mother spent her life dedicated to. My ambitions for the future of the organization are just as lofty as the high expectations she always had for me, herself, and everyone else she ever met: I hope to have a documentary about Rusty made, and perhaps even a biopic for the movies. But perhaps most importantly, we will continue to positively touch lives and show people they can overcome whatever obstacles stand in their way so they too can achieve their goals. Goals don't have to be gigantic. They can be as simple as getting dressed and going outside; and no matter how small, you never can tell what little goal might just end up changing the world.

Despite the ambitious road Rusty found herself on, her world wasn't always so high-stakes. Her drive to win started with the little victories. Finishing school. Getting that first job on the up and up. Finding love. Walking out onto the mat. Winning a match—both as a woman, and in spite of it. Standing tall when the gatekeepers denied her that first victory, and every time they tried to deny her the next one, and the next one after that.

Each goal is individual. Rusty respected that. As long as a person tried to give it all they had, they had Rusty's respect. Conversely, Rusty did not fare well with those that easily gave up or elected weakness over digging deep inside and grabbed on to their own inner strength. She didn't have time for those who couldn't stomach a challenge in the face of adversity.

"Kick their ass!" she would often exclaim to anyone and everyone who dared attempt to block her path, or the paths of her compatriots.

Rusty encouraged every child, every adult, every human, and perhaps even some animals, to dig deep inside to find the footing they needed to take the next step. If she were here today, she'd give you this directive: Find *your* voice. Find *your* strength. Make *your* life happen.

I will continue her legacy by embracing what she stood for and telling her story. I will continue her support of the Women's Sports Foundation, as they continue fighting for equality—in sports, and outside of it. I will continue to push people to follow her legacy, encouraging them to always do better.

Rusty was my coach, confidant, mother and, clearly, my Yoda. She lives on in these pages—in the memories we hold of her, the stories we tell, and the tenacity and fervor we continue to bring to our lives, on and off the mat, every day.

The next time you find yourself facing a seemingly impossible obstacle, I challenge you to do what I have done for so much of my life: ask yourself, "What would Rusty do?"

As you might expect, she'd say, "Kick their ass!" But in order to do that, you must first place both feet firmly on the ground and then—you guessed it—get up, and fight. I continue to keep my promises to Rusty.

– Jean Kanokogi, PhD, a.k.a.
"the Daughter of Women's Judo"
July 2025, New Jersey, USA

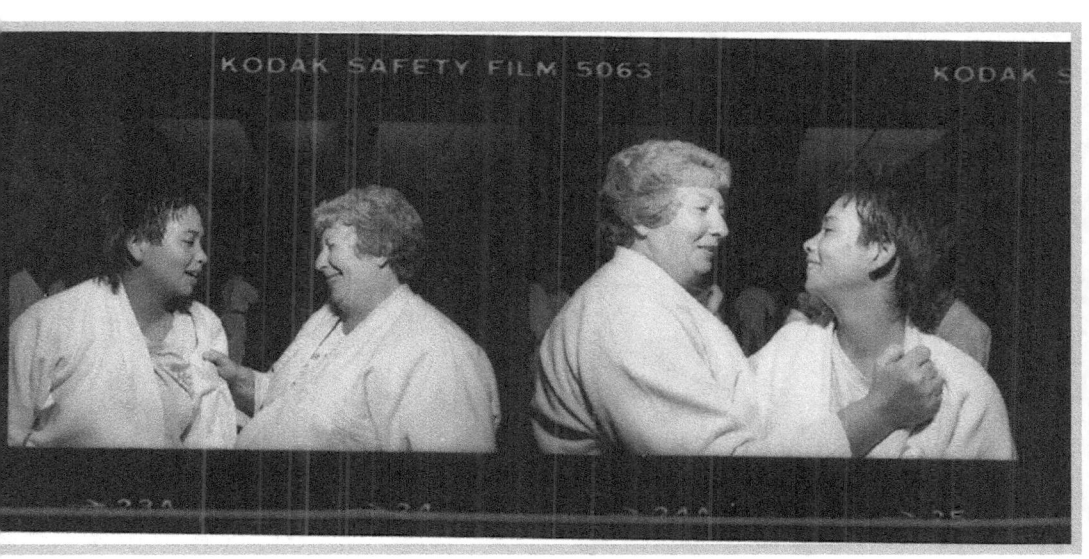

PHOTO CREDIT: PETER PERAZIO.

PROLOGUE

MY STORY BEGAN WITH HARD SCRABBLE LESsons learned in the streets from pitchmen and hustlers. It's about a ghetto kid who was on the way down, and was saved by the sport of judo.

I grew up in Brooklyn, where in the late '40s and early '50s my Coney Island neighborhood was as tough as any in the borough. Teenagers joined gangs for protection and for belonging. Women in my neighborhood didn't train so much as they brawled. I had that undefined charisma associated with leadership, so I formed and ran my own girl gang. What else could I do? I was a five-foot-nine, big, strong young woman, and had a chip on my shoulder. I knew, even then, that this life would only guide me downhill.

Then, the girl gang leader became a lady. At least that's what I thought I was when I got married and had a child. I took off my Apache gang's chartreuse jacket and pedal pushers to wear more traditional, married woman clothing. I had escaped those mean streets of Coney Island—where I regularly indulged in the gang fights, the dodging of zip guns and cops—to become a wife and mother.

This new role did not bode well; I still had uncontained energy, the kind that had gotten me into trouble for all those years. Being a newlywed gave me a sense of belonging, though the shine wore off rather quickly. I went from one tumultuous household into another, almost seamlessly.

At first, I was wowed by this gentleman, but pepper the wow with a lot of alcohol and irresponsibility, and you have the makings of the disastrous and inevitable demise of a relationship.

I had wanted the marriage to work—I had to; divorce wasn't legal in New York at that time, so I didn't have much choice. I also wanted to give my son a chance at having parents, together. I didn't want to be my parents, always fighting and screaming.

In seeking ways to help my new husband I joined Al-Anon—an organization that provides support for family and friends of alcoholics based on the same fundamental twelve-step philosophy offered up by Alcoholics Anonymous.

I really did all I could to try to get Charlie and I right. In the path of this effort, I found judo through a mutually commiserating friend.

Al and I met by chance at an Al-Anon meeting one day. I'd gone to the meeting after a particularly rough run-in with Charlie. I had wanted to vent and ask for help. I didn't realize that Al too was a recovered alcoholic, who just happened to be attending the meeting that night.

He was compassionate, generous and wanted to help. Sure enough, we became friends. Having coffee with him after the meetings was very comforting. He looked like he worked out, which he did, lifting weights.

When he told me he was taking up judo classes at the Brooklyn Central YMCA, I responded, "What the hell is judo?"

He told me it was a Japanese art that helped you defend yourself, as well as compete.

All I ever knew about the Japanese was Pearl Harbor—and in amusement parks of Coney Island we would try to hit Tojo, Hitler, or Mussolini in the face with a baseball at several of the pitching concessions. At that time, I believed all the Japanese were very sneaky, looked like Tojo, and had buckteeth, squinty eyes, and little bodies. *Why would I want to learn this judo thing?*

Then Al said he wanted to show me a throw. I went along with it, always happy to show up a strong man with my learned-in-the-streets fighting skills. He proceeded to pick me up on his hip like I was no heavier than a piece of paper—I was ready to go flying.

That was it! I forgave Japan for all their misdeeds. This single experience completely changed my preconceived notions about the country and its people, and catapulted me to delve into a whole new world where I wanted to know everything there was to know about judo.

It was the beginning of an almost five-decade career and whole new way of life.

I was wowed by judo. This time the wow came with the good stuff—working out, legally fighting and some kind of magic where you could fall and effortlessly get right back up over and over again.

Now *this* was the perfect marriage, I thought to myself. *This is where I can get my body back in shape, release all my energy, and allow myself to fight back—on the up and up.*

I had no other outlet from my bad marriage. This judo class at the Brooklyn YMCA, is what would actually start to calm me down.

I'm hooked…

I was enamored and obsessed. It was an uphill battle to even be allowed into that class, but I welcomed battles. It was—and remains to this day—who I am.

The class was, of course, exclusively for men, but I talked my way in, as I've been known to do, both before I found judo and most certainly ever since. I worked out with these forty men daily. I was a sponge, learning not just the new sport and new strengthening exercises, but the overwhelming inequality between men and women, on and off the mat.

About a year into my training, our team from the Y made it from Brooklyn all the way to the finals that were held in Utica, New York. This was big-time for us. It was a team competition where each team was required to produce seven fighters in various weight categories. I traveled to Utica with them, thrilled to cheer the guys on.

After we arrived at the Y, the guys all checked in, weighed in and changed into their judo uniforms, more formerly referred to as judogis. Before any competition, part of the warm-up was stretching, doing calisthenics to get your body warmed up and a little form practice, called uchikomi. Uchikomi is the practice of doing judo throws without full execution, with little resistance from your practice partner.

After the warm-up some of the guys began doing some light randori. Randori is practice where partners attack and counter each other using a myriad of judo techniques with a higher level of resistance, but not in the manner they would if they were trying to win a point like in competition.

I donned my judogi top so the guys could use me as a partner during the uchikomi phase. Boy it felt good to step on the mat, even though I was not scheduled to compete. During uchikomi, I thought how great it would be if women could be part of this competition.

I mean, nothing on the application or anywhere said women couldn't compete.

During the randori part of the warm-up I heard a yelp, looked across the mat and saw one of the guys on our team laying on his back holding his knee. His randori partner and our coach were kneeling down beside him trying to offer him comfort and assess his injury.

Oh crap, I thought, *now we will be down a point even before the competition starts.* I felt for the guys. As I was onlooking, our coach and instructor, Al Evoy, barked at me. He told me to get the rest of my gi on—I was taking the injured guys' place. I guessed, for him to select me, meant I had proved my worth through hard training. At least that's what I told myself.

In reality, they really needed seven bodies to compete. I was close in weight to the injured guy, so that made me lucky number seven.

My internal emotions soared full of adrenaline. I went from thinking that it would be great for women to compete here, to being told to get ready to compete.

Lucky I brought my judogi with me!

I brought my gi with me everywhere back then—I was always ready and eager to learn and fight.

There were no ladies locker rooms anywhere to be found, so I entered the ladies restroom to change. I squeezed into a stall, disrobed, shimmied out of my clothes and started suiting up in my gi, all the while paying attention to not let my belt hit the floor, as I did not want to disrespect the belt. There is a lot of honor and etiquette when it comes to the belt and the gi. While I was donning my undershirt, I thought, *Since I am going to fight a man, I should somehow downplay the fact that I am a woman.*

The judogi covered my body so there were no concerns there, but what about my breasts? I was not that well-endowed, so I used an ACE bandage to flatten them. I had short hair, big shoulders, and a deep voice; no one thought the wiser that I was a woman, or if they did, they figured I would lose anyway.

I saw my opponent. He was about my height, well built, looked strong and a bit heavier than me. He also looked determined and very serious, especially when he was staring me down.

As I was on-deck to compete, Mr. Evoy whispered in my ear, "Don't win, just take a draw. The guys will do the rest." He did not want to call attention to me, since I was a woman.

"Just keep it low-key," he said.

Here I am on deck. I've trained like the men, with the men—and have even beaten some of the men.

The men had the pressure on them to win. I was alleviated of that pressure— because I was a woman.

I felt a surge of frustration, but I was so excited to have a chance to compete. The thoughts swirling around my head were of all my training: conditioning, techniques—and Mr. Evoy's voice telling me to *not* go for the win. I was about to explode inside.

The referee pointed and indicated for me to step forward onto the mat. I courteously bowed, first onto the mat and then to my referee.

As I was walking to my starting point on the mat, my opponent was giving me a very stare-down look to psych me out before we even gripped. I looked at my teammates—I don't know if it was for reassurance, camaraderie or to let them know, *I've got this.*

The referee gave the command to begin. This hulking man, my opponent, took a vice grip on my gi and my Brooklyn attitude kicked in. I took my grip on his gi. I attacked my adversary using foot sweep techniques. He attacked with a shoulder throw. I countered his throw. We stumbled down to the mat and began ground fighting. The referee had us stop, fix our gis and begin fighting from the standing position again.

My teammates cheered so loud, "Go Rusty!" "Go Rusty!"

My opponent gripped my gi, missed a foot sweep and kicked me hard in the front of my shin. I felt nothing but my determination. *Go Rusty* echoed in my head. *Is that my own voice or my teammates?*

Who knows?!

But I followed suit with the command.

I gripped my opponent's gi as he was gripping mine. At this point, it was similar to a fistfight—we battled to get the advantageous grip. I got my grip and—*bam!* I had no reservations. It was do or die. I smashed him with a throw that awarded me the full point and the win.

Holy shit, I won! Uh oh…

I won.

Our team took first place. I felt the jubilation in every bone in my body. I was part of this winning team. We trained. We won. And now we would get our award—the first-place trophy.

The guys and Mr. Evoy were thrilled. They were hungry to win this championship, as was I.

Once we all got cleaned up, we were told the protocol for the awards ceremony. All the teams were to line up to receive the appropriate trophy and individual medals. The smiles, the pride, the sense of cohesiveness was almost tangible around my team. I was so excited—for my win, and for the recognition I was about to receive for it.

We lined up as a team. I was beaming with pride. This was my Olympics at the time.

I'm actually getting a medal for fighting instead of a citation!

The tournament director methodically placed the first-place medals around each of our necks and then presented our coach with the first-place team trophy. After we disbanded, I was walking past the competition mats, smelling the sweat in the air and feeling unbreakable.

Just then, the tournament director approached me and asked to have a word in private. I thought he was going to compliment me on my technique but inside, I felt a level of nervousness, like I had done something wrong. Having done so many "something wrongs" in my life, this was my go-to feeling when someone wanted to speak with me.

"Are you a girl?" he asked in a low tone, out of earshot of all others. "I know you are a girl."

Then he added—in a snide, guttural, condescending tone—that it was illegal for me to compete because women were not allowed. My first thought was that this jerk didn't even give me recognition for being a woman and referred to me simply as *a girl*.

In my head, I mimicked his same snide tone, and I asked him if he was a cow because his question was so outlandish. In reality, I kept my mouth shut; judo had taught me to choose my battles.

My heart was racing. I felt tears welling up in my eyes, not from sadness but from a boiled anger—but I kept listening. I held in those tears. No one could think I was soft—*not even now*.

He told me if I accepted the first-place medal, my team would be disqualified and would have to forfeit their win *and* the trophy we had rightfully earned.

I was shaking inside. My heart dropped to the floor. My breathing was labored. But I showed nothing to him——he and his rule makers did not deserve any emotion from me.

This was all done quietly, no other tournament officials knew about it, but I told Coach Evoy. He exclaimed that the team would all give their medals back. But I insisted that would make the situation even worse, because these medals were all won fair and square.

I went back to the tournament director and agreed, in as casual a way as I could muster. I would not accept the medal—*my medal*—from my very *first* win.

I handed him my cherished medal. At that moment, I felt like I did everything wrong just by being a female. I was heartbroken.

As I uttered the words of declination, I realized that this moment would be one of those pivotal occasions, not just in my life, but in the lives of women in judo and other sports around the world.

No woman shall ever suffer such an indignity again, I told myself. *I will make sure of it*.

I was going to change judo history.

Later that day, I found out that someone had ratted me out for being a woman. I knew that this was not going to be the end of the many sore losers and conniving rats that would throw themselves in my way, as attempted obstructions in my path. In the end, they would be merely speed bumps.

After that competition, every application for judo competitions had a male- only clause in it. I was going to change all that—*this was my mission!*

– Rusty Kanokogi, "the Mother of Women's Judo"
May 4, 2005, Brooklyn, New York

Rusty, the only woman in the room, at the Judo Twins dojo in the early 1960s.

PART 1
CONEY ISLAND KID

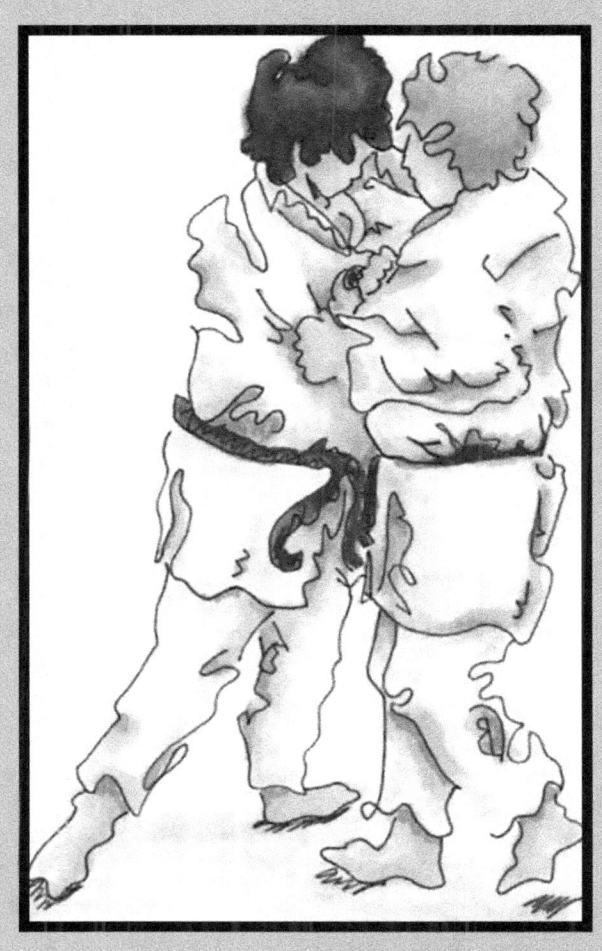

1

THE CLEAN SMELLING BREEZE OF THE ATLANTIC
Ocean, along with the aroma of exotic, garlicky Nathan's Famous hot dogs, were natural fragrances to the eight-year-old girl roaming the streets of Coney Island.

I was thinking about what the day would be like. Should I go to Steeplechase, one of the most exciting amusement parks in the world, or should I go over to the concession stand in Luna Park, another spectacular amusement park where Mom worked?

Mom sold Mr. Jaffe's hot dogs—not Nathan's by any stretch, but the price was right, and those Jaffe's came with fries and a root beer. I learned early on that connections were everything. Mr. Jaffe was Jewish, a little guy that looked Chinese. I could never figure that one out. He was polite to me, but not overly friendly. However, after he gave me a gift of five bucks for my birthday—an unexpectedly enormous sum for just being my mom's daughter—I cut him some slack.

Mom would remind him every year about my birthday. Sometimes she reminded him two or three times a year. He always forgot the date and often commented, "How time flies!" I kept collecting my five bucks a few times a year and was so proud of Mom for inventing, then pulling off this scam. I was grateful for the ruse—the extra coin meant Mom wouldn't have to push me off the trolley car right when the door opened and act like it was all the motorman's fault, an elaborate two-person performance just to snag a free ride.

With Mom hustling the hot dogs and me celebrating my birthday two and three times a year, we were both thriving. The year was 1943. There was a war going on, both in the world and in the mind of my eight-year-old self.

It was an exciting time; all sorts of wonderful things were coming up. Soon the US Army would be raising hundreds of pup tents on Coney Island beaches, from Seagate to Brighton, with most in my favorite bay, West Eighth Street, a block from where I lived. The entire neighborhood was talking about how patriotic they would be by giving cakes, pies and donuts to the GIs. Everyone would bake and buy.

There was a frenzy around the entire event. I was selected as the delivery girl to bring the donuts to the soldiers in the pup tents, as I was the strongest, not shy, and wanted to do anything to help stop Hitler. Keeping the military well fed on greasy donuts was hard work. The box was big, loaded with heavy sugared donuts with a perfect hole in the middle, and dripping lard.

Even though it was only a block away, it was a very long block. First, I had to pass the firehouse, then the police station, and then the barbershop where Joe, the bookie, held court. The box got heavier with each step. Then. I had a great idea.

I'll eat them until the load is lighter!

The load decreased rapidly.

My freckled face was getting a tint of green to it, but I finally made it to the tents. The grateful soldiers looked at me and said, "Look at that poor kid. She's green and exhausted and must have walked ten miles to get us these wonderful donuts." I was a hero. I kept my mouth shut because if I opened it, little pieces of donut would have flown all over the place.

Upon recovery a few days later, the excitement of the Mardi Gras was on us.

Wow! More work, money, a celebration, and best of all, Mommy and Daddy will have to talk to each other.

Business was business.

2

THE SEASON AND THE HOOPLA WERE WINDING down, and fall and Public School 100 was approaching. I had my experiences of the past summer to think about. Mom bought me some clothes for school.

Going back to school meant waving goodbye to the transients and the warm breezes that left Coney Island at this same time. The transients would be back next year if they weren't in jail. I wouldn't miss them. I only had a warm place in my heart for my real Coney Island buddies: Milo, the mule-faced boy, and my beloved Pinheads.

Milo had made me a star the summer before when he picked me out of the audience to sing *Let Me Call You Sweetheart* by Bing Crosby to the large crowd in front of the freak show where he worked. The pitchman was telling the mesmerized group how a mule gave birth to Milo, while I dazzled the crowd with my vocal chops. What a thrill for me, getting all this attention and being singled out by this extraordinary star.

Many years later, after Coney Island folded and died, I figured out that my friend Milo was just a very bucktoothed, mentally disabled man who was making a buck or two. It didn't matter to me. The warm place in my heart remained.

Oh, would I ever miss the Pinheads! They worked in Luna Park at another freak show. Not only were they the sweetest, kindest, little people—they also used to babysit me!

They, and everyone else, knew me as "Rosie's girl." When Mom was extra busy and they were between shows, I'd stay with them. We never taught each other anything, just giggled and giggled. That was good enough for me. Come to think of it, I may have learned a thing or two from them. They looked and sounded different from most, but that didn't matter to me. Their character mattered more than anything. I kept that throughout life.

School was okay. I ate the same lunch for years, not by choice. It consisted of tomato soup, plain whole-wheat bread smeared with some kind of margarine, milk and an apple. Still, I liked it and looked forward to returning to my public-school gourmet banquet. I had eaten hot dogs, fries and root beer every single day, all summer long.

Mom went back to Bonnamos, the candy factory in the neighborhood. Daddy continued his daily trek to the racetrack. Things got back to normal, as they didn't speak to each other again except to fight. But when they did, I continued to learn new words from it: "whoremaster," "hophead," and even a Yiddish word or two, like "*kurva*."

I didn't know what these words meant, but I certainly knew they weren't praising each other.

Rusty at two years old, Coney Island, New York.

3

THE APARTMENT AT 6 KISTER COURT WAS NOT unlike most of the houses on the block. However, what was contained within the walls may have had something to do with making this particular two-family house unique.

We shared the first floor with the landlady, Sophie Dennis, and her husband, we referred to as Joe, "the Nazi." Joe was a small guy with slicked back hair. He always appeared cordial to us and the rest of the tenants and neighbors, but there was a monster lurking under his sly guy disguise.

We shared the same bathroom, which was all the way down the hall, close to their kitchen entrance. It was a nightmare for me to go to the bathroom when I was home alone.

I hated going to the bathroom was because the Nazi would abruptly open the door and yell at me to scare me and see how high he could make me jump off the seat.

When his wife wasn't around and I was home alone, which was nearly all the time in those days, Joe waited for me to use the bathroom. As I exited the bathroom, he scooped me up and gave me lap rides. I was around five years old – at this age, I didn't know the difference between male genitals and a hot dog. His lap rides entailed having his privates out and bouncing me up and down for the *ride*.

I thought he was being a nice man. I had no idea there was anything wrong going on until my mother chastised *me*, telling *me* how wrong *I* was. After that, I did all I could to avoid Joe, especially when going to the bathroom.

As years passed, he continued to lurk, and once he became aggressive and grabbed me by the arm and dragged me into his apartment. I shook free and ran back to my apartment and locked the door behind me. I was scared. I did not like this feeling. This fueled my decision to be physically, emotionally and mentally tough as nails—was central to my survival.

4

MOM ALWAYS BEFRIENDED HER FELLOW hustlers when they were down and out with a few bucks between their paydays, no matter how she may have got the money.

When she did, I was always the little princess of Luna Park to them. I could go on any ride I wanted to, as often as I wanted to during the hot and exciting summer. I was also privy to the Luna Park pool.

Even though we had an enormous beach area, I always liked going to the pool. It was closer to the concession stand where Mom sold Mr. Jaffe's hot dogs, fries and root beer. It made me feel like a big shot, because everyone else had to pay to go to the pool. I was not like the kids that had to go to the beach.

Roaming around the park was fun since all I had to do was select the ride I liked and stay on it for hours. One of my favorite rides was Shoot-the-Chutes[1]. It was a water roller coaster, like a water flume ride, except this one was so high up that even the sailors screamed on the way down. But not this kid. *Not me.* Different emotions had been developing in me. It seemed I was becoming immune to any fear of rides, the constant fights between Mom and Dad, missing my brother, and worrying about Gypsies kidnapping me—a common rumor from old European folklore that parents often used to scare children into behaving[2]—at any given time.

Other than that, life was a joy! I had the best rides, food and the most special friends in the world. Who needed love anyway?

5

STEEPLECHASE PARK, LOCATED RIGHT ON SURF Avenue about two blocks from the hot dog heaven, Nathan's, became the most impressive fun center in the world, short of Tivoli Gardens in Denmark.

From Surf Avenue it went back to the beach area, several city blocks wide with what was supposed to be a happy, inviting, huge sign with a face smiling from ear to ear. That's how I viewed it until my perspective changed—I traded a child's youthful naivete for a streetwise kid's tough exterior; everything and everyone looked suspicious. Then I saw a bizarre face offering me a challenge.

With Luna Park in ashes from a recent fire, this was the best game in town. I had already toughened up and had been working on my reputation of being as fearless as my brother. One didn't see many little kids on these rides. Those that were there were mainly teenagers and adults. I was tall, at eleven or so, and savvy; I hung out with older kids. All my friends were Christians since, by this time, all the Jewish girls were not allowed to play with me anymore.

The rides in Steeplechase Park had people thrashing and flying all over the place. Major sexual abuse occurred at the park. Molestation was thought of as entertainment by several mean dwarfs who had the same sleazy sneers on their mugs as the leering clown welcoming all at the entrance to the park. I had begun to see him for what he was; a bizarre symbol of the monstrous acts featured just inside the park grounds.

The ride that ended in sexual harassment by the dwarfs in front of a packed audience of spectators began innocently enough with the horse ride that was named after the park. The Steeplechase was a kind of race where one mounted a small wooden horse on a rail. There were about six horses across. One really didn't have any control over the horses as it was run by electricity, but someone always came in first. There wasn't any prize—not one you wanted, anyway.

When the ride finished, the only way out was through the stage, known as "The Blow-Hole Theater[5]." It had a moving floor, so most unsuspecting people fell down. As one ran past the blowholes scattered over the thirty-foot stage, the nasty little dwarfs would use an electric type of prod or a wooden pincher to get a young girl or woman's hands away from holding down her skirt or dress. In those days women wore only skirts or dresses.

As the women were shocked or pinched, they would let go of their clothes and their skirts would fly up over their heads. The crowd would roar and whistle as the poor woman became disoriented and kept running in circles with her body and underwear exposed. The loudest howls would occur if she had on no panties. Although this was rare, sometimes an excited female patron might pee in her pants because of the thrill of one of the rides and then ditch her bloomers.

From the onset, I hated these miserable little creeps, so I sought revenge.

I was well prepared. I wore jeans and had my usual fragrance on, which my mother made me wear most of the time—kerosene, embedded in my two pigtails, to keep the lice away. The bag of camphor tied around my neck with a piece of cord was to prevent me from getting polio. The garlic placed in my pocket was, I can only guess, for keeping the werewolves away.

I had nothing to ward off mean dwarfs, only my friends. We turned the tables on them big time and gave the audience the best show they had ever seen. One of my crew laid down flat. I pushed "shorty" over his body...one down. Then I grabbed the electric gizmo and chased the other pest.

I got his pinchers as my two friends and I stung them, pinched them and harassed them unmercifully. They spat and cursed us. When the cops came the show was over, but the best theatre ever had already taken place. And best of all, we had avenged womankind.

6

THE NEIGHBORHOOD BOYS WEREN'T A REAL thrill, as I had grown up with them and played all the street games with them. Actually, they always picked me first, before any of the other girls. I was the most daring and had proved myself many times.

One of the proofs was jumping off a beam about thirty feet up in one of the old, burned-out Luna Park buildings. On the beam hung a rope with a big knot that I put between my legs as I swung out and then jumped. It was great fun! One day I swung out of the window and hit the charred wall on the swing back. It was so weak that I knocked the wall down. It was tough explaining to my mother why I was now charred black, as well as black and blue.

Another fun thing we did when the rides would close down for the winter and there had been a good snow day, was to sneak into a roller coaster ride, climb up the scaffolding, and then go down the hills with our sleds. After those kinds of cavalier feats, the boys knew they wanted me for Johnny-on-a-pony, ringalevio or any other evening events.

Oh, yes, they wanted the other girls too, but for different games.

The Jewish holidays were coming up again. I knew we were going on our trek to grandma's house. I was so excited as I wanted to tell Aunt Lee and her boyfriend Igor about my artful experience during the past summer. Both Aunt Lee and Igor were artists.

Well, did I get a surprise when we arrived at Grandma's. Igor wasn't with Lee. Some goofy looking guy by the name of Jackson was with her. My mother could read my mind and told me to shut up before I asked for Igor.

What the hell kind of name was Jackson Pollock? I thought to myself. *Igor was so handsome and debonair, and this schlep isn't even good looking at all. Oh, well.*

Now I knew why Mom always referred to Lee as "the mashugana artist." Jackson was pleasant enough; however, he kept pissing me off by calling me

Renee instead of Rena. Rusty was for outside of the family.

This was to be my last year at PS 100. How exciting it was with graduation, plans for high school, and having to make my graduation dress. Making my dress turned into a disaster. Neither my mother nor I could sew very well, so as spring neared, we knew I would need a dress to graduate. My mom hired the neighborhood-sewing woman who also happened to be the neighborhood drunk. As it turned out, during graduation rehearsal, Joel Baker, the boy sitting behind me in the auditorium, pulled my pigtail. It wasn't the first time. He sat behind me in class also. In fact, sometimes he would dip my braid into his inkwell. Well, pulling my pigtail that day was the last straw. I had to get him. I stood up, turned to him, and punched him square in the mouth. Everything stopped.

The principal flew in to see what was going on and viewed Joel without a front tooth and Rena Glickman looking real happy. It didn't last for long. I was told I would graduate, but not receive my diploma, only an empty envelope. With the drunk making my dress out of old window curtains, and an empty envelope, I had the feeling graduation wasn't going to be much fun.

Oh, well, what the hell!

I'd work on my next life in high school.

7

I SELECTED BROOKLYN HIGH SCHOOL FOR Homemaking[6] to attend in September and was accepted. They offered a nursing course and I thought that being a nurse was what I wanted to be. I didn't know that you had to take six months of exploratory courses before you even got to first aid, let alone nursing.

The high school was near Prospect Park; not downtown, but pretty close. It was a good forty-five—minute subway ride. Just like most kids, I felt so mature because I was going to high school, but the disappointments were coming in rapidly. I tried to make friends in this all-girl school where white girls were in the minority, but my need to prove myself as the toughest girl in the halls didn't win me any popularity contests. To me, this didn't matter, but interracial friendships were not favored by either race during this time. I saw the person and what was inside, not the color of their skin. You can be any color and be a good person or bad person—what's inside is all that counts.

In high school, my day was filled with the usual subjects. Most of the time was spent on the special subject of waitressing. Some of us had to take that before the beauty parlor course. I could sell confetti, sew names on hats, engrave on jewelry, hustle ice water, be a barker, but now I would have to balance a tray and be sweet and polite.

It was really asking too much of me.

There was another division of the school that was for cooking. That was where we waitresses picked up the teachers' lunches to serve them in the dining room. Day one was a disaster. Not wanting to make so many trips back and forth, I overloaded the tray. *What the heck?!* I was strong and could carry it.

It wasn't bad until I got to the table to serve. Not only were the teachers at my assigned table, but the principal was also there. One little slip of my tray and they were all wearing their lunches. I was rushed out of the teachers' lunchroom and out of waitressing.

They now installed me in the beauty parlor school. As I mentioned before, white girls were in the minority at my school, so when I arrived in the beauty department, the other girls took one look at my long pigtail and all wanted to work on me. It was fun. They fussed around me, trying to decide what style to do. They experimented and all I had to do was sit there and be a head.

I did have to choose one girl who would do my hair for her grade. After I selected my favorite, it was a tough life. The disappointed girls would take the subway to where I lived to try and beat me up. I said *okay*, but I would only fight two at a time.

They left quickly after getting hit harder than they expected while hurling some derogatory remarks my way. All that helped me decide it was time to say goodbye to homemaking and hello to Lincoln High, which was right in the neighborhood.

It also made me realize that I had to organize my own gang.

Terry, Annamay, Carol, and Lila all agreed to join. I proudly named it the Coney Island Apaches and donned by Indian head signet ring I'd bought with my wages at the souvenir shop the summer before.

Our mission was to defend our turf, help the needy (for a small price—*kind of like Robin Hood*), be tough and daring, and arrange fights with other girl gangs. We didn't want any part of the boys' gangs because they already were packing zip guns and switchblades. But I had a few surprises of my own. My brother had given me his Marine bayonet. Our gang's reputation skyrocketed when the other gangs heard I kept it strapped to my leg.

8

HOORAY FOR LINCOLN! STINKIN' LINCOLN! FLY
thy banners high!

This was the first introduction to my new high school by one of my friends that was already there. I transferred in the middle of the first term in January, and by February I had already created chaos. My Capone image was surfacing. All the other areas of my life seemed out of my control, but when I acquired that Capone persona, I was the one with the power. One day, I was using the stapler too long for one of the boys in English class. When he came over to me to take the stapler, I got out of my chair and told him to get the hell away from me or I would staple his balls together. After I slapped his head by surprise, he meekly walked away. I was in control, even if just for the moment. This felt surprisingly calming to me.

I began my strengthening plan and I had started lifting weights at home. I didn't have access to weights so I used the heavy bus stop signs.

They were somewhat awkward, as the metal triangle on top (with the word "bus" on it) and the heavy round bottom base made my weight lifting lopsided. I switched around enough so I wouldn't give my natural left-handed side too much more power than my right.

The extra strength, coupled with my aggressiveness and a large chip on my shoulder, was going to rule my destiny for a while. I had finally realized that my life was getting more and more dysfunctional. Rather than feel sorry for myself, I decided to become the hammer and not the nail.

There was a sweet shop right across the street from Lincoln with a great jukebox, super egg creams and an easy-going staff. The management pretty much let us hang out, providing we didn't break up the place. It became my headquarters. We danced to Teresa Brewer's

"Music, Music, Music"—"*Put Another Nickel In. In the Nickelodeon*"— and other hits.

We girls danced with each other as the boys only wanted to do the slow dances like The Fish, which was similar to a dry hump. I loved The Jitterbug and always wanted to lead. *The hell with the boys!* The jump was better than the hump.

All scheduled fistfights took place in front of the sweet shop. They were arranged in school earlier in the day or a few days before. My opponents were mostly boys or sometimes a girl who thought she could handle me. We agreed on no weapons and I didn't consider the big Indian signet ring on my finger anything but my club identification.

I was the champ, as I didn't wait for the mouth fight to go first. As soon as I saw my opponent, I swung. The Indian head made a nice mark on their faces. There was no stopping me. I liked the feeling of being a winner, even though it was winning in a bizarre way. I liked the respect and felt part of a family that cared about me, the other street punks.

I must have gotten a glimmer of sanity somewhere along the way in high school as I tried to get into some school sports.

There weren't any organized girl sports teams so once again I had to try and get on the boys' teams. The first was football, then baseball, and then on to basketball. None of the coaches would even let me try out. They told me to go home and play with my dolls.

Well, someone would have to pay for that slur!

Step by step I egged on some of the boys that were on these teams into a fight in front of the good old sweet shop. I proceeded to beat them up and put the mark of what could have been Geronimo on their heads.

My gang and I wanted to snazzy-up our dress style, so we got black and chartreuse satin jackets with a big Indian head on the front right side and APACHES written across the back. We wore black pegged pants, chartreuse socks, and black penny loafers. We looked sharp!

We didn't wear these clothes during actual gang fights. Under my advice, the clothes to go to war consisted of denim bell bottoms, a navy mock crew sweater that was real army/navy store equipment, sneakers and Vaseline rubbed all over our faces and arms.

My rationale was that we would be so slippery no one could get a grip on us. The sweaters were strong and wouldn't rip even when pulled hard and they wouldn't be able to tear our tops off and make us try to cover ourselves up rather than fight. And of course, the sneakers were for running from the cops. We also had our hair tied back tight as this could have been another weak point.

We had our new war uniforms. Now it was time to suit up and fight.

We went looking to start shit. It didn't matter who they were, where they came from or why they needed a beat down. If there was a fight to be had we had it, and I was throwing the first punch. The only rule was allegiance—the other gang was the enemy.

My tribe against yours.

One day we had a fight scheduled in the schoolyard of old PS 100 with the Scarlets, a newly formed black girl gang. This was going to be exciting since we had never had a beef with black girls before.

I couldn't find my gang anywhere. It was close to the time of the battle, so I figured they were already in the schoolyard waiting for me. I proceeded to the yard. When I got there, I saw about seven black girls in red satin jackets, and not one Indian head in sight.

Shit!

I knew I was in trouble.

Where the hell are the cops when you need them? I couldn't back out now.

What's more important than your reputation?

As I was walking over to where the Scarlets were, they were walking toward me. I was hoping that they thought I was nuts and would leave or forget about it. But my thought was *no way*—and certainly not with their boyfriends looking on. *Here we go.*

I tried to transform my fear into mad-dog mode. It kind of worked. They circled me and I wasn't going to throw the first blow—*not this time.*

Bang! Boom! Bash!

It happened. Fists were flying. I was swinging wildly as there were just too many directions to try and hit. Then the next big weapon came out—of all things, a damn umbrella! One of the girls was trying to swing it around like a crazed samurai. That's when the boys began to step in.

I got a fast look at the zip gun one of the guys was packing. My bayonet was inaccessible.

Suddenly there was beautiful music in my ears—sirens, and they were getting closer. One of my adversaries was yelling to her gang, "Chickee, the cops!"

They took off. I was too tired to run.

When questioned by the cops, I told them I was cutting through the schoolyard and some people attacked me. I hadn't seen what they looked like and couldn't remember anything special about them. That's just the way things were then.

I was fuming at my own gang. One by one they would be punished for putting me through this alone. I got my revenge, but not after I realized that you had to depend on yourself in this life—and that I needed to get with a more committed, tougher group of kids. I was getting more hardcore every day.

Again, it was time to move on.

9

SCHOOL WAS INCIDENTAL AT THIS POINT IN MY life. Most days, there was no supervision or structure to fit into at home, so I was basically on my own. I felt that way for a while. My father was long gone, my brother in the military somewhere out there in the world, and my ma preoccupied with her own problems. At age 15 I felt like I had done it all already. I had outgrown the street games, went past tough and had become hard, in body and personality. I didn't have to look too far to find a community of fellow ruffians. I was hooking up with characters like myself—cavalier and frustrated.

It was 1951, and I was on the cusp of my "sweet" sixteenth birthday. I was looking forward to sixteen, when I could work legally and get out of school, at least during the day. I was getting wilder every day. I picked fights with strangers just because I didn't like the way they looked at me. It didn't matter to me, male or female—I brawled with anyone I could.

My inside connections at Coney Island had dwindled by now, so I would pick up guys near the ride or at the boardwalk to have fun with. I didn't give them too much in return, just a little feel. It was their dime, after all.

I liked this guy—"Jingle Bells"—who surfaced near my neighborhood one day. We used to climb up the outside of a place called the Velodrome, where wrestling matches were held. We had a good time together and I liked him more every day. I thought it was mutual. After all, we were making out.

One day I saw Jingle Bells paying a lot of attention to one of the better—a.k.a., more traditional, "ladylike"—neighborhood girls, literally across the tracks. Jingle Bells was a tall, blond, good-looking guy, in a sort of Kirk Douglas sort of way. I knew I had a prize. I also knew that Barbara, the attractive debutante that he was warming up to, had to go.

I waited for the right time and proceeded to beat her up. I thought this would fix it—she would go away and leave me and my prize alone. She didn't. The next time I saw Jingle Bells; he walked over to me like a man with a mission and popped me with a punch square in my jaw. My plan had completely backfired.

I didn't drop—I was enjoying the multitude of colors. I felt dizzy, but remained standing. I believe he was giving me a message. My heart wasn't broken. In fact, it added a new dimension to my reputation. Jingle Bells was five years older than I and was supposed to be stronger and he didn't even knock me out with his best punch. Who would want a guy like that anyway? She could have him.

It wasn't difficult to get my hands on a switchblade knife. Mine was real sleek, sharp, and had about a five-inch blade. It sure was easier to tote around than the rusty old bayonet I'd been playing girl gang leader with for years. The zip guns had a bad rep—they blew up when you shot them and would cause more wounds than your opponent. Before the summer was over, I had a lot of fights still depending on my fists to do the job, but I felt good knowing I had my blade as a backup if my opponents tried to surprise me with their knives.

My next boyfriend, Johnny, was also my partner in crime. Back then, being my partner in crime was now a prerequisite for me, from a trust point of view. He was a local kid, another bored, misguided street urchin that was probably looking for some excitement. *Well, here I am.* Plus we were pretty much in the same boat. I didn't realize until sometime later that day that his boat was a sinking ship, and mine was about to get a huge hole in it.

One day, we were walking down the street about a mile from where we lived and a woman passed us. She was close enough so he could grab her handbag. As fast as I could blink, he grabbed her handbag and yelled at me to run. We took off like bats out of hell. I heard screaming from afar, and then something from not so far too.

"Halt or I'll shoot!"

Twice. Just like in the movies.

Then I felt something burning and wet on the right side of my neck. We kept on running. We reached the train station and jumped over the turnstile. Luckily the train was coming into the station just in time. We hopped on and both of us collapsed in our seats.

Johnny saw the blood. I was busy calling him every *dumb bastard, freaking idiot, and stupid son-of-a-bitch!* name in the book I could think of for thrusting this surprise robbery on us. After we calmed down, I asked the *moron* how much was in the bag.

It was about two dollars and change.

When we got off the train, we went to a drugstore to spend most of the loot on peroxide and bandages to take care of my superficial flesh wound. I had been shot by the cop.

Enough of this crap!

I decided to go straight from then on.

10

TERRY SULLIVAN AND I HAD STAYED FRIENDS even though we didn't hang out a lot anymore. She had settled down by now. She was almost 18 and I was 16.

She told me she was going to try and get a job with the telephone company, near Canal Street in the city. I told her I would go with her, as I wanted to be legit now.

We did good at the initial interview. This was followed by some tests; one was the length of your arm—because switchboard operators had to plug and unplug cables all day long, having good reach was a prerequisite for the job. Next was a test of your voice. I didn't realize at the time that they very rarely hired Jews because of their "singsong voices." No one in my house had that affliction. With all the yelling and swearing we did, we sounded like any other good American, Italian or Irish family in Brooklyn.

We both got hired but were separated. She went on to learn to be a telephone operator right away, but because of my age and the fact that I was in continuation school, I could only be an in-house messenger. I felt a sense of accomplishment, plus I looked forward to becoming a real telephone operator in a few months.

I liked receiving a paycheck and got two major perks. We couldn't afford a telephone prior to me working for AT&T, but with my employee discount we could now have a telephone for half price. I also signed up to take a couple of bucks out of my paycheck every two weeks to buy the company stock at half price. Things were going well until one fatal day. I was off of work on a nice Saturday afternoon and took a stroll on the boardwalk with a friend. We were just shooting the breeze when two girls passed us, looked me up and down and laughed. I did an about face and followed them until I caught up.

"What the fuck is your problem?" I asked Miss Giggles.

She was obviously scared and looked straight down. Then her friend started to cry.

I asked the jerk how much money she had, and she shakily said a quarter. I demanded it. She readily gave it to me. I told them to get the hell off the boardwalk and never come back. As they turned, I kicked Miss Giggles square in the ass.

What a bummer!

I was on my day off, had almost gone from the switchblade to the switchboard and then this shit happened.

Oh, well. The hell with it!

I returned home to Kister Court to change my clothes and to get my Apache jacket. It still looked good. I was going to meet another friend out of the neighborhood and knew it would be a good idea to have some colors on.

I was walking to the West Eighth Street train station and had to pass the police station en route. There were the two girls from the boardwalk and a bunch of cops. Our eyes met and she pointed at me and yelled, "There she is!" All hell broke loose.

I should have kicked her harder, the rat!

I took off running to the train, going up the two platforms with all those cops chasing me. I ran up and down, but they split up in two groups and blocked all exits.

They got me! I was taken back to the 60th Precinct.

The interrogation began. The cops acted like they'd just caught Dillinger. I wasn't going to make it easy for them. They didn't know who they were messing with...

I was pretty familiar with the 60th Precinct by this point in my life.

As a young kid I had turned over my dog, Blackie, to the precinct when they were collecting dogs for the war effort—heartbreaking for me but I knew it was important to America. Until this day, I still don't know why they needed Blackie or what they did with him, but I was just bursting with pride. I was a member of PAL (Police Athletic League) and actually got to carry the flag when the cops took us on a boat trip to Bear Mountain State Park in the Hudson Highlands.

As we marched off the boat, I carried the flag with dignity and pride all the way up the mountain. Then I realized how quiet it was.

When I looked over my shoulder, I saw that I was an army of one—I had gone the wrong way.

Another memory of the 60th Precinct was when I was a kid playing hide-and-seek in the neighborhood. I decided to get the best hiding place. I pushed open the back door of the precinct and slipped in. I heard my name being called.

"Rena! Rena! Come out, come out, wherever you are!"

Hah! They would never find me! And they didn't.

I had proved my wonderful hiding ability but it was time to get out. *Oh, my God!* Then to my chagrin, I heard the click. It was the loudest click ever because I knew what it meant. It was the door automatically locking behind me. Worse, it had locked me in the morgue. Terrified and stuck with all the dead bodies, I pulled as hard as I could—but that door just wouldn't give. Next, I screamed my guts out. A few cops heard me and came to the rescue. They opened the door and scolded me soundly for hiding in the morgue.

The detectives went to my house to ask the landlady what kind of person I was. The *bitch* told them that I was a *robber* and threw in every kind of vile lie she could conjure up. The dicks were happy. They were going to turn this into a big case.

It wasn't long before I was in the paddy wagon on my way to general lockup in downtown Brooklyn. I remember the ride; no springs, bouncing all over the place. It was strange I didn't feel scared or angry. My ability to repress my feelings was getting stronger—I felt I had a role to play.

My fingerprints and picture were taken. I had the bend-over physical. Then I was put neatly into a cell. The next day was the court appearance in front of the judge. My mother came to court with her cousin, Willy, the lawyer.

The charges against me were assault and robbery, all for a quarter and a kick in the ass. The prosecutor said they had to make an example out of me and that I would probably be the first girl in the electric chair in New York. Well, the judge agreed. He called me a "wayward minor" and I was sent off to the Women's House of Detention in the Village.

Cousin Willy was useless. I waved goodbye to my family and told my mother to bring me cigarettes when she visited – I knew they were great barter tools in the can.

I was off on another adventure. When I arrived, I had another bend over exam, had some powdery stuff put on my head, was made to scrub down and given some blue rag that resembled a dress.
They gave me the rules and routine and marched me off to my cell. It was small and came with a toilet and a bed. At least I could sleep alone—at home I had shared a bed with my mother since I was born. I met a few women that were interesting. They loved telling me their stories. They were very impressed with my credentials of assault and robbery. Of course, I had to make it much bigger than it was because it was embarrassing to tell them the truth—that a kick and the two bits had landed me here.

11

THE CELL HAD A PAPER-THIN MATTRESS THAT WAS

fairly clean. The toilet came without a seat, and there was a small shelf for a minimal amount of possessions.

There was a communal shower area, and us inmates would pick up our little pieces of soap en route. Everything was scheduled. You were in your cell unless it was open for all. I didn't have a watch because we weren't allowed to have one, so I figured out the time of day by my stomach being hungry.

We all had the same simple blue dress; I don't remember what I had on my feet.

An announcement was made, the cell doors were opened, and we were off to the commissary. The food was simple and filling. When you're hungry, anything tastes good.

I learned an interesting fact on the first day of this jailhouse brunch. The inmates at Rikers Island, a men's correctional facility in New York, made the bread we were eating.

What a spirit lifter! Maybe a murderer or bank robber was pulling on this dough and turning it into a lovely breakfast for me.

All kinds of women were grouped together, and I met some real, funny, tough and dangerous women there. Recreation time was when we had the chance to chitchat.

One woman I met was a prostitute, did drugs on the outside, and told some weird stories. One that I still remember was about the time she gave her pet monkey a shot of some drug, then watched as he jumped out of the sixth-floor window and became very dead. She laughed her head off telling the story, and all I could think was, *I don't belong here!*

I believe I was the youngest inmate at the Women's House of Detention, but happily, not the smallest.

I had mixed emotions, even though no one bothered me. I made sure I kept a low profile, had a strong presence, and minded my own business. The nights gave me some serious thinking time and after about a week or two the novelty of being in jail was wearing thin. I wanted to *get out*.

I was getting really pissed at the process. It was too slow and now I felt that I was wasting time.

When my mother came to visit me, we had to speak through this thick glass window with small holes in the bottom, which was reinforced with metal. To make matters worse, my mother was hard of hearing, so I had to shout all the secrets I was telling her.

One important thing was to notify my boss at AT&T that the reason I wasn't at work was because I was in the hospital with double pneumonia–*or is it triple?*

It worked. In a few days my mother received lovely get-well cards and a bunch of flowers to bring to the hospital when she visited me. They asked if the boss and my coworkers could visit. My mother said absolutely not—I was in a special unit. When they asked the name of the hospital, Mom's deafness worsened.

After a couple weeks, we finally got a court date. It was set for two more weeks out, so in the meantime, it was back to the grind and more thinking.

I didn't like being incarcerated. I was missing my job and the street. I knew my reputation was going to be super escalated when I got out, because I would be an ex-con—and I'd seen enough gangster movies to know that added up to respect in the street.

Even though it brought me more recognition in the neighborhood, I knew in my heart that this kind of life was for the birds. My next dilemma was figuring out how to get out of it without losing face.

The court date arrived. I spiffed up for my big appearance. My mom met me there. Finally, I went in front of the judge and was asked if I was sorry and if I had *learned my lesson?*

"Yes," I said, though it was only half true.

The judge gave me one year of probation and that was it. My time in lockup was, gladly, over.

12

ON THE OUTSIDE, I HAD TO REPORT TO OFFICER
O'Neil every week or so. Her nickname was Ma O'Neil, and she was a nice, old Irish woman who was easy to talk to.

Ma told me to get myself together, as I had lots of good qualities, and suggested I become a policewoman like her.

I thought about that suggestion for one fat second and decided it wasn't for me. Policewomen in those days took care of lost children and became quasi probation officers—certainly not enough action for me. I had now made my way out from punksville, and found I could keep the street respect and have a good reason not to screw around too much anymore.

Hey, man, I can't. I'm on probation and don't want to do any more time.
Easy out!

I went back to the phone company and thanked everyone for their good wishes, cards, and flowers. My boss was happy to see me back as I was a good worker. She informed me that I would be moving out of the messenger department and would learn to be a real long-distance operator. It was just what I needed.

I felt the life shift happening. After all the grief I gave my mother, she would now be so proud of me. I would be making more money and could help support her a little better now. As an in-house messenger for AT&T, I got to meet many of the bosses. They were fond of me since my delivery was on time and no load was too big for me to carry. Of course, I got a lot of, "Atta girl!" from them when I returned to work.

During the Christmas holidays, I volunteered to be the Santa Claus for the entire building, all 16 floors worth. I was to go around—in full costume—and give candy canes and little gifts to everyone. It was fun, especially when the president of AT&T invited me into his office to take some photos.

At last, I was going to be taught how to be a real telephone operator. I was a good student, and it wasn't too long before I was assigned to the switchboard. I was in the division called Inward; when someone somewhere in the country wanted to reach someone in New York, they had to go through us.

The switchboards were all lined up together, about thirty in a row. There were several rows. We each had thirty-two cords, sixteen in the front and sixteen right behind them.

What a thrill it was for me to put the tip of the cord into the light up hole, say "New York," take the other cord and plug it into a hole and dial the number the out-of-town operator requested!

The job was exhilarating to me. It was murder answering the southern belles as they drawled their numbers—I was always in a hurry. Nevertheless, I loved the challenge of trying to be helpful when the operator or her customer had only a partial name or number. I dug until I got it.

The supervisors were pleased with me as all my cords were in use. When I saw the incoming light, I pounced on it. I enjoyed the praise. As I got more confident and the supervisors didn't have to look at me so hard, I began to entertain myself.

I figured out how to monitor incoming calls after they were connected and became a major nosey body. Some of the most interesting conversations were between Spencer Tracy and Katherine Hepburn. They really adored each other. Jerry Lewis received lots of calls when he stayed in New York and Billy Daniels, the singer and showman, invited me to the Copacabana.

I made phone friends with lots of the rich and famous, but the best was Marlon Brando. He lived with a few guys: Sam Gilman, a nice guy, and Wally Cox, an asshole.

Marlon and I kidded around a lot via the switchboard. He didn't know my age and made a date with me. I never showed.

I made some excuses and we spoke many times after that. In fact, I gave him my home number. He called at three a.m. to ask me what I had on. Of course, I told him my peekaboo black negligee. He wished he were there with me, he said. Little did he know that I had on my Mickey Mouse pj's. Then my mother blew the whole mood by yelling, "Who the hell is the dumb bastard calling this time of night?"

I absolutely delighted in connecting Mom, Aunt Lee, or Uncle Jackson, Aunt Ester and Aunt Ruth on the same call. It would go like this.

"Hello?"

"Hello, yes."

"Who do you want?" "Who's this?"

"Why are you calling?" "I didn't call you."

After a few minutes they all recognized each other and figured out I was the culprit. It was comical.

13

THE JOB WAS GOOD. I WAS RECEIVING A DECENT differential for working split shifts and weekends. As a rookie operator, I basically had to take the shifts assigned. I liked the split shift as it gave me time to go to the movies when it was less crowded and cheaper.

Often, I would go to hear a great band at Neary's, a joint on Eighth Avenue and a regular hang out for the military men. Bernadette, a friend from the phone company, and I would go to Neary's as often as we could. We both liked the rhythm and blues that the all-black band would play from their soul.

When they played my favorite, 'Night Train," there was no holding me back from my bumps and grinds. Bernadette and I rocked the floor. She was as adventurous as I was. No shame, no shyness. We always got a round of applause and drinks. We had to play it cool with the booze though because we had to go back to old AT&T in a few hours.

Dancing the afternoon away was fun. It was a good work out after plugging away at the board all morning. It also gave us a chance to meet the servicemen and select whom we wanted for a later date.

Sometimes when we arrived at Neary's and found our soldier boys fraternizing with some hookers, we would bounce the hookers out. We were only being patriotic and protecting our boys from cooties. Plus, it made us good girls more popular.

I was burning the candle at both ends, working full time and going to continuation school (it was the law!), and partying as much as possible. My seventeenth birthday was approaching, and I thought it was time to go for another challenge: I decided to join the Air Force on my eighteenth birthday.

It wasn't wartime so I couldn't get away with an early entry. I would have to go through the normal process and bone up for the initial exam in order to be accepted. I would let them know that I wanted the job of pilot, bombardier, or machine gunner—you know, something I could use in later life.

I told Mom of my plans, and she encouraged me. In her simple way, I knew she loved me but could never really do much for me.

14

MY PROBATION OFFICER, MA O'NEIL, TOLD ME my reporting time was just about up. She liked what she saw: I was working, finishing up continuation school, and preparing to go into the Air Force. She still tried to convince me to be a cop. I didn't want to hurt her feelings and tell her I didn't want to babysit wayward minors like me. The rule regarding not entering bars and fraternizing with ex-cons didn't apply to me—I glamorized my criminal past, and the justice system really didn't give a damn what I did or with whom. They simply wanted to teach me a lesson, and they did!

I never had trouble with getting a boyfriend. If I thought someone was cute, I would tell him and let him know that he was my boyfriend, whether he liked it or not, but I know usually it was mutual. I never let any romance last too long because I didn't want to ever get serious with anyone.

Those were famous last words!

I had managed on my own for a long time and just wanted to play the field.

I had several good friends at the phone company. One of the latest gal friends was Mary, a nice Italian girl from Bay Ridge who already had a few years with the company. She was about five years my senior and sort of became a big sister to me.

Her father and mother owned a bar/restaurant on Fifth Avenue and Fortieth Street. She invited me to her family's place for a bite and a beer.

They had an outstanding jukebox with terrific music, so I was back to my kind of exotic dancing. I went on the floor by myself and proceeded to do my Gypsy Rose Lee schtick but didn't take off my clothes. Somehow, I fancied myself as a sexy tease. Granted, I did have an audience as the bar part of the place was always busy—with my weekly act, the place was packed.

I was enjoying myself but didn't want to make my gyrations into a career, just entertaining for the food and beer at Mary's pop's place. There were a lot of guys around, just the usual bar fly types, nothing interesting.

Then one night this guy comes in, catches my act, and we start talking. He was nice looking, very intelligent and gave me the impression that he had plenty of dough. He asked me out. We went on a few dates. Then I took him home to meet Ma and Grandma. Well, I almost fainted as he brought candy, flowers, and perfume, just like I used to see in the movies. He charmed the family, and they were immediately encouraging of the relationship. I think they wanted me out of their bed as much as I wanted to get out of it.

He was from Bay Ridge, which was a fancy-schmancy neighborhood at the time, and seemed to be related to Rockefeller, the way he flashed his money around. He spent money on me like crazy, and even bought Mom and Grandma matching umbrellas.

Most of the guys I would run with were my age or a little older. This guy, Charlie, was seven years older than I was. My eighteenth birthday was right around the corner. I had met with my advisor from the military who was setting up the date for my entrance exam to be a WAF (Women in the Air Force).

I was getting ready to leave AT&T. My friends at the company had a farewell party for me and gave me a gold-plated ID bracelet as my goodbye present since I had told them I would soon be leaving for Lackland Air Force Base in Texas for my training. Test day came. Everything went well.

My friend Charlie took me out for my almost eighteenth birthday and what I thought was our saying goodbye for now. We were in this Italian restaurant in Little Italy having a great lunch and then he springs it on me. He takes out a box from his pocket, hands it to me and tells me how much he loves me and that he can't live without me. *Would I marry him?*

It was just like in the movies! Oh yeah, there was a diamond ring in the box. I don't know what the hell came over me but suddenly we were on a train to Elkton, Maryland to get married because you didn't need parental consent there.

Goodbye to the Air Force and some of the best years of my life.

15

WE WERE IN ELKTON. WE CHECKED WITH A TAXI driver for his recommendation of a place where we could be married. Soon after we were at a preacher's house.

Charlie paid a couple of bucks extra so I could have a corsage for the big event. There were magazines all around the room and everything seemed to be sanitized. It's possible the preacher was also the town doctor, as I felt more like I was in a doctor's office than a chapel of any kind.

We returned to Brooklyn the next day and were en route to meet his family and give them our good news.

Charlie's mother, Esther, was a sweet woman and her husband Charlie Sr. had a job with General Motors in New York and made a very good salary.

I spent a lot of time with Esther and was often present when her husband would come home from work. His greeting was always the same, never hello or hi. "Where's my eats?" he would say. I found out later that he collected Nazi-Gestapo memorabilia. I reminded myself never to take a shower in their apartment.

Charlie's sister also worked for General Motors. She had the looks and personality of a washrag. When we met them all for the announcement, his mom seemed happy, the sister giggled and babbled, and his father grunted, so I figured the odds were in my favor. They knew he had a serious drinking problem—maybe they thought I was the cure—and never bothered to tell me. In all fairness, it was too late anyway.

They gave us a nice chunk of change to start out and wished us well. Then it was off to my place to give my clan the exciting news. We received the congratulations, and they helped me pack.

We had already made a tentative agreement by phone with a landlord for a little basement apartment on Ryder Street in Flatbush. It was furnished so I would only have to buy odds and ends. I felt so grown up and excited that I was going to be setting up my first household. This was going to be the perfect life and marriage. We had good jobs, and Charlie enjoyed being a bellhop at the famous Algonquin Hotel in the City. His salary wasn't a big deal, but the tips were.

16

I RETURNED TO THE PHONE COMPANY RIGHT away because I didn't want to have any of my pay docked. I thought it was amazing that I received more praise and congratulations for eloping than joining the Air Force. They didn't even ask me to return the gold-plated bracelet!

The married women would cozy up to me on break time to chitchat about homemaker things like what to make for dinner or how to decorate the apartment. I enjoyed being considered a woman now and not a wild girl anymore.

I thought I was in love, and maybe I was, or maybe it was just fascination with the whole deal. In any event, I fell into my new role without any reservations. It was nice to be met after work, go out to dinner with my husband, have a romantic meal in nearby Little Italy, and talk about plans for the future.

Little did I know about the drinking Charlie did after he had taken me home when we were dating, or the binges he went on.

I was familiar, to a certain degree, with addiction to prescription drugs through Mom's activity and addictive gambling through my father's romance with the racetrack.

I really wasn't suspicious of my husband for a few months. I tried to be a good homemaker with my cooking skills, which were sad because as a kid I had been too busy to ever watch or be curious about the fine art of cooking. My first try at pancakes was a disaster. I took the entire box of mix, added milk and some water and put the concoction into the frying pan, figuring I'd save time with one gigantic pancake that I would cut up and share with my spouse.

We ate out a lot.

I didn't dwell on the family's reaction to the marriage, as I really didn't care. I knew Aunt Lee was already married to a Christian, and so was my brother. They were still around. God didn't strike them dead, so no problem.

When I spoke to my Uncle Jackson by phone, he invited me out to East Hampton—he wanted to give me a wedding gift, one of his paintings. I thanked him and told him when I got a car I would come out. It wasn't a big deal to me, as Mom would say, Aunt Lee had a mashugana husband—meaning an artist, generally not known for earning a good living—like herself, so I figured I wasn't in any great hurry to get the wedding gift.

If I knew then what I know now, I would have carried the gift on my head and walked the hundred miles back and forth.

After a few months of marital bliss, the shit hit the fan. Charlie started going on binges with his paycheck. He spent any small savings we had and showed his true colors of being a full-fledged alcoholic. After the binge, there was the swearing up and down of *never again, I love you, I'm sorry*, and the tears, over and over again.

At first, I believed; then I got angry and started to fight back hard. Unfortunately, I believed that having a baby would cure him. It made things worse. Even during my pregnancy, we were in physical battle. I hadn't taken crap from anyone, and I wasn't going to start now.

One time in my sixth month of pregnancy, he got so abusive that I tried to call the police. He grabbed the phone, put the cord around my neck, and tried to strangle me. I reached over the counter in the kitchen, grabbed a knife and stuck it in him. It was on the side of his shoulder, but enough to neutralize him.

He went to sleep on the floor. When he awakened from his drunken stupor, he asked me what happened. I told him he passed out and fell on the knife. He usually blacked out and didn't remember much anyway. I didn't tell my friends at the phone company what was going on, nor my family, I didn't want opinions or to be judged.

I felt I was really stuck. With the baby due soon, I would preoccupy myself with thoughts about motherhood. I worked up to the very end and then requested a six- month leave of absence, which was the norm for the phone company. Everyone wished me well. I received the usual baby gifts, then took my time off.

We had a cat at this time and as I was walking across the room in the apartment, my water broke right on him. I got myself to the hospital by taxi on Friday evening, got prepped, and went into the labor of hell.

I remember the nice intern who stayed with me for what seemed like days, trying to comfort me. The only painkiller was this metal gas inhaler with a rubber bulb that you squeezed when the contraction was coming. It became useless and I hurled it across the room. I know women yell out crazy things when they are in labor, but my curses were real. "Get me a lawyer. I want a divorce now!!!" I yelled over and over.

The baby was born on Monday morning. The father was off on a binge. My mom and the rest of the family were not aware that I had given birth.

The baby was big and beautiful. Welcome into this crazy world of mine, Christopher Charles Stewart!

My emotions were on overdrive. What the hell was I going to do now? I didn't know then that the baby had already been cursed with so many of his father's genes.

17

VERY SOON AFTER I RETURNED FROM THE HOS-pital with the new baby, Charlie's family helped us relocate to a ground floor unit in their apartment building. They purchased an entire nursery set for us and we ordered a bedroom set. With that and all the hand-me- down furniture, we had a decently furnished home. I really believed things would change for the better.

For the first few months, I did my motherly thing. I went up to the fourth floor to visit with my mother-in-law every day with the baby. It was pleasant enough, and in her motherly heart I felt that she also thought that the marriage and baby would change her son's ways.

Well, the change wasn't happening. It was like a merry-go-round: the binge, the apology, and the tears. I threatened to call the cops all the time. If I had him thrown out, *big deal*. He would go upstairs and sleep at his parent's apartment.

I found out about Alcoholics Anonymous and told him he had to attend, or it was over. I joined Al-Anon which offered support to the hurt person connected to the alcoholic. I bought every book, recited every slogan, hung them all over the apartment and became a true believer in the program. Unfortunately, Charlie didn't.

The support helped me get through many of the emotional abuses while I was waiting for him to see the light. I must have said, "God grant me the power to change the things I can, serenity to accept the things I can't, and wisdom to know the difference," at least a hundred times a day. Finally, I was granted the power and I threw him out permanently.

The baby was six months old when I got a job in the city as a switchboard operator at a private clothing manufacturer. The only babysitter I could get was a woman that lived ten blocks away and would take care of Chris in her apartment five days a week. I would bundle him up, walk the walk, drop him off, and take the train to Manhattan.

I knew I needed more in my life besides the soap opera I was living and wanted to get back in some sort of post baby shape. When I heard about a women's fitness program at the Prospect Park YMCA, I jumped on it.

Wednesday was ladies' day at the Y. I got a babysitter and was off to my workout, which consisted of learning how to hang and do rollovers on the rings, tricks on the trampoline, basketball, medicine ball, and pull-ups on the chinning bar. I was a happy camper.

The physical fitness director told me I was overwhelming the other ladies with my aggression and ability. He must have liked me so he made me a deal, if I became his fitness assistant, he would work out with me and spot me, plus be my partner on the medicine ball.

It was a better workout for me than before. We tried to wear each other out, smashing the fifteen-pound ball at each other in sit-up position as well as standing. He liked the way I encouraged other women, and I became gentler with them.

Going to work every day to get a paycheck to support Chris and I was tough. Charlie's folks bought things for the baby and gave us food from time to time. They wanted to stay on my good side as I had the only grandchild and heir to the Stewart throne, which was just the honor of their progeny as they had nothing much else to leave to him.

> My mother came over on occasion and sometimes baby sat. A few things happened to persuade me not to ask her back again. The first was when she sat too close to the playpen, watching my round-screen, hand-me-down, blurry TV. Chris was playing with pegs that he had to knock into the pegboard with a wooden mallet. As and ma was partially deaf, he couldn't get her attention fast enough, so he clobbered her with the mallet, knocking her out. I arrived home, saw her lying on the floor and accused her of sleeping on the job.

The more serious incident, however, was when she emptied her ashtray into the trash bag in the kitchen, not realizing the butt was still lit. She nodded off and I came home to a blaze with the baby in the next room. I threw Mom out but of course, we made up the following week, and agreed - no more babysitting! One day Charlie came by. I had a court order, so I didn't let him in. He was bombed as usual. He got really pissed and threw the gift of some frozen food and canned food through the window. Fortunately, the baby was in the crib in the nursery because most of the broken glass landed in the playpen.

> I had the comfort of a warm cuddly baby. Little did this tyke know that his father had an illness that according to the guru of AA, Bill Wilson, would end his life after much turmoil and sinking to the bottom.
>
> Getting to the bottom is supposed to be the turning point in your life, where you finally admit you're an alcoholic and the sun shines through. Well, it didn't happen like that. The disease lives on, even when the initial carrier doesn't.

I kept it as it was to make sure his family would see it; then maybe I could get more moral support from them—but I didn't hold my breath. Standing up to your own kin and refusing to continue to enable their addiction is a step that can take some years to make. The community I found Al-Anon supported this already raging fight within me—one thing I had never been a victim—but everyone who lives inside the tornado of a loved one's alcoholism is strong enough to dig their heels in and weather the storm.

> I met Al by chance at an Al-Anon meeting after a particularly rough confrontation with Charlie. I went there desperate - for clarity, for strength, for something I couldn't name. Al was kind, grounded, and generous. I didn't know he was a recovering alcoholic himself, just quietly attending that night. After the meeting, we grabbed coffee. His calm presence was a comfort I hadn't realized I needed. He looked strong, he lifted weights and carried himself with quiet confidence.

CHAPTER 17

One evening, Al mentioned he had started taking judo classes at the Brooklyn Central YMCA. I blinked. "What the hell is judo?"

He explained it was a Japanese martial art, part self-defense, part competition, part philosophy. At the time, all I knew about the Japanese came from war stories and Coney Island carnival games where we'd throw baseballs at caricatures of Tojo, Hitler, and Mussolini. My mind held crude stereotypes, remnants of a post-war America. I didn't know any better, and frankly, I didn't think I wanted to.

But Al offered to show me a throw. I figured - why not? I had learned to handle myself in street fights. Let him try.

The moment his hip lifted me off the ground, it felt like gravity shifted. He tossed me like I weighed nothing, like a rag doll, and I was stunned - not by pain, but by the power, the precision, and the control.

That was it. Right then, everything changed. One throw, and I let go of decades of prejudice. My world cracked open and judo stepped in.

I was hooked. This was more than fighting - it was art, it was strength, it was therapy. It was a place to release my anger, build myself back up, and learn to fall… and get up again. Over and over.

Judo became my salvation. It gave me purpose, resilience, and the discipline I didn't know I craved. That single class I planned to attend at the Brooklyn YMCA, would become the unlikely beginning of a five-decade journey - one that would shape my body, my mind, and my life.

Now I was determined that I must join!

18

I WAS REALLY LOOKING FORWARD TO attending my first judo class. When I arrived at the Brooklyn Central YMCA, the strange looks were already happening. I had to take the elevator up to the sixth floor where the class was held. Women never went past the lobby.

It took quite an ordeal to get me into the class. Mitch from the Prospect Park Y told me he would go to bat for me on the condition that I would teach what I learned to the women at his Y. The following week of class, I agreed.

René Kearn, the director of the Brooklyn Central Y, was hesitant about having a woman on the premises and for reasons I'm sure were outdated even then. Mitch didn't bother relaying those reasons to me; he knew it would be a waste of breath. Instead, he worked his own magic and finally convinced René to give me a shot. Who knows what he said - maybe he painted me as some kind of Amazon warrior. Either way, it worked. And that's all that mattered.

The instructor's name was Al Evoy. He had on a judo uniform with a black belt and that was enough credentials for me.

There were about twenty-five advanced guys and a group of fifteen potential beginners, including me. The mat was a typical wrestling mat. We first had to watch a practice session and then decide if we were going to come back to class. My friend Al, from Al-Anon, was on the mat and gave me a fast wave. I was thrilled that somebody there knew me.

As the advanced group—yellow belt and up—practiced, I became mesmerized by what I saw. They did exercises like they were in boot camp. They took falls from every position and direction. They knocked each other down. They continued to fight by immobilizing their partners or trying to choke them. They even stretched their partners' arms out, putting pressure on the elbow until their opponent tapped out.

WOW!

I could go back to fighting and not get in trouble. I wanted to learn all that good stuff! I wanted to bow to the world and tell everyone I would be okay! I would work hard in judo, take care of my kid, and get to my job. What a great life I was going to have!

Mr. Evoy spoke with us before the formal practice ended and asked who was going to be coming back next week. We all raised our hands, but all eyes went to my arm.

When my hand sprang up with vigor and enthusiasm, it was the first true indication that I was committed to returning to class, and to the study of judo. That day changed my life and the course of many other lives. I never dreamed that years later I would raise that same arm again to award an *ippon*—a full point, the highest score a fighter can achieve in judo—to a competitor at an international competition as an official referee. (The ippon is as close to the judo equivalent to a home run as it gets.)

Mr. Evoy told me I was not entitled to wear a judo uniform yet, so I was instructed to get to an Army/Navy Store and buy fatigues, cut off all the buttons, and have the pants and jacket cut and sewn up similar to a judo uniform. I asked about the belt. He said I should obtain a clothesline rope long enough to go around my waists twice with some to spare on either end.

I couldn't wait for the next week to come. I told my mom what I was getting into and as usual with her hearing affliction, she told everyone she knew very proudly that her daughter was, "doing Judy."

PART 2
THE FIGHT—ON AND OFF THE MAT

19

I WENT TO THE ARMY-NAVY STORE AND BOUGHT my fatigues from a salesman who had a puzzled look on his face. It wasn't the typical purchase for a young woman, so he asked me if they were for my husband or boyfriend.

"No," I said. "They're for my mother."

Women's roles had been mapped out a long time ago, and I had never dealt well with the mold.

I was off to judo the following week. I was so excited that I breezed through my day at home. The women in my building were the evening babysitters for judo and the in-laws sat for my Al-Anon meetings.

My first judo session gave me a rude awakening. I was strong, well-coordinated, somewhat agile, but the falling down was murder because of the way the instructor taught. All we did was fall, fall, fall on the cushioned wrestling mats.

I wasn't the only awkward person in the class. From the time I was a kid, someone would always be telling me to be careful and not to fall down. Now this judo teacher/drill sergeant was yelling, "That's no good. Do it again!" Translation: fall down again.

Nevertheless, it was a great workout. I was drenched in sweat, sore and dizzy. When I got home, I staggered in, took my shower and fell asleep before my head hit the pillow. I was glad the baby was sleeping and didn't want to play.

The next morning, as I began the usual routine, besides being sore as hell, I had purple, basketball-sized bruises on both hips. I never thought for a moment that it wasn't worth it.

The turmoil with my mostly estranged husband continued. This kept me away from many people, but I did see my mom on occasion.

Since Aunt Lee and Uncle Jackson were way out in the country in East Hampton, the family hardly ever saw them. It seemed that they made themselves scarce and didn't want to be with anyone but each other. Both of them were engrossed in their work and I could appreciate that, as all I could think of was this painful judo art I was involved in.

As alcohol was almost ruining the lives of both Chris and I, it also took Uncle Jackson's life away. Lee had been away in Europe when the tragedy happened. Two lives were lost—a young woman in the prime of her life and the uncle who had always called me Renee.

Lee was devastated. There was a lot of confusion. The date of the funeral was mixed up and not many family members got to be there. I thought "death lurks behind the bottle" would be the prophetic message to my husband. But no.

Hell, no!

Even though he hardly knew Pollock, he went out on one of his longest binges yet to drown his grief.

Yeah, sure!

20

TOTAL DESPERATION SET IN. I HAD TO RESOLVE this emotional roller coaster of a marriage one way or another. Kings County Hospital in Brooklyn was starting a treatment center for alcoholics and was looking for volunteers. Naturally, I volunteered Charlie.

They treated patients with a drug named Antabuse. The medicine was benign until the patient took a drink of alcohol, then they got very sick. Symptoms included heaving and the potential loss of control of normal body functions. This extreme reaction was supposed to discourage drinking.

It worked for a little while and there was a glimmer of abstinence in him. Then he took all the money that was in the apartment, anything hockable, and went on a super binge. Little did I know that he only faked taking the Antabuse, just so he could stay at the apartment.

I wanted to teach Charlie a good lesson and maybe even cure him. When the dust settled on the last binge, I made believe everything was hunky-dory. I cooked a nice dinner that included mashed potatoes (unbeknown to him, loaded with powdered Antabuse). After dinner he said he was going out to get the newspaper. I knew that was bull—he was going to the local watering hole. I quickly got my neighbor to look after Chris and got to the bar just in time to watch Charlie guzzle down his first drink of the evening.

When he saw me, he put it down, waiting for me to have a fit. "Go ahead," I told him. "Don't let me stop your fun."

He chug-a-lugged his drink despite a somewhat puzzled look on his face. Now it was just a matter of time.

It didn't take long. He turned green, began throwing up, ran to the men's room, and staggered back with a purple glow.

CHAPTER 20

It was a very colorful experience for me, but not the answer. The question now was where could I get a divorce—and where would I get the money to pay for it? It was late 1956 or early 1957, and the great state of New York did not grant divorces at that time.

21

AFTER A YEAR STUDYING UNDER MY INSTRUCTOR
Al Evoy, he passed away. He had a bad ticker, and I don't think having me in the class helped him there.

Though I did the unthinkable and won, the moment was bittersweet—one I'll never forget. Al had wanted the entire team to give up their medals in protest, but I wouldn't go that far. Instead, I volunteered to be stripped of my victory, knowing deep down that the real fight was only just beginning.

When Al passed, I felt a deep sadness. I genuinely liked him. More than that, he had been a friendly gatekeeper to the world of judo—a rare kind of person who opened a door and asked for nothing in return.

And then the selfish thoughts crept in.

What about practice now? What do I do without him?

Fortunately, I was still teaching at the Prospect Park YMCA, which allowed me to continue to train with my own students. Up until then, I had been demonstrating techniques to my students that I had learned the previous week in Al's class; now we would have a review until I learned more. We spent a lot of time practicing randori—a good way of testing one's skills without the cooperation of a partner. It was good, old-fashioned free fighting, judo style.

At the startup of my classes, it was only women who participated. Then the boyfriends or husbands came to watch. Obviously, they liked what they saw, and before not too long, the class was opened to men as well.

> **Judo Classes For the Gals**
>
> Judo classes for women at the Prospect Park YMCA, 357 9th St., will be resumed at 7:30 P.M. Oct. 3, under direction of Mrs. "Rusty" Stewart. Instruction will include "defensive measures to take against undesirable elements stalking city streets," according to Loren Mitchell, physical director. Women wishing to join the classes may phone MItchel at SO 8-7100.

To learn more judo, I found a club in Manhattan. It was run by two six-foot-four masses of muscle, both partially bald and wearing glasses, named Bernie and Bob Lepkofker.

They had both been in the Air Force stationed in Japan where they had studied judo.

They had never had a woman at their club before. I explained my past training, my teaching experience, and that I had a child who would have to come with me if I came during the day.

It was lucky for me. I found a new home.

It worked out perfectly. Bernie and Bob wanted me to teach afternoon classes to beginners. This barter forgave the monthly dues and I could bring my kid.

Rusty performing a judo demo, Prospect Park YMCA, circa 1960.

The new routine began. There were several guys that worked nights and came up to practice during the day. They were brown and black belts, so I knew I was going to learn more plus have good sparring partners for randori.

Elliot Farrell, who belonged to an all-black judo club in Brooklyn came up during the week for a workout. We hit it off right away. Elliot looked like a younger Louis Armstrong. He always had a joke, a smile, and his presence would light up a room.

Elliot and I thought we were the judo twins. When prospective clients would come up to inquire about judo and Bernie and Bob weren't around, we would call ourselves as such.

As if that wasn't bad enough, one time Elliot gave Chris and I a lift back to Brooklyn and stopped for a light with the car windows opened, and Chris called Elliot, "Daddy." The light turned green, and we moved on, but the car next to us stayed in the same place—probably in shock. This was 1960, and at that time communities were still commonly segregated.

Elliot really helped me improve in judo. We also did a few newspaper interviews together with photos and it wasn't long before he invited me to St. John's recreation center.

Wow! A dozen smooth judo players on the mat at one time!

It was great. No lessons, just continuous randori. That was a lesson enough. These guys were fast and furious. I was up in the air more than standing on the mat. The mutual respect was obvious from the onset. Here I was a female, strong and didn't complain when I got thrown. I was adding on judo training sites for myself and I began to get a reputation in the small, local world of judo.

22

A JAPANESE BUSINESSMAN CAME BY THE JUDO club, which I learned was called a *dojo*, and inquired about training. The twins immediately recruited him to teach an evening class for the advanced students. There were a handful of young Japanese instructors in New York under contract to Jerome Mackey, a Juilliard graduate, concert pianist who had the distinction of having performed a piano recital at Carnegie Hall, and judo entrepreneur.

Mackey, opened one of the first commercial judo schools in New York in the 1950s, and was one of the first Americans to franchise martial arts in NY State at the time. The die-hard judo community frowned on that as not being in the tradition of true judo. However, it was the American way, so it not only worked, but also excelled. If one had the money, Mr. Mackey had the time. The instructors were paid a fair salary and were able to get the American experience.

Mackey, who was a good judo player, went to Japan every so often to practice and recruit the crème de la crème of up-and-coming judo stars, usually from Nihon University, one of the top schools with the best judo teams. It was comparable to our top football universities.

I liked Mackey's model because it defused some of the New York knuckleheads from believing they were the very best. Once they visited Mackey's place, played one of the Japanese powerhouses, scraped up their bodies, false egos and left, their self-evaluations were a bit humbler, although a few were dumb enough to believe they just had a bad day. Whenever I went to see the new guys from Japan, I only wanted to learn what they did and how they did it.

Mackey's school was upscale and pricey. He spent a lot on his investments. I felt like a fish out of water there—all I really wanted to do was to study the art and craft of judo. This place was way out of my reach and budget, and I knew it—it seemed very clear to me, with all the great talent there was there, that when it came to teaching, they needed me like a third eyeball.

At my dojo, Judo Twins, we were thrilled to get our Mackey assigned instructor who was a little older than the young bucks at Mackey's instructor stable. He was Japanese so he had to be good—he came from the homeland of judo. Mr. Mamoru Saigenji became my sensei—or martial arts teacher, which had more powerful overtones than instructor; I would now begin learning true judo, including the philosophy and way of life. He was my Yoda.

The class was packed with guys from all over the place to train with our new Sensei. Training was hard and I remained the only female.

Everyone, including my Sensei, considered me an exception; I was not the typical female—I was an equal and treated accordingly. There were no derogatory remarks or hard feelings when I knocked the guys down, nor did I brag about being equal to a man. It was an unwritten rule. I just became one of the boys.

'Y' Judo Classes

The Prospect Park YMCA at 357 9th St., Brooklyn, will resume its judo classes for women on Monday, Oct. 3, at 7:30 p.m. under the direction of Mrs "Rusty" Stewart.

Our YMCA team did well. The women trained exactly like the men and as I played judo with all my students, it was making all of us stronger. It was amazing to me how easily our sensei could demolish all of us without even breaking a sweat. I yearned to learn the secret.

What compounded the hurt to our bodies and pride was that before class ended, we all had to sit in *zarei* position— sitting on your legs with your butt on your heels. Mr. Saigenji would also sit the same way, facing us, although he could not see us since he was blind. He told us old war stories of how we blew up

a ship he was on during World War II and how he had to spend thirteen hours in the sea near Shanghai before he was rescued.

It was always a long story so he could get revenge on our American long legs. We didn't dare look at each other for fear we would crack up and he would kill us.

Rusty and her fellow judo classmates, early 1960s.

23

MY LIFE, THOUGHTS, AND DREAMS WERE COMpletely wrapped up in judo. It seemed to fulfill so many of my needs and gave me a sense of belonging, structure, pride, and discipline. Judo guided my energy in the right direction and enabled me to defuse lots of hostility and channel it. The challenge for me was not the rank or the win, it was a means of inner change. I attributed this metamorphosis, as I transitioned out from behind the angry lens I had previously viewed life through and in how I handled challenges that arose, to following a great philosophy, even though I only partially understood it at this point.

Besides practicing and teaching, I bought some books on judo. There were not many to be found. One of my first, *Illustrated Kodokan Judo*, was like the bible of judo. History, philosophy and techniques were all documented in this one book.

I had known that judo was from Japan and developed by Dr. Jigoro Kano in 1882, but through this book I learned that judo was derived from jujitsu and Dr. Kano and his students had to kick a lot of jujitsu ass to get the Japanese government to approve judo as the official martial art of Japan. Dr. Kano was a little guy who did a big job. He won my respect and devotion immediately.

I liked the translation of the word judo, which literally means "gentle way." Understanding both the physical and mental aspects of the gentle way, in my view, is the most difficult aspect for a new practitioner, and it takes the longest to learn. Because the techniques of judo are based on the philosophy of gaining maximum efficiency by using minimal effort, judo is often referred to not only as an art but as a science; there's physics involved, such as leverage, gravity and momentum.

I was obsessed. I was falling in love with a sport that wasn't really Americanized, and I was reading and trying to follow in the little footsteps of the great professor Kano with my big Brooklyn feet—size eleven and a half, triple E.

Saigenji Sensei was pleased with my continued enthusiasm, especially since my recent return from the busted shoulder injury from a previous open mat fighting session (randori). He gave me special attention, but no praise, which only encouraged me to do better. New York did not have an official promotion board.

The Kodokan Judo Institute in Tokyo, Japan, founded by Dr. Kano is often referred to as the Kōdōkan, is considered the Mecca of dojos and the headquarters of the worldwide judo community. The Kodokan indicated to the New York judo community and leadership that a black belt organization, known as *Yudanshakai* had to be formed and we would have to join the national organization, which was the Judo Black Belt Federation of the United States. With these new regulations, New York judo formed its own board of directors, and promotion board examiners, and was deemed an official entity.

The first official promotion competition and examination was going to be held in the spring of 1962. This event was for black belt promotion. My sensei entered a group of us up for the test, including me. Going for the rank of first-degree black belt—known as *shodan*, which literally means "beginning degree" and represents the lowest black belt rank in judo. As much as I wanted it, I thoroughly enjoyed being a high-ranking brown belt. I could clean most everyone's clock and even throw black belts during randori and not feel bad when a black belt threw me. After all, weren't they supposed to be better? It was obvious that not a lot of the philosophy was kicking in yet.

24

THE DAY OF THE PROMOTION COMPETITION DAY

finally came. I wasn't sure who or how many were in my division or who the officials would be. This was the first-ever competition and belt rank examination in New York State, maybe even in the United States. Several of my students were going to attend to cheer me on.

The event was held at the Academy of Music in downtown Brooklyn, which had a good-sized mat area. My sensei was there, as were several of the Japanese instructors who had branched out after their contracts with Jerome Mackey, expired. My pals from the Judo Twins club were taking their tests also and greeted me as I walked in. After all the good luck wishes to each other, I checked out my opponents.

The referee for my consecutive matches was Shiina Sensei, a Nihon University alumnus and one of the best judo practitioners around. Although I never practiced at his dojo, he heard about me through the judo grapevine.

My first match was against a woman named Ruth, who claimed she was almost mugged but pulled out her judo membership card and flashed it at the mugger he allegedly ran away. If I were the mugger, it certainly would take more than a membership card to make me run away or lose in this instance.

Another opponent was a large Asian woman who practiced at the American Buddhist Academy in NYC. I didn't know anything about her or the pretty blond who seemed to materialize from Mars that I was matched up with after. All that mattered to me was that these women were all that separated me from my black belt.

My name was called, then my opponent's. This was the first time I was competing against other women, rather than men. It was a very strange feeling. Practicing with my female students was just play. This was going to be a fight!

Poor Mr. Shiina refereed our first match. I could tell he was bewildered, never having refereed women before and not knowing our capabilities.

When Ruth and I bowed and began the match, Mr. Shiina mumbled something in his thick Japanese accent along the lines of, "be careful; don't hurt each other. Remember this is only randori and not a real match." Primarily, he was looking at me.

Coming out of the bow, I made eye contact with my sensei. He gave me the nod, which I interpreted as, "seek and destroy." I ended my match very quickly with a full point.

My students carried on and cheered like lunatics; they knew the mugger story. The unknown Asian woman appeared to have the verve of a direct descendant of Genghis Khan, was a very different story. She had a thick body, thick legs and thick feet, and she only attacked with leg and foot sweeps. There was a lot of action during this match. It was tough to get under her center of gravity. I heard some shouts from my students that gave me the extra zip that I needed. My attack wasn't pretty, but it was fierce, and it knocked her down and out.

Mr. Shiina was beside himself.

"I told you we would have trouble with girls!" he was yelling to his colleagues. That was it for my part of the competition, except that I would have to demonstrate the *Nage-no-Kata*, fifteen formal throwing techniques that had to be demonstrated on both the right and left sides very precisely. I had been practicing these techniques for months and had a great deal of confidence with my form. I received a perfect score, which was the highest score of the day.

I was promoted to first-degree black belt.

What a good day!

We went out to celebrate and during the toasts I told my sensei I wanted to go to Japan to study judo. He looked at me very deeply and realized this wasn't idle talk from the joyous moment—I was dead serious.

He said we would speak again, and he would check out the feasibility.

25

SAIGENJI SENSEI GAVE ME HIS BLESSING TO GO to Japan - oh my God! Not only that, he offered to write a letter of recommendation to the Kodokan, the global Mecca of judo at the time. It was the legendary home of the Honorable Professor Jigoro Kano and his disciples. Although Professor Kano had passed, his son, Riesi Kano, now led the Kodokan, and I knew I'd be surrounded by masters who could help guide my journey.

Sensei also planned to introduce me to his good friend, Dr. Kobayashi, and would request that I stay with the doctor and his family while I trained. It was still 1962, and I hadn't yet received my first-degree black belt certificate from the Kodokan—I figured I could pick it up while I was there.

There was so much to do. I didn't have any money, plane ticket or passport. What would I do with Chris? I got the wheels in motion. First, I got a passport, which wasn't easy since the plane ticket was not going to be in my name for a while, and at the time you needed to show proof of travel in order to apply. But just like always, I found a way to hustle around the rules.

My buddy Cowan had a student who worked for Pan Am. He was allowed to get a pass for his wife to fly free, so I became his wife. I got the in-laws to foot the bill for Chris' sleep-away camp in the Poconos, managed to get the passport and visa, got injections of some sort, and left the Red Hook maniacs in charge of my judo program at the Y.

My students all chipped in for my luggage. They bought me two Amelia Earhart suitcases. *Were they trying to tell me something, like maybe this was a one-way trip?* I packed very conservative clothes, as I was told to do: no Apache jacket or bell-bottoms. I got an advance on my YMCA class stipend and had about $200 all told, which wasn't bad at the time because the exchange rate was 360 yen to a dollar. I wasn't going over to shop, and I would live like a monk if that's what it took.

Hawaii was still another country at this time, so I had to buy my ticket round trip from Hawaii to Japan. I could be Mrs. Pan Am from New York to Hawaii, but from there on I had to do everything legit. That's when the paperwork and passports were checked.

As a bonus, my sensei made arrangements for me to stay in California for a couple of days and practice at San Jose University with their unbeaten judo team. Mr. Yosh Uchida and his brother George picked me up at the airport and were very hospitable. I guess they were told I was a poor but determined judo girl from Brooklyn.

I noticed I was the only female on the mat during practice. *What else was new?* I played hard, got caught a few times, but dished it out as equally as I got it. In later years I found out that one of the guys I did a number on was a big shot with the government. He always sends me his regards, from a distance.

It was pretty cold on top of San Francisco's Golden Gate Bridge when the Uchida's took me for a little sightseeing, even though it was the beginning of June. I was happy with their efforts. The Uchida's were American big shots in judo and were well known. I was happy and grateful they took the time to help me.

The following day I was off to Hawaii. I was to meet a guy by the name of Sam Fujiyama, my sensei's friend, who also happened to work for customs in Hawaii. Of course, he was also a judo guy.

Sam got me squared away and told me where to go to practice the following day. Never mind sightseeing when there was all this judo around.

The dojo's name was Shobukan. It was home to a fast-moving mat with speed demons all over it; if you stood still for two seconds, you would be thrown. I never moved so fast in my life just to survive.

The head sensei was a Hawaiian legend of sorts. This was my introduction to Asian culture, lots of Japanese people, and dynamic judo. I wondered if this was planned so I wouldn't freak out when I arrived at the judo Mecca in Japan, or was it just the way it went?

Two days later I was off to the land of the rising sun for the most prolific, painful, and wonderful experience I had ever had in my life.

26

IN THE FLIGHT TO TOKYO, I CONTINUED TO HAVE the chills. I didn't pay too much attention to them as I was caught up with the excitement of the adventure. The time zone change, with day going to night in a flash, had me bewildered. I was completely unaware of such amazing feats of nature.

The meals that were given to us on the plane were primarily Japanese. My only experience with Japanese food up until this point was sukiyaki, a delicious meat and vegetable dish that Saigenji Sensei prepared as a reward for us at a party at his apartment in Manhattan. The plane food was a mystery. It was served in a bento box with several different items in it, from the recognizable cooked fish, to seemingly familiar vegetables prepared in a way I had not experienced before. There was some clear colored stringy stuff that could have been anything. Determined to conform and take everything in my stride, I finished all of it, including the clear rubber band-looking things I assumed were noodles.

We finally landed in Tokyo. On the way down all I could think about was the film *Thirty Seconds Over Tokyo*, the story of the historic Doolittle Raid, America's secret bombing mission and first retaliatory strike back against Japan after the attack on Pearl Harbor in December of 1941. I was hoping that they had forgotten. I was looking forward with great anticipation to being met by my host and sponsor, Dr. Kobayashi, at Haneda Airport. After going through the major customs ritual, I moved on to the reception area. At the time, I had had very limited exposure to Japanese people and because of this, I had a hard time distinguishing one Japanese person from another. It wasn't really that difficult so much as that, at five-foot-nine, I didn't expect to be so set apart—not just in my obvious Americanness, but in stature as well as appearance; my bright red locks were easy to spot in a sea of brunettes.

I towered over most of the people I saw around me. Japan was a whole new, eye-opening world for me—one in which I was woefully naive to the vastness of culture outside of my then still very homogenized American experience. Years later, when visiting Japan as a family, my daughter, Jean, experienced something similar, turning around in a shopping center and losing sight of her own father in an ocean of five-foot-seven men all wearing baseball caps—so I suppose I can't be too hard on myself for this one.

I was looking for a sign with my name on it. All the signs being held up were in Japanese.

Shit!

I figured they or he would easily spot a five-foot, nine-inch, 175 pound redhead in the incoming crowd of Japanese people and a handful of elderly tourists. It didn't happen.

After several hours and still no Dr. Kobayashi, I knew I would have to get out of the airport and fend for myself. I felt rather warm and a little dizzy, but I didn't dwell on it, as I was preoccupied with figuring out what to do. I didn't have Dr. Kobayashi's address or telephone number and his name was as common as Smith in the States. I did know he lived in a place called Nakano and that would be helpful later.

I managed to partially communicate with a few people who spoke broken English and were somewhat embarrassed to speak to an American with their limited vocabulary. I managed to find out about the transportation into Tokyo proper. I also got the address of an inexpensive hotel. Everyone I met was so polite and really tried to be helpful. Even if we couldn't communicate verbally, they would go out of their way to take me in the direction I had to go. I was most grateful and knew I was never going to see Brooklyn the same way again.

After I got settled in the mom-and-pop hotel, I went for a walk to check things out and try to figure out how to find Dr. Kobayashi. I had never felt so lonely in my life. I thought I felt a real depression setting in. What it was, in fact, was my temperature, which was sky-high. I didn't know what the hell to do. I went back to my room to lie down—I didn't have much choice; it was the room or the street. The mama-san came up to the room to bring tea, as part of the daily ritual, took one look at me and called for papa-san to come up. They had a very hurried conversation about my condition and me. I didn't have a clue what they were saying, but I did recognize certain words—names of certain throws and some minimal counting, which was part of our regular warmup routine—because all the Japanese I knew at the time was based on judo terminology.

They made gestures for me to get out of bed and go with them. I was sweating profusely, and the sheets were soaked. They put a towel around my shoulders as I followed them to a nearby hospital. Fortunately, the doctor that took care of me could speak some English. I told him why I had come to Japan—to study judo—and he passed this on to my rescuers. Altogether, I heard the biggest *"ah, so desu ka,"*— which translates to "is that right," and is interchangeable with "ah, so"—and there was a new look in their eyes toward me, a look of great respect.

The doctor told me I had pleurisy, something like a super flu. I needed medicine and rest. I told them my tale of woe about not finding Dr. Kobayashi and the doctor said he would help me locate him.

I was first given an injection and then packets of powder to mix with water, to be taken three times a day. I felt so weak, but pleased that I did get help and would have a chance to find my host. After three days I was feeling better, not tip top, but a hell of a lot better than a few days before.

The good news came via the mama-san that the doctor who saved me had managed to contact Dr. Kobayashi. He would be coming to get me later that day. He had been waiting for me at the airport, however on the following day. It was a big mix up, with time zones. He was beside himself and very embarrassed about the confusion.

My strength wasn't up to par yet, but I put on a real happy face and attitude as I felt everything would be good from now on. Dr. Kobayashi was a small man with a pleasant face who could speak a little English. After all the apologies and pleasantries, he indicated that he would like me to teach his brother English and I would be his guest at his home and medical clinic. The family lived above the clinic and I was welcome to stay as long as I liked. I immediately agreed to teach his brother English, since basically it was mostly conversation. I laughed to myself, as I knew this kid would be the first man in town to have a Brooklyn accent.

I met the family and was escorted to my nice clean, adequate room. I proceeded to put my things away in the closet. Then I saw this humongous bug and called for help. My future student, Yukio, ran into my room and started laughing, as it simply was a cockroach. He started to knock it down when the damn thing flew at us.

I couldn't jump on Yukio as I would have killed this tiny guy, but I was in a major panic. I couldn't help but compare it to a New York cockroach. This sucker must have been nuked when we dropped the bomb—similar to a Florida palmetto or the New York water bug, the Japanese roach was alarmingly more aggressive, and it could fly! I decided I would have to keep one eye open while I slept because otherwise, I feared "Gigantor" and his family might carry me out at night while I rested.

It wasn't hard to keep one eye open because unbeknown to me, the medical clinic that was below us was a legal abortion clinic, which was Dr. Kobayashi's specialty as a gynecologist. The walls were paper-thin so you could hear the blood curdling screams very easily. At first, I didn't know what the hell place Saigenji Sensei had hooked me up with—all kinds of things were going through my mind— and I was strangely relieved when I found out. A lot of women got themselves knocked up. Dr. Kobayashi's business was good.

27

THE DAY HAD FINALLY COME. I WAS OFF TO THE Kodokan. It was my dream being realized. I was on my way to Seidobashi, where the Kodokan was and I would be in all my glory.

Dr. Kobayashi's sister-in-law walked me to the train station to point me in the right direction. My station's name was Nakano-ku, and I was going to Seidobashi Station, ten stops away. I had on a conservative white blouse and dark skirt. I carried an umbrella that would come in handy not only for the rain, but to allow me to count ten spokes so I would know when to get off.

I didn't have a seat at first, nor was I looking for one. I was enjoying being the center of attention. When I had boarded the train, every eyeball was on me checking out my size, coloring and who knows what else. As a pretty confident person, it didn't bother me. When the train filled up a few stations later, the standing room was tight. Since the average height of the businessman was five feet four inches, no matter which way I turned, my bust was in someone's face. I wasn't that big, but compared to the average young Japanese woman, I was enormous.

Finally, there was a seat. I wanted it just to get my knockers off the marketplace. I sat down quickly, resorting to the New York style of attack, and once again was the star of the show. The seats were so low that when I plopped down, my knees and chest connected—not a lovely sight. I hardly ever wore skirts or dresses, and having big legs to begin with left me in an awkward position once again. I'm sure I gave the train travelers plenty to talk about when they got to work. I held on tight to the ninth spoke from my umbrella and was really happy that number ten was coming, where I would get off.

I asked directions to the Kodokan and was becoming used to people taking me rather than telling me, as it was useless anyway. It was a muggy day, as it often is in Japan during the summer. The sun peeked out occasionally, just enough so that when I was standing in front of the life-sized bronze statue of Professor Jigoro Kano, the father of judo, admiring the exquisite work of art, I had the feeling that we would be together forever. The sun did its quick peek-a-boo and I could swear I saw the statue smile.

The foreign office on the right side of the entrance was where I was to report and register. There he was: Diago Sensei. He was much larger than his photos in the illustrated Kodokan book that was my bible. I had a little crush on him just from the book, and now was completely tongue-tied seeing him in person. The gentleman in the office introduced us. He grunted ahem and I babbled a *hai hai* which means yes in Japanese. Now I know why I became so popular—I was agreeable to everything. I took care of business and of course they had the letter from Saigenji Sensei with his good recommendations. There were no problems

...yet.

A guide took me on the tour to get me familiar with where I would be practicing the next day. There was the place where you took off your shoes and carried them to the shoe check-in place. The long, solemn hallway was a beautiful polished wood. It felt like I was in a holy place.

About fifty feet away two large blurs were walking toward my guide and me. As they got closer I could see that they were two sweaty judo players about six feet four inches or more who had just finished training so the smoke was still coming out of their bodies. They passed us and almost knocked us down without even being aware that we were there. I could feel their power, see their size, and wanted to look at my guide and say, "What nice mess have you gotten us into now, Ollie?"

My goodness, I must have been duped by all the World War II movies. I thought back to Coney Island, where I used to throw the ball at Tojo to win a prize. None of these Japanese judo players looked like that stereotype.

We proceeded to the different dojos; we went to the children's dojo where a bunch of adorable kids were trying to knock each other down. It was obvious they were having fun with their jovial and good-natured sensei. We then went into the foreign dojo where a small class was going on. I was introduced and knew I would be back with them soon. The next dojo was the women's. There were lots of girls and women doing forms of kata, randori and looking pretty busy. The women's sensei indicated to my guide that they would see me the next day. The best was saved for last.

"The Meat House," as I affectionately called it, was the main dojo, about half the size of a football field. At least a hundred guys at a time were playing randori. They were the elite judo athletes who came from colleges all over Japan. They were of Olympic and national caliber. Watching them train was like witnessing a coordinated work of art in motion. Bodies were flying all over the place, and yet no one was colliding into anyone else. I was drooling. I couldn't wait to get in there. The tour was over after I saw the mini restaurant and girls' locker room. We had a little tea. I thanked my guide, got my shoes, and was on my way back to Nakano. I got on the train and got the umbrella ready: one, two, three...

28

MY FEELINGS WERE CLEAR: I WOULD TURN myself into a sponge and try to absorb as much as possible. Certainly, I wasn't going to impress anyone at the Kodokan with my judo skills. It was the day of reckoning, my first day of training.

After I took off my shoes, I proceeded to the check-in area, still in awe of the immaculate wood floors. The women who took care of the shoes recognized me from the day before and greeted me with a sweet refrain of sorts and a very low bow. I remembered that my sensei had said that to show proper respect, one must bow lower. I made a noble try, but as they were four foot, ten inches and I was a foot taller, I almost fell on my head. *How embarrassing!* I almost got hurt before I even stepped on the mat. It was, however, the beginning of a nice friendship.

I went to the locker room to put on my judo gi and proceeded up to the women's dojo where I was assigned for now. I did a standing bow as I entered the dojo. Then we lined up and bowed in from the formal sitting position. I loved all this. Even though we did the same respect ritual of bowing upon entering the dojo, bowing onto the mat and bowing to your partner in New York, this was taking it to the max, as I felt such a deeper meaning being in Japan.

The women sensei's were lined up in front of us. One of the senior women led the warm up exercises. At home it was pushups, sit-ups, and stretching. At the Kodokan, the warm up was like a cheerleader's dance with the movements of kabuki and sumo all jammed together. Don't get me wrong. It wasn't easy and I looked like Clara the Klutz trying to imitate them. I did my best and no one laughed at me. If it had been the other way around, I would have been hysterical and rolling on the floor. These women had great self-control.

The art of falling, known as ukemi, was a very important part of their training. My falls and rolls were alright, but these women were possessed with falling. Primarily, they practiced forms of kata, which they did exquisitely, and played randori with lots of movement and finesse. It wasn't easy for me to lighten up on my not so technical techniques; I still depended a lot on power, which was a no- no here in the big leagues.

When I moved around with the younger girls, I would let them catch me; with the older and stronger, I gave in as much as I could. I wanted them to like me and not get the reputation of a big bully from the West. I suspected they all had a big brother like the two I saw in the hall the day before and didn't want to die, not yet anyway.

This was the daily routine for a while. It was fine. I was getting my health back. One day I showed up for practice and I saw another foreign woman working out with the girls. She was killing them. Oftentimes randori partners jump when their opponents are executing a throw on them to add a little extra zest to the move; the result is a more magnificent, grand looking throw. This new, French judoka, however, gave no aid to her practice partners: no jumps for them, and no mercy from her. They couldn't say no when she asked them to play randori. It was an unspoken rule; when you were asked to engage in randori, you had to trust that the asker wasn't intending to kill you—or if they were, it was up to you to survive, politely, of course, and with a show of mutual respect.

I could feel the tension in the air. It was time! After she trounced the last girl, I went over to her with my John Wayne walk and asked her to play. We went at it. I don't think the Japanese women had seen such vicious attacks between two female competitors before. She was good and had more skilled technique than me, but I was a fighter and smashed whatever way I could. After five or so minutes of strenuous randori, we were both exhausted, bowed out, and walked to different sides of the dojo.

The young women looked at me with thanks in their eyes and were my pals from then on. The stormtrooper I'd just worn out on the mat was from France, one of their best judoka. She was studying in Japan before returning home to become an instructor at the police academy in Paris. That day was her last day of training in Japan, so she was set on giving payback to the other judokas for reasons I didn't understand. All I knew was I would not be going to gay Paris any time soon.

Rusty and the women of the Kodokan, Japan, circa 1962.

29

SPECIAL SUMMER TRAINING AT THE KODOKAN was quickly approaching. I wasn't sure of what it was going to entail but that didn't stop me from signing up for every course. The Judo Twins from New York must have contacted their sensei in Tokyo, Mr. Nakabayashi, and alerted him that I was going to be training in Japan, because Mr. Nakabayashi soon found me at the Kodokan and asked me if I would be interested in training other places as well. Naturally, I jumped at the chance. And just like that the police dojo, the US Air Force base, and the Japanese Coast Guard dojo—all places that Mr. Nakabayashi taught—were added to my training itinerary.

The only downside was that another judo rat would be frequenting all these places with us. I didn't mind sharing the mat, but the guy who was training with us was a real immature, spoiled, 19-year-old brat by the name of Ron Hoffman. Ron was from Chicago, and was a good judo player, but extremely self-centered. We didn't like each other from the onset. I didn't know if it was because I was a woman, from New York, or that he would have to share the attention of Mr. Nakabayashi that gave him his negative attitude toward me. Had we been in Brooklyn, I would have kicked his ass immediately with my former martial art, street fighting.

It was a first for females to participate at these training sites so, once again, I did my damnedest. I enjoyed the police dojo the most, even though it was the roughest place in Japan. The cops in Japan had to stay in good fighting shape because at that time many of them didn't carry guns.

The large judo training area was side by side with the almost mirrored floor of the kendo practice dojo. Kendo is similar to samurai sword fighting, except it is practiced using long bamboo sticks. They wore kendo uniforms, called hakama, and had full head and face gear

Rusty & her fellow women of the Kodokan, Japan, circa 1962.

on. The face mask looked like a baseball catcher's getup.

Part of the kendo martial art involves excessive screaming while taking headshots with the shinai. We yell—called kiai—in judo, but only when we really need it. I could have used some of that protective gear because every time I got thrown in the police dojo and landed half way on the mat and half way on the kendo floor, one of these screaming kendo killers would whack me. But I never complained; I knew that rotten Ron was watching me and laughing.

This routine, as much as I enjoyed it, was put on hold. We began special summer training. The day began at 9:00 a.m. in the main dojo of Kodokan, a.k.a. "the meat house," with instruction from the great Daigo Sensei, assisted by the notorious Iso Inokuma, one of Japan's best fighters and soon to be Olympic gold medalist. The fact that I, a woman, was invited to practice in the main dojo stunned the entire Japanese judo community. This was a first in Kodokan history.

None of this occurred to me to be a big deal at the time. I was just going to train. Besides instruction, we had an abundance of randori. It seemed everyone wanted a piece of me. As we bowed in to each other formally, on our knees, we would say "onegaishimasu," which I understood to mean please help me. In my mind I just added another word before it—*God, please help me*.

It is the philosophy of judo that one learns by one's mistakes. I sure learned a lot at summer training.

Rusty & her Kodokan practice partner, Japan, circa 1962.

30

TRAINING WAS INTENSIFYING DAY BY DAY. THE instructors at the places where I practiced knew I could take it so several of them were investing some good time and techniques on me. At the Kodokan they were told by Saigenji Sensei in his recommendation letter that I was in a unique situation; not only was I a student of judo, but I was also a teacher. They recognized the situation of not having enough instructors in New York as an opportunity for me to carry the skills and traditions of judo home. Therefore, I was able to participate in classes that were reserved for only the highest level of senseis in Japan.

One such class I participated in was a special summer training kata seminar that ran for about ten days, where the big shot senseis from all over the country came to practice together and hone their skills. The ranks of these senseis ranged from fourth-degree to eighth-degree black belt. And there I was: somewhere between a brown and black belt, since I hadn't received any promotion papers as of yet!

I was standing on the mat with the men (let's face it) that were basically the makers of the history of judo at that time. I was amazed at the ages of a lot of the old timers in the class. I'm sure they were amazed at my presence. The teaching senseis were living legends in the sport. It was awesome having the chance to learn at this level. My eighty classmates and I got down to business. I didn't have a problem getting a partner. In fact, I was so popular, I almost needed a dance card. During practice one day, a man started to walk toward my training partner and me. Everything stopped. There was a hush in the huge, half a football field- sized dojo. My partner took a bow down to his ankles, stepped aside and gave me up to this man. He was about five feet, six inches tall, maybe seventy years old, and had the physique of a Mack truck. Without a word, he continued to work on the techniques and forms my partner and I had been working on. The transition was smooth, not a beat missed—almost like I was in the middle of doing a slow methodical technical tango and a new dance partner cut in seamlessly. But this new dance partner was a judo god. I didn't know if this was punishment or reward for me.

I found out later on that my senior citizen samurai was Igarashi Sensei who came down from the mountains up north, by horse, to attend this practice. He had been the 1932 All Japan Judo Champion. In those days, they almost fought to the death. *What an honor!* I was a *made* woman! He decided to be my sponsor, telling one of the women in the women's dojo that he had been watching me, liked my spirit, and wanted to help me. From that point forward, Igarashi Sensei gave me a weekly allotment and paid for my lunch at the Kodokan lunchroom daily. My newfound godfather never asked for anything in return. The significance of this relationship didn't hit me until many years later.

I was so devoted to practice and learning that I hadn't taken a break to see beautiful Japan. One Sunday Dr. Kobayashi and his family were having none of it, and kidnapped me to take me sightseeing. We all stuffed ourselves in his tiny car and went on a trip, visiting temples, and more temples, Buddha's and many great sights. It was overwhelming to see it all in one day. If it weren't for the photos, I would never have remembered any of it. I was so punchy, and out of it, it felt like it was all a dream.

It was good that Dr. Kobayashi had a small car because he must have hit at least one or two people a day. He was a horrible driver. He never really hit them hard, but he did hit them. I was with him on one of these occasions. To my amazement, the guy that he had knocked down got right back up, brushed himself off and apologized for getting in the good doctor's way. In turn, the doctor apologized to him. They kept bowing and bowing until they parted. *What a pleasant way to live. This would NEVER happen in Brooklyn!*

I added to my physical training by going to a local pub with the bad boys of Nichidai college at Nihon University, drinking beer and teaching them the latest American craze, the twist.

One by one we did our gyrations. I was so happy to find that in Japan it was okay for men to dance together; it also got me off the hook a little bit. This judo group from Nihon University was extraordinary and tenacious on the mat, but I could take them on the dance floor.

Rusty posing outside the Kodokan with the other judoka/students, Japan, circa 1962.

31

A FEW CALAMITIES WERE IN STORE FOR ME during my Japan adventure. One has remained still vivid in my mind ever since. I was looking for a bank en route to my judo practice session to cash in an American Express check. As I got off the train at Seidobashi, I went over to the first person I saw, an elderly gentleman, to inquire about a bank.

With my best Japanese, I said, "*ginkō kudasai.*" The grammar was incorrect, but I thought he would easily figure it out. "Please, give me the bank," was what I thought I was saying. The man looked at me in amazement. I thought he was hard of hearing, so I got closer, waved the check, and repeated it, louder this time.

Now he appeared terrified. He started to back away. Still not getting it, I followed. He made a sound like *aaaaye* and ran. This commotion made the police officer that was standing nearby take a look. I once again asked my question, this time louder and slower, as if it were to miraculously translate with the elevated volume. The police officer's eyes met mine and he calmly pointed me in the direction of the bank. I still didn't understand what exactly had just transpired.

That evening when I returned home to the Kobayashi's, I told them about the incident. They became immediately hysterical. I had used the slang word for penis, *chinko*, instead of *ginkō*, the word for bank. I had literally been telling the old gentleman to do me right there and *do it now*. Can you imagine what he must have told his wife? She probably had him committed.

Rusty, wearing the yukata and getas her host family gave her for her birthday—before she fell over, Japan, circa 1962.

Staying low-key was certainly not in the cards for me. I was practicing with another early bird in the women's dojo. She was a strong, tenacious teenager. She had come from a tough, poor neighborhood so I could pretty much relate to her. She wasn't very tall, but Eiko Saito had a strong body.

We played around a bit, sparring. I came in for my favorite throw, *harai-goshi*[8], which means hip sweep. With your back half to three quarters to your opponent, standing on one leg, fully balanced, you proceed to reap your other leg backwards, taking out your opponent's leg. Because of Eiko's great balance and power, I didn't hold back on my attack. As a result, we both went up in the air. She landed, and then I landed on top of her.

Next, I panicked! We were alone, she was only slightly conscious, and I thought she might die. Thinking that a warm compress would be helpful, I ran down to the locker room, grabbed the big teakettle, ran back to the dojo and placed the kettle on her chest. Fortunately, she had on her thick cotton judo uniform or I would have burned her as well. The poor thing was very winded. I had deflated her lungs and left her partially unconscious from the unintended kamikaze throw.

After a rest she was alright. I apologized profusely. Wonderful true judoka that she was, she forgave me. We remained friends; however, we did bow out from sparring together.

My birthday was approaching. This would be the first time in my life that I would be out of the US on this occasion. It's not that it was such a big deal. I did have a little bit of home-sickness set in but it was very quickly eliminated. The Kobayashi's had a birthday party for me with a special dinner and gifts. In fact, it was much better than I ever got in Brooklyn.

After dinner and a few rounds of saki, they insisted that I don my gifts for the camera. I put on the summer kimono—*yukata*—with the obi around my waist; then the high standing platform sandals, called *getas*. I had never worn high heels, let alone these geisha shoes. I posed in my precarious, feminine gear in front of their exquisite wooden and fine silk paper garden door. Then, seconds later, I lost my balance, fell through the closed door taking it with me, and landed in the house on the tatami floor with my kimono over my head, my feet up in the air, and legs wide open. It was a party that none of us would ever forget for the rest of our lives.

32

I WAS GETTING EXACTLY WHAT I CAME TO JAPAN
for: skills, knowledge, and the in-depth study of judo as a sport, tradition, and way of life, though not necessarily in that order.

I felt a transition of sorts taking place every day. When I thought I understood a technique, I tried it. My mind and body were not always ready, so it was easy to get frustrated. It wasn't in my personality to give up. I believed the respect my fellows had for me in Japan wasn't due to my skill, but my perseverance. On some days I got so battered in the main dojo that I couldn't make the stairs to take the train home and I had to blow what little money I had on a taxi. Fortunately there was another famous sensei that seemed to care about me, Mr. Hosokawa. When we left at the same time, which was usually at the end of class, he would offer me a lift in his car. I always gratefully accepted.

Takata Sensei was in charge of the foreign dojo where many men from all over the world took lessons, in addition to their practice in the main dojo. The foreign dojo was primarily for honing one's techniques. I remember meeting Mr. Glahn from Germany, Mr. Anton Geesink from Holland, and Mr. Rogers from Canada.

Takata Sensei was a specialist with the technique of *hane-goshi*[19], a difficult throw accomplished by lifting your opponent on your hip with your leg in a slight bent position, using your leg as a guide. Well, Takata Sensei had the spring of a powerful cat and would literally lift both his body and his opponent's at least a good foot up in the air en route to the completion of the throw. He seemed genuinely pleased that I wanted to study with him.

I don't know for certain if I was the first female he taught or not, but I suspect that I was. He told me I was depending on too much power and had to change my ways. He was going to help me. One of the most important things he did for me was to blindfold me and have me move around with him, attacking with my favorite technique, *harai-goshi*. It was in the same family as his favorite throw, but the leg was placed differently. In mine, the leg was straighter and not turned into a V.

My main focus was trying to get the timing right. Every time I came in wrong, which was most of the time, Takata Sensei would throw me with a technique called *sukui-nage*, which involves grabbing the person between the legs from behind, then lifting and turning them in the air and throwing them from above your head. I cursed myself for being a slow learner, as I was paying the price of these constant flying lessons. If that wasn't bad enough, this guy was plucking me bald, if you know what I mean.

The coffee shop/restaurant at the Kodokan was the unofficial meeting place for us foreign judo players. It was a refreshing break to become undisciplined for a few minutes and clown around only as we non-Japanese could do. It was always good to see the guys and have some laughs. I can't remember what was so funny but maybe it was because we all had come so far to get beat up so often. Aunt Lee, the painter, had what is known as the New York School with all the high and mighty artists coming together to schmooze. I went to a coffee shop.

One of my group's high and mighty was Ben Campbell, now United States Senator Ben Nighthorse Campbell. Ben was an outstanding member of the first US Olympic judo team in 1964. He had practiced quite a bit at Nihon University, especially with a guy by the name of Ryohei

Ryohei was one of the Nichidai guys who sort of caught my eye. He had a presence about him. We nodded at each other in the dojo and enjoyed going out with the group; but there was something more. I couldn't put my finger on it. When I saw him and we nodded at each other, I felt a celebratory spark inside me. He was very good looking, even boyishly handsome and didn't look like a killer, compared to his colleagues. He had a medium frame, was about 170 pounds, and had the speed of a cat. No wonder he managed to beat up the big boys.

Another of our judo group's royalty was Jim Bregman. He was deadpan, super-focused, and trained like a machine. And it all paid off—just a few months later, Jim won us a bronze medal in the first Olympics to include men's judo. It was a long time before the US won another medal for judo at the Olympics.

Hayward Nishioka from California looked more like he belonged at the Kodokan than any of us. He was personable, dedicated and predisposed to be an educator and judo historian, as well as a hell of a judo player.

Don Draegger didn't impress me with his fighting credentials; he was more of a true student of the judo philosophy and of kata forms of judo. Kodokan kata forms are the essence of demonstrating techniques that fall into several categories: throwing, mat work, self-defense and samurai movement. We all wanted to learn some of that good stuff, but not as the majority of our training. But Don was excellent at his calling. He had the respect of all the traditional senseis and was the only foreigner asked to teach at the Kodokan. He went on to author many books on kata.

There were several outstanding people from other countries that would hang with us in our click. Anton Geesink, the huge Dutchman who usually made everyone fly, was a likable chap. He would go on to make history. In 1964, he was the first person to defeat a Japanese at the Olympics. He beat Akio Kaminage, one of Japan's superheroes in judo. Anton became an international hero overnight; his win made the judo fighters realize for the first time that they also had a chance to beat the untouchable Japanese. Anton did it with style and technique, even though some people would like to say it was because of his six foot, six inch height and 285-pound weight. Later, after his competition career was over, Anton became a hardworking member of the International Olympic Committee.

The kid in the group was a reddish-haired, crew cut, feisty youngster from England, Brian Jacks. Early on, after watching him work out, I wondered to myself if his mother knew where he was. He had a baby face, but the heart of a lion. He definitely could handle himself. Brian went on to win at the world championships and became a major role model for British Judo.

I feel so fortunate that I got to meet and know these guys. As big and famous as they got, they always had time for their friend Rusty. There is an amazing thread that ties us all together—we have all played randori with Ryohei Kanokogi and got dumped.

Rusty & Ryohei, January 1964.

33

I WAS RUNNING OUT OF TIME IN JAPAN, SO I overdid my training, trying to get in as much as possible. It got to the point that the shin of my right leg was so swollen that my leg from the knee down was the same size as my thigh. The hospital that I visited indicated that I had big blood clots in my leg, and they wanted to perform surgery. Hell, with the language barrier, I didn't know if they wanted to cut out the clots or cut off the leg. I knew it was only a matter of weeks before I would be back in the States, so I decided to tough it out. My leg got so large and painful that Dr. Kobayashi started applying this gray cooling glop on it and wrapping it tightly with a few rolls of gauze. It seemed to work well enough so I could continue to train.

It was now my daily routine in the morning to first have my instant Nescafe coffee, then my bowl of miso soup and rice with small pieces of fish, get glopped up and then trudge off to the train station. One morning when I got off the train, as I was walking across the platform to get to the down staircase, the people on the train were smiling and laughing as they pointed at me. I was used to being looked at, but not laughed at. Unknown to me, my ten-foot-long gauze bandage had unraveled, and was trailing along behind me like a streamer, held on by the sticky glop. In later years when Gary Smith did a story on me for *Sports Illustrated*[10], he referred to that scene as "Rusty appeared to be the crazed mummy."

Bad leg and all, I still managed to get to the little bar and dance place with my Nichidai friends. One night after practice we went to the bar. It was dark outside and almost as dark inside. It was the custom to have little crunchy snacks on the bar for the customers. I wanted to put something in my stomach before I had a beer because after training, one beer to me was like six. I proceeded to eat the familiar rice cracker munchies, along with some little dried vegetables. Then I spotted the tiny dried fish and packed them away. I wanted to be as Japanese as my friends were. I thought I was eating the same way they did.

Before the owner closed the bar for the evening, she put on the regular lights. My friends looked at my dish in amazement and said, "Ah, so, Americans like to eat fish heads." When I looked at their little dishes, the fish were gone, but there were all the heads left on the plate. All I could do was smile and nod yes and try not to throw up on them.

Toward the end of my training time in Japan, one of Ryohei Kanokogi's close friends asked me to meet with them at the Kodokan coffee shop. I couldn't imagine what the heck for. Turns out his friend's English was better than his own, and he'd wanted a backup for translation. The big meeting was to let me know that Ryohei had been selected to go to Africa, Europe, or the United States to teach— the choice was his.

They had lots of questions for me. I assured them that if he came to New York, I would help him, plus there were already some of his university judo teachers in the area. Ryohei had also been appointed to be on the Japanese Olympic team coaching staff, so he had a lot of decisions to make. I knew he had been working with the Japanese team. He decided to go home for a while and then make up his mind.

One day when he was home in the southern part of Japan in Kumamoto, Kyushu, his father called him to come into the family room. He was watching the news and they were showing this American woman practicing at the Kodokan, telling a good story about her. Ryohei was busy and called back to his father, "It's ok, I already know her." The father then said, "She looks big and strong and can make big babies."

It seems Mr. Toraki Kanokogi was a cupid shooting the first arrow. Soon after that Ryohei made up his mind; he was going to America.

There was so much to do before my trip to Japan was over. I didn't have much money left and I wanted to get gifts for so many people to thank them for their kindness and patience with me. I went to the best department store in Tokyo and bought up their handkerchief department. They were lovely and not expensive, but the salesgirl wrapped each one like it was a rare and luxurious jewel.

I was invited out to dinner quite a bit now since folks knew I was nearing the end of my stay. One of Saigeni Sensei's friends, Mr. Wada invited me to dinner and shopping for my farewell gift. This was going to be a doubleheader.

First, we went to a fabulous private restaurant that I could have sworn was a geisha house, if I'd known what one looked like. Dinner was delicious, and after we went to the department store, the same fancy one where I had bought the hankies. Mr. Wada led me directly to the jewelry department, had the salesgirl show me some trays of exquisite pearl rings, and told me to pick one. I couldn't believe it. *What a wonderful surprise!*

I picked a knockout. Then, Mr. Wada placed it on my left-hand ring finger. I didn't know what it cost—I sort of looked away when he paid—but I knew it was gold with a pearl.

Mr. Wada also insisted on getting my child a gift. I picked something that I thought Chris would like: a large kabuki mask made from paper mâché, in the form of Tengu. It was red with a long nose and scary eyes.

After our evening out, Mr. Wada dropped me off at my home. We bowed at least fifty times, as I was thanking him so very much. His English was pretty bad, so I just kept saying, *hai, hai*, meaning *yes, yes,* and nodding my head just to be polite.

As he was going off into the night, a lightbulb went off in my head.

Holy shit, did I just get engaged to a sixty-year-old, five-foot, two-inch, 120-pound non-judo player?, I thought to myself.

Worse than that, I forgot to give him his gift—a beautifully wrapped handkerchief.

34

TIME WAS MOVING VERY QUICKLY NOW. IN A way, I was glad because I wanted to get home to see Chris and give him his wonderful gifts. I wanted to see my students and begin to share all that I had learned, especially the philosophy. I wanted to see my family. I never really got homesick while in Japan; I just missed Chris and Nathan's hotdogs. The wannabe hot dogs in Tokyo were white and mushy tasting.

There was so much to do. I had been invited to go to Osaka with the little superstar Masako Chinin, her friend Habu san, and their legendary sensei, Mr. Hamano. They invited me for a weekend of training at their dojo, the New Japan Dojo. When they left the Kodokan after a special training session, I went back with them. Hamano Sensei was a ninth-degree black belt, so it was a thrill to be traveling and training with him and the young women.

Ninth-degree was so high up in the clouds it was almost impossible to get in Japan at that time, unless you died. Of course, nowadays the ranking system has been greatly prostituted in the United States, so it's no surprise that some people are walking around with their John's Bargain Store rank, even a ninth-degree black belt. The stringent requirements to achieve high ranks seems to have gotten lost in translation somewhere between integrity and money.

The training in Osaka was fun and I got to see a few more castles and drink beer on rooftop gardens. My friends put me on the train back to Tokyo, and as I said my *sayonaras* both my little buddy Chinin-san and I were weeping, the two big bad wolves of women's judo.

The following day there was to be a reception for all the senseis that attended the summer training at the Kodokan. I felt bad that Hamano Sensei had to leave and couldn't be with us. The party was to be in the private dining room upstairs where only the big shots were allowed. When I was invited, I knew it was going to be special, and indeed it was.

I understood very little of President Risei Kano's opening remarks, but I did recognize my name. The fact that my classmates, all men, were looking at me, smiling, and saying, "Ah, sou desu ka," meaning yes, that is so, led me to believe whatever they were saying was positive.

Before President Kano concluded, I was invited up to the dais. He gave me a lovely gift. It was a wooden box with his name and mine on it. I knew it was impolite in Japan to open a gift in front of the presenter so I knew I would have to wait until later. I thanked him and was so happy not just for the gift but for the generosity; here I was, the lowest ranking person in the room, and I was the only one that received a gift.

Dah!

It was my goodbye present.

After a few more speeches, the head sensei of the women's dojo announced that I was taking my promotion test for second-degree black belt the following day.

Holy mackerel, Andy!

This was turning into the best party I had ever attended. Lunch was served and the beer was flowing. Custom has it that no one's glass should ever be empty, so just as soon as I took a sip, it was filled up again. Of course, I walked around the room and reciprocated. We were all getting pretty happy, singing and toasting each other with '*kanpai*'—the Japanese equivalent of 'cheers!'—and even getting a few '*banzai!*'s in, a battle cry that literally translates to "to live a thousand years" and is used as a blessing.

35

WHEN MY JAPANESE JUDO FRIENDS DRANK alcohol, they tended to turn very red. Most of them looked like Tengu, the red-faced kabuki mask, but a few of them thought they were real lady's men. I managed to fend them off with a gesture or joke even though they didn't understand. I laughed, they laughed. I couldn't use judo on any of these guys; they were the masters! *What the hell?* If I'd really needed it, my Brooklyn street defense would have kicked in, but I never did. It was only some good-natured fun; A pleasant time was had by all.

I had to get home and get mentally ready for my promotion exam. I was floored when I saw President Kano come to the dojo where the exam was going to take place. I had never seen a chair placed on the mat before. They put one down for the president to sit on as he was going to watch my exam. Just what I needed! I was nervous enough.

I had to demonstrate three different katas, do a lot of ukemi, and then play randori with a few of the other women. The kata part was tough, as they all were so good. I wanted to shine. Even though I trained a lot with the men, they had me fight women. I had no complaints; I had enough to do.

I was informed I had passed my test and now was a second-degree black belt.

What a thrill!

Later I opened my gift from Mr. Kano. It was a beautiful silk *furoshiki*, similar to a scarf, a golden-brown color with blue cranes on it. His name and mine were in the texture of the silk. It was absolutely gorgeous. I knew I would cherish it forever and I have.

The goodbyes to my Japanese family, the Kobayashis, and my friends were difficult. I truly loved them all. The kindness, respect and education I received in one summer seemed to make up for all the past neglect, cruelty and lack of love that seemed to be a part of my life before judo. I felt so fortunate because of the insight I got into another culture, and the philosophy of this beautiful martial art I had found. It continued to change my life and I knew in my heart I would go on to give back for this wonderful deed that was done for me.

I needed almost two cars to go to the airport, one for me and my luggage, and one for the more than eighty gifts I had received. A whole crowd of my judo friends came to the airport to see me off. I was so damned impressed. *My god!* They made me feel so good.

Ryohei Kanokogi was there too. He handed me a slim box that I put in my purse. I would open it on the plane. We waved and bowed and cried and suddenly I was in my seat en route to Hawaii. Thank goodness the flight crew allowed my ton of gifts on the plane and helped me bring them on.

After we took off, I opened Ryohei's gift. It was a lovely purple and white flowered fan with a stunning note in broken English. He said he wanted to be friends forever, and that he would never forget me.

Yippee!

I felt the same way. I hoped he would choose to come to New York.

It didn't seem long before the plane landed in Hawaii and the sweet aroma of the pineapples was being inhaled by all. It was hot in Japan but the heat in Hawaii was pressing. Fortunately, the ocean breeze, even at the airport, was a great neutralizer.

A gentleman that had been at the Kodokan, who I occasionally practiced some kata with, was also traveling back to the States. His name was Wakabayashi. He was a professor at some university out West.

What a guy!

His name should have been Professor Klutso. When I had practiced the forms of *Nage-no-Kata* with him at the Kodokan, it had been a disaster. One of the techniques required me to pull him three steps forward, drop down on my knee continuing the pull, and off-balancing him to the point of making a successful throw. His part of the technique was to fall on the other side of me. However, instead of going past me, he dove straight toward me and caught my nose with his knee. I heard a crack and felt the warm flow of blood, which flowed like water from my already unglamorous nose. The mats were a mess. My judogi was saturated with my red American blood while Professor Klutso just stood there saying, "Ah, ah, ah."

I was cleaned up and helped to clean the mats. I came out of it with a break on the right side of my nose that left me with a deviated septum and the snore of a dragon.

A mutual judo friend picked us up at the airport in Hawaii, as we were both staying overnight. Our friend, Irwin Kawano dropped us at an inexpensive hotel, waited as we got squared away and proceeded to take us sightseeing. *Never a dull moment!* We parked the car and walked over to this wonderful sight of a waterfall flowing upside down. It was magnificent and completely had our attention.

As we were walking back to the car, we saw a guy reaching into the passenger- side window, where I had been sitting ten minutes before. He had my handbag, which I had foolishly left in the car with the window open. When I saw him with my purse, I yelled, and he jumped into his car with my bag. I only had a few bucks in it, but it also contained my passport and plane tickets.

I pursued him but he hit me with his car door on his escape. We jumped into Irwin's car in pursuit. Both of us actually picked up Klutso and threw him in the back. He was nervous; I don't think he could harm a fly unless it was by accident. Irwin, being a tough Hawaiian kid and a good judo player, drove like a maniac. We caught the crook, cut him off, dragged him out of his jalopy and beat the crap out of him. He said he couldn't help it because he was a junkie. Hopefully, we were part of his cure.

With the bag secured, we took off, almost forgetting the professor who wasn't part of the action. He did, however, encourage us with his words. "Ah, ah, ah."

Thank goodness I would be on my way to Brooklyn the next day.

36

THE FINAL LEG OF MY JOURNEY WAS HERE; BACK to New York via California and back to my phony plane ticket. I was much more honorable now, so cheating wasn't easy, like it had been on the way to Japan several months before. I had changed.

I tried to inhale the sweet smell of pineapples and gardenias before I boarded the plane in Hawaii because I didn't know if I would ever have a chance to return. It was a bittersweet feeling. I was getting further away from Japan and, now, leaving the Land of Oz.

Chris and I were so happy to see each other. I had kept him in postcards from Japan, but when I got back he wanted all the stories and his gifts. What a big boy he was for a seven-year-old. He seemed to have grown up a lot over the summer. He didn't have any hard feelings or resentment toward me for my several-month-long trip to the orient—not openly, anyway. He knew it wasn't a vacation and that I was going to study hard and get better jobs teaching because of it.

The public relations guy from the Prospect Park YMCA sent out a press release regarding my adventure and returning with a second-degree black belt. It wasn't long before the press got in touch, and there was story after story, including photos.

They treated me like some kind of hero. Chris was in the photos with me, so the headlines read: "Mother Defeats Japanese and Brings Black Belt Back to Her Son."

Oy vey, the press!

The extra press packed my classes at the Y, plus some colleges and private schools contacted me as a result. I assumed they were probably thinking in terms of self-defense. *So what?* I thought. *Get them going and they will love judo the way I do.*

I was most looking forward to getting back to my down and dirty class at the Y. It was 1963, and I was a whole new me.

I lined all my students up, male and female alike. I went through the line, cooperatively sparring with all of them one by one, almost without breaking a sweat. I was fast, clean and in superb condition. Too bad we didn't have the Olympics for women's judo yet. I felt there was a gold medal out there with my name on it. Men's judo had not yet made it to the Olympics either; however, it was on the schedule for 1964 as an exhibition event. Before his demise, Professor Jigoro Kano had convinced the International Olympic Committee to have judo's first entry be in the Olympic Games that were to be held in Tokyo. I even mentioned to my students that my friend Ryohei Kanokogi was one of the Olympic coaching staff in Japan, and there was a slim chance he might be coming to New York after the Games.

The students were very impressed with the techniques I brought back from Japan, and they would work hard to master them and be better competitors. I let them know that while their progress was good, much more than winning would now be expected from them. It was good to be home.

The Prospect Park YMCA public relations director did a good job promoting my voyage, training and return. Something about judo or me was in the press every few weeks. The coed classes at the Y were packed. Other places were getting in touch with me, offering me teaching jobs. I was a quasi-celebrity of sorts and that always attracted schools.

I was hired by Pratt Institute's physical education department as a judo instructor. My boss, Wayne Sutherland, was the athletic director. I was really happy about this job, and it was during the day when Chris was in school that I could be a college teacher.

Aunt Lee looked at judo with different eyes now and so did my mother. Pratt Institute was a world-renowned art school, as well as engineering and architecture. This was big league for me.

It was still unusual to have a woman teach men anything physical at that time, let alone judo, so I knew I would have to impress my class of twenty male students with something. After a few weeks of having them learn falls, throws, and pins, I lined them up and we played randori. This was impression time!

I threw them, pinned and choked them and generally made a point to dispel any reservations they had about me doing the walk and not only the talk. After that session, it was full steam ahead. I had to make them good to prove I was good. I'd always had a need to prove myself.

The students were a mixed bag. The guys were from all over the United States and sometimes a foreign-country or two. In most academic institutions the students of the same major hang together, but this wasn't true in judo. The clean- cut engineering students became best buddies with the longhaired artists and so on. They practiced four times a week. Once in a while, I would have some Prospect Park Y students come down and work out with the Pratt class to accelerate their learning. The Newark School of Engineering had a judo team and wanted to compete with us. I knew that their instructor was a famous Japanese judo guy and figured this was going to be a major challenge. I didn't have to think twice about it. I told the Pratt team that I would select the best students who were practicing judo with me. Competition was in one week. They had never competed before except against each other in class and with me so they were a little apprehensive, though they didn't show it too much.

We worked on the brain first. I had convinced them the Newark boys were coming to kill them. Instead of getting scared, they were getting mad. I had to take away the anger as it would make them too tense, and screw up their judo attacks. The final preparation was to compete. I told them to go in, with a cool head, then we went over the rules, and some strategy.

The competition was held at the Prospect Park Y on a Saturday afternoon right after my regular class. In walked the captain of the Newark team with his strong looking, well-groomed competitors. They all wore blue blazers, gray trousers, white shirts and striped ties. He asked where the locker room was, so I sent someone along to assist them.

My grungy group showed up at about the same time. I could hear some laughter from the Newark "hit men," as I called them, as they passed my longhaired, unkempt, mangy-looking team from Pratt. I noticed Newark's instructor was not with them. I figured he would show up later but he never did, which was a break; a little less pressure on everyone.

The teams were in their judo uniforms now, warming up and getting ready for World War III. When they lined up against each other for the team competition, I noticed Pratt was short a man. In the excitement of the day, I hadn't noticed it before. This would be an automatic win for Newark.

The students from the class at the Y were sticking around to watch the competition and cheer for their brother team. My student Kenny Pollard, twelve or thirteen years old at the time, volunteered himself to fill in. I checked it out with the Newark captain. He agreed and snickered as he walked away. I told Kenny to just pull a draw, and not lose a point. He was a strong kid, but he was going up against a man.

Kenny wasn't playing with a full deck, but I knew he would do his best. The other team wasn't concerned in the least about him. Actually, I don't think they were concerned about any member of our team, especially because they had a woman instructor.

Crash! Bam! Slam!

Yea, yea, and *hooray, we won!*

As it happened, Kenny threw his opponent for a full point. You would have thought it was the Olympics. Everyone shook hands after bowing out. Newark went down to the locker room to put on their fine school uniforms and left Brooklyn with their tails between their legs.

The following week there was a big story in the newspaper regarding the competition. The headlines read: "Brooklyn Woman Defeats Japanese Judo Instructor." The Newark instructor didn't speak to me for years.

Hey, I didn't write the story!

Life was good. Chris was in Lutheran Elementary School, doing well. I was teaching all over the place, building my reputation as a teacher, making some money and encouraging both judo and my students.

Kenny and I got closer every day and I knew he was going to be a challenge for me to help, both in life and judo—he was an angry kid, who'd been tossed on meds and neglected by those around him. I took him on as a student and felt a fondness for him as if he were another son to me.

Kenny's story is forthcoming, and it will make you laugh and cry, just like it did to me.

37

HAVING BEEN BORN AND RAISED IN CONEY Island probably gave me a sense of acceptance of unusual people. My basic prejudices were not the run of the mill. It seemed that the only time I had zero tolerance was when the person was afraid to try—not only in judo, but also in everyday life. I had very little tolerance for those that I considered weak because they wouldn't try.

There was a leftover feeling of World War II in my head. It fluctuated between disgust, impotence, and anger. Watching all the news as a child at the movie theaters and seeing the Jews going to the slaughter without a fight left a great scar on my heart. I was a Jew, and this was never going to happen to me! I would fight to the death and take some of them with me. *I'd be tough!*

It hardened me. I became tough.

I was tough and it got me in trouble as a teenager. For so many years I didn't understand it, and used this immature philosophy to guide me. Through judo, though, I grew out of this stunted tough girl exterior and I continued to grow as a human being, and even more, I grew into an empowered, tough woman. My tolerance levels increased as I met the needs of my students who required direction, encouragement and, in some cases, love, to grow. In Kenny Pollard's case, a little direction and encouragement was the will he needed to survive.

I had met Kenny a couple of years before, when he and at least another dozen kids came to the Prospect Park Y to have a free trial lesson in judo. He was pretty big for an eleven-year-old.

I invited the group on the mat after the scheduled class was over. Kenny had on shorts and a big Mickey Mouse shirt. The fellows followed along with the exercises, did some falling practice, and learned a throw. Most of them were excited and wanted to come back to join the class. Their parents were present, and it was a good feeling all the way around.

We were just about to bow off the mat when a voice called out from the line on the mat. "I can beat you anytime," it said.

We all looked towards the mouth of Kenny. *I'll teach that big mouth kid a thing or two*, I thought.

"Hey, you, Mickey Mouse. Get out here," I said.

He came to the center of the mat, no bow, just proceeded to jump me from the front, screaming like a banshee. Hell, this was now self-defense! I handled him, threw him down on the mat—not too hard—but he kept getting up and rushing at me again and again. I increased the velocity and force until he ran out of steam and finally quietly got back in line to join in the bowing out ritual.

The parents who were standing around were dumbfounded by this whole deal. I thought they would run away and I would never see them or their children again. Didn't happen! They were impressed and signed up their children for the course. One parent said that what impressed him was not the judo, but my cool head. I'd been pissed off at this kid, but had concealed it rather nicely.

Everyone left, including the big-time bomb.

Thank goodness, I thought, *I never want to see that knucklehead again.*

The new class began the following Saturday. First, I had the advanced class and then the beginners.

Oh, God!

There he was, that wacko kid. He had joined the class. I checked the paperwork five times but no matter how many times I looked, he was still registered.

Oh well.. Here we go!

I lined them up and explained the bowing ritual; It was not a religion but rather a display of mutual respect and a way of greeting each other, as well as a clearing of the mind for the start of judo practice. All the while my senses were on high alert.

I was expecting an attack from Ken at any moment. I didn't even want to look at him, concerned that I might incite him. Finally, I did look directly at him, planning to go through some more explanations. We caught each other's eyes. Kenny's were smiling and full of respect.

This threw me mentally off balance for a moment. What the heck was going on here?

During class Ken worked so hard, more than the others did. He hung on my every word. After the final bow, we proceeded to put the mats away. Everyone helped; it was part of the training. Ken was nowhere in sight. I asked one of the kids where he had gone. I was told he went out to the water fountain for a drink. There he was breaking the rules already; everyone was supposed to wait for a drink until the mats were put away.

I went out to scold him and saw that he was trying to take the lid off a large bottle of pills. I asked him what the pills were for and he said that he had to take them a few times a day. They made him sleepy so he hadn't wanted to take them before class. I asked him what the pills were for and he said were to keep him from fighting with anyone, and to make him sleep a lot.

My instinct told me to dump these pills and become Kenny's cure for whatever they were doing to this kid. That was the last pill Kenny ever had to take for his behavior modification. Right or wrong, I knew this kid needed a lot of help, but it shouldn't come out of a bottle. He needed a firm hand, a role model and a monitor. As I got to know him better I made up my mind: he was going to succeed, no matter what. As I seemed to be the only adult in his life to show him that cared about him, he told me about some of the horrors he had been through. It's amazing what people do to their own children.

I loved Kenny and he became my faithful judo sidekick and an incredible human being, never leaving my side. He babysat for Chris, who tormented him the way kids with a brotherly bond do, and when I had my younger kids, he became their protectors too—and one of my most loyal captains in my crusade for women's judo.

Many years later, after Kenny had moved to Florida and was in the hospital on his deathbed, he told us he was holding on until Ryohei and I got there. When we arrived at the hospital, his last words were, "I waited for you, Sensei." I miss him.

Early 1980s: Rusty, Kenny and Ryohei.

38

WHEN I WAS STUDYING AT THE KODOKAN IN Japan, I knew Ryohei Kanokogi had his choice of where to teach. Not long after my return to the States, he was on his way to New York. As we were just friends, I can't honestly say I had palpitations, but I was looking forward to learning more judo from him.

After he arrived and began working and settled in, I got in touch with him and let him know I would take him sightseeing when he was ready to go. He called and I borrowed a friend's big, old Plymouth convertible and took Ryohei out on the town. He was even better looking than I remembered. We had a great time, went to dinner and hit it off really well as we rekindled our friendship.

As most of the Japanese instructors were here on two-year teaching visas, some went home when their contracts expired. A few changed their status and opened their own judo clubs. As Mackey had a clause that wouldn't allow them to open a club within a fifty-mile radius of New York City, several of them opened up shop in New Jersey and Long Island after they finished their contracts with Mackey. Judo really took off in New York and the East Coast because we had the crème de la crème teaching all over the place.

Ryohei and I would see each other at competitions. I had a good team of kids and adults at the Prospect Park Y. Some of my college boys were working out with us a lot so they had strong practices and were doing well in competitions, which got Ryohei's attention. After all, I was a female judo teacher whose students were regularly beating his and other male instructors' students. *very interesting*, Ryohei later told me he thought, *I want to know more about her.*

Ryohei teaching at Jerome Mackey's, circa 1963.

As aggressive as I usually was, I was a little shy around him. Was it the beginning of love? He taught six days a week. I did the same and attended tournaments on Sundays. It was the basic judo life. We didn't have much time to date. Since I had been totally separated from my former spouse for quite some time, I knew I had to get a divorce and officially end the marriage. The only way I could get the money was to work around the clock. I would have to take on a night job also.

It was around this time that Kenny began to become a great source of help to me. As we got closer, he told me about some of the atrocities that happened to him as a very young child. His father used to put his head in the toilet and hold it there in the water to punish him. After a while his parents put him in a mental institution for children, where he was constantly sexually abused by the male nurse's aides. He was always treated as a bad child instead of a child with a mental disorder. The poor kid must have gone through hell and back. I would never let anything bad happen to him again. I believe in helping people as long as they try to help themselves.

As a teenager, Kenny worked for me. He helped me clean the apartment, went to the store for me, and stayed with Chris on occasion. I, in turn, let him participate in any class that I taught providing it didn't interfere with school, helped him with his homework, fed him, and took him to tournaments, movies, or anyplace I took Chris. It all felt so natural.

Kenny's mother was a hypochondriac and resented me most, I suspect, because I took her slave away from her. He lived at home with her, did basic chores, but got away as much as he could. His two older brothers were useless and left home at an early age. The father split on all of them and finally in later years, his sister came to be saved also. She was a nice girl with a good heart. Her judo skills were limited although she tried hard. She wasn't Kenny.

Proudly, Kenny became the youngest competitor in New York to compete and earn his first-degree black belt in the men's division at the age of 15. He went on to win first place in the high school national championships and became the alternate athlete to represent the United States in the Pan American Games.

Did he drive me crazy? You bet. One time I was coaching at a competition in the city. The place was so packed that it took ten minutes to find my shoes after coming off the mat and another ten minutes to go up to the telephone upstairs. Kenny was watching Chris for me that afternoon. I gave him the telephone number to call me only in the event of an emergency. A call came and I became frantic.

I turned the twenty minutes into twenty seconds.

Winded and scared I asked what was wrong. Kenny replied that Chris's baby turtle was having trouble breathing so he had to take it out of the box, massage it, and pump its heart. At that point, the turtle's eyeballs popped out and it died. Chris was so mad that he wouldn't stop hitting Kenny and he wanted to know what he should do. I was fuming and my first response was to tell him to jump out of the fucking window. Then I hung up. As I started to walk away I realized what I had just said and called back immediately because Kenny usually did everything I told him to do. I began to have zombie-like symptoms due to getting very little sleep. I worked a night job in Bushwick, one of the hellholes of Brooklyn, as a lone telephone operator on a busy switchboard. One of the clients was an ambulance service. I always wondered if I fell asleep on the job, how many people would die

Ryohei & Jerome Mackey, circa 1963.

waiting for the ambulance? But I earned enough to get to Alabama and get my divorce. I made arrangements with a New York lawyer who contacted his colleague in Montgomery, Alabama and I was on my way.

39

MOST OF MY KNOWLEDGE OF THE SOUTH CAME from the movie *Song of the South* with Uncle Remus, Br'er Rabbit, Br'er Bear and Br'er Fox; and my impression was confirmed when I took a taxi from the airport to a small hotel in Montgomery, Alabama. The driver asked so many questions— what was the purpose of my trip? Was I visiting family or was I there on business? I felt I was being interrogated by a Klansman.

"Divorce," I said, honest and direct. That in itself put me in the shady area of his mind. Can you imagine if he knew I was divorcing a white boy with a drinking problem, and pursuing a relationship with a Japanese foreign national judo player? He might accuse me of snagging an enemy of the United States for marriage. So I kept that tidbit to myself.

The lawyer told me I would have to stay in Alabama for a few weeks while this divorce was processed. I looked up a YMCA that had judo and went to work out to keep busy and pass the time. I had my judo uniform with me—I never traveled without it because the opportunity to work out might arise.

There was only one guy working out by himself, doing form practice, reviewing his throws against the air. It was sort of like shadow boxing. I introduced myself. His name was something like O'Riley. He said he was in the military and was home on leave. He wanted to practice but no one showed up during the day, just he and I.

After warming up and doing some cooperative form practice, we agreed to do randori. During form practice, my Coney Island con mind kicked in and I only went in with half power so he would think I was weak. When we started to move around in randori, I opened up. He was surprised.

Well, that was the idea!

I threw him one after the other. He caught me once or twice too. What I liked about him was he didn't get pissed off. He seemed to enjoy the practice, including the surprise.

When we both had had enough, we bowed out and shook hands. He was gracious enough to buy me a Coke. We said goodbye and went our merry ways. I liked this guy. He had a lot of freckles, much more than I, and he wasn't a mean competitor. He was fast, strong and handled himself with good judo spirit, better than I did before my pilgrimage to Japan and the judo philosophy awakening it brought about.

The next time I bumped into O'Riley was at the United States Military Academy at West Point where I was coaching my team from Pratt at the Eastern Collegiate Championships. We recognized each other immediately. All I knew him by was his last name, but we stood and talked for a long time. All the nearby cadets stood at attention, as this full bird colonel and I took a walk down memory lane.

I had a few lasting impressions of Alabama. One was drinking bourbon for the first time and another was beating up some military brass. However, the saddest memory was when I was sitting at the counter on a stool at some local diner having breakfast while a black woman who was obviously the cleaning lady carried a big trash can outside for the rubbish collection. No one paid her any mind.

As she passed me, I could hear her sigh with the struggle of lifting something heavy. She approached the door but couldn't open it, as that would have meant putting the heavy can down and then trying to lift it again. I jumped from my stool and went to open the door for her. She gave me a suspicious look as she passed by with her burden and didn't utter a word. Although there were at least twenty men in the diner, no one bothered themselves to help her—not Br'er Rabbit, nor Br'er Bear, nor Br'er Fox.

I sat down to finish my breakfast and heard the nasty words coming down the counter directed towards me.

"Hell, why don't that Yankee go back where she comes from? Nigger lover."

I wanted to strike out at them both physically and verbally, but I knew it was going to be a lose-lose situation. George Wallace was their governor at that time, in 1963. I could have gotten hanged.

I made believe that I hadn't heard the remarks, paid the tab, and eased out of the diner, checking my back.

Then my big mouth got the best of me and I let them have it, preparing to run back to the hotel.

"The war is over; dummies and we won!" I shouted at them all as I raised my middle finger.

After that, I stayed close to my room until I got the call to pick up my long-awaited declaration of independence. Then I took a cab, got the documents and headed straight to the airport.

Free at last. Free at last.

40

ZIP-A-DEE-DOO-DAH, ZIP-A-DEE-AY!

Now I would be able to get on with my life, whatever that would be. Being officially free, however, did not escalate the dating between Ryohei and me. We had a few problems. There was a bit of a language barrier, a cultural interaction, and the fact that his friends and other Japanese judo instructors would constantly remind him that I was a divorcee with a child. Why *on earth* would he want to get involved with someone *like that*?

I guess the fact that I was a judo competitor and an instructor whose students often won against their students had nothing to do with it.

Yeah, sure!

The additional pressure against this romance was that Ryohei only planned to be in New York for the length of his contract with Mackey, which was two to three years at most. Also, his family In Japan had made a tentative marriage agreement with the Mitsumoto family for Ryohei and their daughter. Ryohei was somewhat traditional and would have honored the pledge, were it not for the lure of becoming a judo champion in America.

I wasn't promised to anyone, nor in a major hurry to make another commitment. My only responsibility was to Chris and my mother. Being one of the only women in a predominately male sport did put me in a big candy box, but I was immersed in working out and training others.

Ryohei and I dated. I knew things were changing because I was easily annoyed when I thought someone was hitting on him. That didn't last long though; I could be a major force to reckon with and any girl with even half a brain didn't want any part of me.

As time went on, I felt that I was the one pushing the relationship. Then there was a turn of events. When I walked away and was ready to dump the whole idea about us being a twosome, he started pursuing me. I guess the game is played the same way despite cultural differences.

Chris and I were sharing an apartment with Kathy, a woman who was dating one of the other Japanese judo teachers, Mr. Ito.

We shared expenses and housework. Kenny helped out so the place was immaculate. Her boyfriend Ito would come over and bring Kanokogi with him.

Everything was going well until Ito told Kathy he was leaving for Japan, as his contract was up and he wanted to go home. He did not ask her to get married, or wait for him, or come to Japan. She was devastated.

This was a wakeup call for me. I wasn't going to let the same thing happen between Ryohei and me. I was no Kathy!

The apartment the judo instructors shared on Riverside Drive in Manhattan would be raising the rent sky-high and several of the guys were going back to Japan or moving to another neighborhood, so Ryohei and I decided he should move in with us.

Chris and Ryohei got along really well. Ryohei had an easygoing personality. He always had a smile and found time to play with Chris. I was falling hook, line, and sinker. Still, it was hard to know if the feelings were mutual because the Japanese are very conservative with their emotions. It's a throwback from the old days of the samurai.

One day Ryohei came home to our humble Brooklyn apartment, walked in, called me over to him, and opened his hand to show me what he had found on the train. It was a modest, but exquisite diamond engagement ring, exactly my size. Of course, he didn't actually find it on the train—he'd gone out and bought it, but true to his nature, he downplayed that part of the story. He'd always been more understated, the inverse to my overtly stated.

He put the ring on my finger. I looked at him and said, "Does this mean we are engaged?"

"Don't talk about it," he said. I presumed that meant yes.

Zip-a-dee-doo-dah, zip-a-dee-ay! Wonderful feeling, wonderful day!

41

WE HAD OUR BASIC ROUTINE GOING ON IN January of 1964, teaching judo, coaching judo, and speaking, living and breathing judo. Then a new word was entered into our conversation: marriage. Ryohei thought it was time.

First, he would have to shock his family and friends with the news. There wasn't much of a problem with my family because they really didn't care too much about what I did as long as I didn't go to jail. But there was another little problem: Ryohei's visa was going to expire.

Jerome Mackey wanted him to continue teaching because not only did he have excellent judo skills, but also his students loved him for his kindness and caring personality. No one wanted him to leave, especially Chris and me. But Mackey was limited in what he could do; he didn't want to hinder his agreement with immigration. So, it became my responsibility.

I dug into my mental filing cabinet to see whom I knew. At that time, the United States had a quota on how many Japanese could be in the country at one time and they were very strict. I knew I would need a federal friend.

A few years before, I had made friends with a man by the name of Rene Varley. I don't even remember who introduced us or why. His mother was some kind of countess. He worked for a large real estate firm and wrote children's books. I may have given him some private judo lessons.

One day Rene contacted me and asked if I would give his friend some lessons. I agreed. He gave me the name of someone who I didn't know but the address was on Park Avenue. That did mean something to me. I called first, set up the appointment and then proceeded to my new private lesson. The apartment was fancy. The man who greeted me at the door was my new student, an obviously wealthy man by the name of Fred.

He was very gracious and offered me a drink and food such as pate, crab, and beluga caviar. He then opened this shiny, exquisite box with about a half pound of marijuana in it. I thanked him but refused all of it. I didn't even want a drink of water at this point. I thought to myself that I might have to fight my way out of there.

Fred was a big guy. Unknown to me, however, was Fred's kinky obsession: he got his rocks off by being dominated by women.

Shit!

What had I gotten myself into this time?

I kept my cool and showed him a few throws. I absolutely insisted he keep his clothes on when he indicated he was warm and wanted to take them off.

When the hour was up, I told him I had to go. He wanted to know when I could give him another lesson, maybe something more advanced. I said I would call him.

Right!

He gave me a crisp new hundred-dollar bill. I was really excited, but I didn't dare show it. I knew I wasn't going to return to this place.

I called Rene and told him what had happened. He laughed but didn't seem surprised. I was far from devastated but told him he owed me one—a *big* one. I wanted to meet his friend United States Senator Jacob Javits.

Rene made the arrangements. It all fell into place, so we set the date for the wedding and through some Japanese connections, we were able to have our reception at the prestigious Nippon Club in Manhattan.

Rusty & Ryohei, Brooklyn, 1965.

42

PREPARATION FOR THE WEDDING WAS NOT too big a hassle. The most important thing was to make sure we had our classes covered so the students wouldn't have to miss a practice session. The date was set: November 29, 1964.

We signed the agreement with the Nippon Club for our reception and met with the Buddhist priest, went to City Hall and got our license. We made our guest list and sent out the invitations to the families here and in Japan, to Senator Javits, and most of the judo community. The best man was Mr. Kiyoshi Shiina and the bridesmaid was one of my students, selected so she would look good next to Mr. Shiina.

My mother was excited. She liked Rychei. Chris was happy.

Aunt Lee wanted to buy my mom her dress-up clothes and accessories for the big day. She told us to shop and give her the bill. I don't ever remember my mom in anything else but a housedress or some other *shmata* she had adorned. This was going to be fun.

Mom and I went to the best department store and selected a lovely taffeta skirt and jacket with a satin blouse. We got her shoes wide enough to accommodate her huge bunions and a petite beaded handbag to finish off the outfit. My light blue gown was in the works at a local bridal shop.

Getting shoes for my large hooves was a real challenge. I ended up getting men's ballet shoes in white and having them dyed the same color as my *Cinderella* gown, it would be the first gown of my life.

The big day was upon us. I don't recall how we got to the Buddhist temple in uptown Manhattan. The place was packed. Ryohei and Mr. Shiina, along with my bridesmaid, were standing in the front of the room near the reverend in the formal area.

Rusty & Ryohei's traditional wedding ceremony, November 29, 1964

Reverend Seki had on the traditional garb of a fancy Buddhist priest. It was orange brocade, interwoven with gold in a lovely Japanese design. He had a dark headdress on that I had seen in samurai movies. He looked better than I did!

My brother had on a dark suit and the groom and best man wore tuxedos. The entire ceremony was in Japanese. I didn't understand one word of the Shinto ceremony. The reverend might have been talking about the history of Japan for all I knew.

While the ceremony was going on, there was a huge urn with lots of incense smoldering. The smoke rose out of it with a strange but not unpleasant smell. I was a little lightheaded. I didn't know if it was the excitement of the moment or some leftover opium in the urn.

Then it was onward to the Nippon Club. There weren't many Japanese restaurants in New York in 1964. At our wedding, sushi was in big demand by the judo community, so much so that our waiters could not even get the trays to our tables before our aggressive judo pals, who had stationed themselves at the swinging doors to the banquet hall, emptied them within two feet of the kitchen exit.

The booze was flowing and people were having a good time. When they brought the cake out, I invited my mom to help Ryohei and me to cut the first piece. She did, but her pretty beaded handbag locked onto her wrist and proceeded to swing directly into the cake and got full of icing. I would not have expected anything less. We had a good laugh and ate it anyway.

Finally, we were back in our simple railroad apartment in Brooklyn. We changed our clothes immediately and sat on the bed and looked at our gift bag with the envelopes to see what a killing we had made. Chris helped us. We then read the telegrams from Senator Javits who could not attend but wished us well, and from the president of the Kodokan, Reisi Kano, giving us his blessing also.

We were so hungry because we hadn't had a chance to eat even one morsel of sushi or anything else at the reception. We decided to go to the local diner and have a celebration meal. We both ordered steak. Chris had a hamburger. We will probably never forget this meal. The steak was as hard as the shoe Charlie Chaplin tried to eat in one of his classic films. We gave up, went home and got to sleep—we both had to be back on the mat the next day.

I was now Rena "Rusty" Glickman Stewart Kanokogi. What a hell of a road I had traveled!

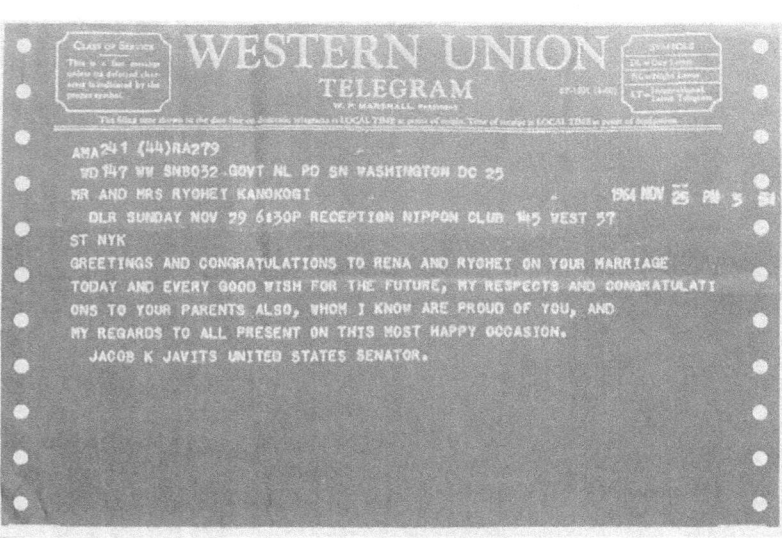

43

WE SETTLED INTO OUR ROUTINE AS A FAMILY. WE taught our classes, went out to dinner, had folks over for a meal now and then, helped Chris with his homework, and went bowling, to the zoo, and to the beach with Ryohei's Japanese judo colleagues. Every so often, a friend would come from Japan and stay with us, such as the high-ranking judo sensei Mr. Takata who was notorious for his *hane-goshi*—the hip throw that requires the spring of a mountain lion.

Takata Sensei had no problem with his spring. In fact, right smack in the center of our small combination living room/bedroom, he did a forward roll over my five-foot, nine-inch head as I stood there watching him from below.

I really worked hard on perfecting my Japanese cooking because I wanted to surprise our guests. On one occasion we had a visit from Mr. and Mrs. Tanino from Toronto, Canada. Mr. Tanino had a club in Toronto and when Ryohei had to leave the United States for visa renewal purposes, he taught at Tanino's club for a month or so. In any case, Mrs. Tanino and I spent some time together and she gave me pointers on Japanese cooking. I didn't realize that the advice coming from a *sansei*, or third generation Japanese person, would be much different than that coming from an *issei*, or first-generation person.

I decided to surprise Ryohei with one of Mrs. Tanino's recipes for tempura. I bought a ton of shrimp and vegetables. I spent the whole day cleaning them and preparing my batter. About an hour before Ryohei was set to arrive, I started the cooking process.

Chris was doing his homework and I had a large kitchen table full of food to dip and fry. Everything I dipped and fried came out huge. It didn't look like the tempura in Japan or for that matter anywhere else. Mrs. Tanino had told me to use Aunt Jemima Pancake Mix if I couldn't buy regular tempura mix. Well, I couldn't get the fancy mix so I followed her backup plan.

I had about thirty pounds of shrimp and vegetables along with dipping sauces to serve. Chris was really happy. He said, "Mom, these pancakes with the stuff in it are great!" Ryohei could see how much effort I had put into the cooking so he ate and smiled even though he seemed to be gagging. We had a lot left over so I shared it with some of my students who thought it was great, especially Kenny. After that though, it was back to my specialty—spaghetti. No more damn tempura!

We had an unusual guest from Japan. He wasn't a judo person, which in itself was abnormal for us. Instead, he was a friend of a friend and we were asked to take care of him. Naturally, we agreed.

When Mr. Yukio Yanagida first arrived in New York. He went to a YMCA to stay until we got him and brought him to our place in Brooklyn. Ryohei had a class to teach and asked me to pick him up in the city. I brought one of my female students with me in my old beat up jalopy. We found Mr. Yanagida, loaded him and his bags in the car and proceeded to return to Brooklyn via the Brooklyn-Battery Tunnel. I wanted to show off this wonderful New York site to our guest.

As we entered this very long tunnel that connects Manhattan and Brooklyn, my water hose broke, I got a flat tire, and ran out of gas. There we sat in the middle of the tunnel until the tow truck came to get us. My student and I sat in the front of the truck with the driver. He hoisted the jalopy on his towing boom. I laughed all the way through the rest of the tunnel as Mr. Yanagida just sat there in the back of the car in a regal position with arms crossed as if this were the normal way to travel through the city. I thought to myself that he was a hell of a guy.

I was right, too.

He went on to Columbia University where they couldn't teach him anymore, as he was so smart. They sent him on to Harvard. He is now one of the best attorneys in Japan. His law firm, Yanagida & Partners, is ranked in the top ten. He's still a big shot with Harvard and we have remained friends.

I kept organizing tournaments for women and getting the instructors nervous. They felt it was okay for the women to stay in their clubs but it was not okay to compete. I was genuinely impressed with the girls' and women's abilities and felt the need to do more about getting them in the limelight. For such a long time I had been the exception to the rule and now I had even more exceptions training hard, thriving, and ready for more.

Could I be the self-appointed warrior who would get them to the next level?

Before or even while I got to that next level, I had to redirect my energy and focus on another soon-to-be warrior. I was now pregnant and had to concentrate on that for a while. I was lucky since my gynecologist was also my student, Dr. Bauersachs. His children also studied with me for several years.

I felt good that my doctor was usually on the mat with me. My black belt was getting smaller and smaller; it's supposed to go around your waist twice, but mine could now only make it around once. Spectators would look at me with interest because this sport is supposed to keep you in shape, not give you a big belly. Of course, they didn't know I was pregnant.

44

IT WAS 1966; ON THE CHINESE CALENDAR, THE year of the Horse, and I had started to feel exactly like one. I continued to teach and enjoyed being a little pampered by Ryohei.

One night, after I taught some of the finest doctors at Methodist Hospital in Brooklyn, I developed the worst thirst ever in my life. My student, Dr. Bauersachs, who was a member of the judo program in the hospital, accommodated me by having some juice brought from the hospital kitchen. One quart, two quarts, three quarts—I was guzzling it down. It began to occur to me that I might drown the baby.

My thirst was finally satisfied, but I was uncomfortable and the juice sloshed around in my stomach when I walked. When Ryohei picked me up to go home, I could hardly sit in the car. There was no way I was going home. This ocean of juice had to be walked off! The poor guy and I walked up and down the streets in this lovely park-like area of Bay Ridge near the ocean. We spent the entire night there and both dozed off on a park bench.

I had some serious judo to take care of. I had requested that the Amateur Athletic Union (AAU) allow girls and women to compete in judo at the National Championships. Each time I called or sent a letter, I was told ridiculous things such as, "Judo is not for girls."

Hey, dummy, I thought, *I can kick your ass!*

The next excuse was, "There isn't enough interest by females."

Well, doofus, how would you know if you don't have a competition and include them?

The same crap went on for too long. My pregnancy hormones must have been going into full swing, because I was about to declare war.

The plan was to hold a competition in New York, invite the East Coast women, get some publicity, and then go after the AAU again. We had the competition at Jerome Mackey's large judo club in Manhattan. There was a decent turnout of about fifty women with at least seven from my clubs.

The competition used the rules and regulations of the times, which were men's rules since there weren't any for women. The matches went well. The women had good technique. I was convinced that women had to compete nationally. Now it was a matter of convincing the AAU.

There was a gentleman by the name of Joe Speyer who was some kind of big shot with the Daily News who also practiced judo at Mackey's place. He was also my husband's student. *voila!* We got three pages of coverage and a good story in the Sunday edition of the magazine section of the *Daily News*. My students thought we had a good turnout because I didn't compete. They all knew I was pregnant. In any case, I did lead the warm-ups, belly and all.

The nine months of pregnancy flew by. It got kind of slow at the end so I asked Ryohei to drive up and down some bumpy streets to help bring on the labor. All it did was help me get rid of gas.

One muggy evening in September, we were lying in bed watching the Jerry Lewis fundraiser on our little TV. All of a sudden drumsticks started rattling in my spine, not my stomach. I thought I was going to give birth through my rear end. I called Dr. Bauersachs and he told us to meet him at the hospital.

He examined me and said I was not in labor yet, but it was close enough that he could induce. We both told Ryohei to go home, not to worry, and the doctor would call him when there was some news. Reluctantly, he left.

I was prepared and then brought to the labor room. It was so different from the last time. I didn't go in with divorce on my mind—only good thoughts. It was a little hard to settle down because there were two Latina women on either side of my room who were both in full-blown labor. They were calling their husbands every name in the book as well as giving a running monologue on what a male could do with his rotten penis for putting them through this hell.

The doctor was going to take his examination for his black belt in a few weeks and needed to brush up on some of his forms. We had nothing else to do so I coached him while I sat on my legs with the usual mini hospital gown on. While he did his kata forms, I corrected or praised the demonstration, but the pain was getting worse. I rocked back and forth until he finished and then he gave me another checkup and decided it was time to get into the delivery room.

It didn't take too long for Jean Sumiko Kanokogi to come into this world. She was big, beautiful and healthy; truly a bundle of joy. The doctor called Ryohei to give him the good news, however because of Ryohei's excitement and language barrier he misunderstood. When the doctor announced the good news telling him that we had a baby girl, Ryohei replied, "No. Rusty is in the hospital and I don't know yet if it's a girl or a boy."

After a few minutes it was straightened out and he was at the hospital in a flash. This would add a new and wonderful dimension to our lives. I felt warm and loving, and thought it would be a while before I wanted to fight again.

Rusty visiting with Aunt Lee Krasner in The Hamptons.

Rusty, Chris & Lee Krasner, Rusty's aunt, in The Hamptons.

45

WE SPENT SO MUCH TIME LOOKING AT OUR bundle of joy. Like most parents, we were in awe of every burp and motion of our new baby.

Chris seemed happy to have a little sister in his life. We were almost the average family, with one exception—both mommy and daddy were judo instructors.

The next two years flew by as I continued my judo quest, spending my time training, competing and teaching locally, and when I wasn't doing that, playing my familial part. I continued to fight for women's equality in the world both on and off the mat, but my battles were smaller—local to my life, my town, my experience, as a woman, mother, wife and judoka.

While I had always had strong leadership qualities, in my younger years they had usually led right into trouble. I had never considered myself a true leader and teacher—until judo. To me, the work I was doing during this time didn't necessarily seem revolutionary; it was natural for me to jump into whatever I had in front of me with both feet.

In retrospect, anything a woman did that was equivalent to a man's profession made her stick out like a sore thumb. I think it was not only society's fault, it was also our fault, as women. Because so very few of us decided to be different, it was too great a stigma; one had to pay too large a price. It was easier to simply go with the flow—"don't make waves" and "just enjoy your family and family life."

Well, I didn't get all that. Throughout history all over the world there have been strong women with great intelligence. Did they just pop out when they were needed to overcome some major challenge and then go right back in the closet again? Why have women been so suppressed throughout history? What is so wrong with trying to do it all? I found out that a woman *can* in fact do it all—but she will definitely have to pay the price for it, over and over again. We decided in 1968 that it was time to go to Japan and visit Ryohei's family. My father-in-law had a glimpse of me in 1962 from the TV, but that was all. It was time to meet them for the first time, and I had the very best gift of all for them—their granddaughter.

Chris stayed with his grandparents and then went off to summer camp. It was better for him at this time. It was a long and arduous trip, but we gave the baby so much attention during the journey, she was pretty comfortable.

Rusty & Ryohei at a dojo in Japan.

When we finally arrived in Kumamoto, the hottest place I had ever been in in my life, we went to Ryohei's sister's house. She shared it with her husband, children and Ryohei's beloved grandmother. They were thrilled to see us and the feeling was mutual. There was laughing and tears. It was wonderful. I felt that they loved me even though they hardly knew me. That was the last day for a few months that I got to change a diaper, feed Jean, or do any of the mommy stuff myself; the aunts showed up to continue playing "pass the baby" and love her to pieces.

Ryohei, Jean & Rusty on a boat ride in Japan, 1968.

We then went to Ryohei's parents' home, where we would be staying, and had a joyful reunion. With all these babysitters, I had a lot of time for judo. My father-in-law, Toraki Kanokogi, was a former boxer and pretty funny. We really hit it off.

Ryohei and I worked out at many different dojos in the area. Because he was very famous in that part of Japan, we bowed in from the front of the dojo where the senseis bowed in. I think Toraki was pitting me against every guy in the dojo. He was basically showing me off. I had to fight like hell to keep him proud of me.

Oh why, oh why wasn't I just a demure American geisha girl?

An important day was coming up for us in Yatsushiro, Ryohei's hometown in Kumamoto. His sensei, Mr. Shinje Tsuchiya, had invited us for a practice. I had heard so much about this great man. Many of his students became excellent competitors and judo leaders, such as Osawa Sensei from the Kodokan. What I didn't know was that sensei was blind. I wasn't told because it was considered irrelevant.

When we arrived at the small dojo, I noticed that it was pretty dark inside, just one forty watt bulb hanging from the middle of the ceiling. The tatami floor mats were the original ones that Ryohei had practiced on as a youth. He showed me where sensei had his listing of his best students. The names were marked on a piece of wood and placed in the order of honor and hung on an elongated panel with hooks. Ryohei was very proud that his name was first; of course, I was proud too.

Rusty practicing at the dojo in Japan.

While we warmed up a bit in this very tiny, very hot dojo with kamikaze mosquitoes biting through our thick judo gis, the word must have gone out that a New York steak was in town. As I bowed to Tsuchiya Sensei, I was apprehensive because I had never played a blind person before. I was quickly cured of this symptom as sensei moved like a swift ocean wave, hitting me and picking me up and carrying me where he wanted.

I was no slouch, so I went after him and continued to attack. Each time he would say "good, good" in Japanese. After we finished the randori, I asked him to please help my judo. He said the most important thing to fix was my foot sweep. It seems I was turning my foot up to sweep too soon. I was flabbergasted that he could tell me this without seeing my big feet and just feeling them. He told Ryohei that I was strong and he was glad he had married me. To me it was more important to have a good foot sweep than to be sexy.

We had lunch and a nice visit together. Sensei presented me with a beautiful natural stone that he sanded down into an abstract wave, like himself.

We were having a wonderful time in Japan, including experiencing my first earthquake. It was about 2 a.m. We were sleeping on

Rusty performing kata techniques at the dojo in Japan.

our cuddly futons when all of a sudden I began to roll around the room. I suspected an earthquake and woke Ryohei. I was nervous, but Ryohei's reply was, "Be quiet and go back to sleep!" I guess it was okay because the house was still standing in the morning.

The vacation was almost over and the farewells were beginning. There were a few doozies. The Yatsushiro judo community hosted a senseis-only party. There had to be at least fifty of them in attendance. The small lacquered tables were lined up in a large oblong square with comfortable seating capacity on the tatami for all.

The food was already arranged on each table along with several bottles of Kirin beer. One was supposed to walk around pouring beer and making toasts to each other. *Kampai, kampai!*

The folks were really loosening up and they began their own entertainment. The funniest was this rather large-bellied sensei who took off his pants and had the largest colorful shorts I had ever seen. He proceeded to put cigarettes in each nostril and do a Japanese folk dance. As the only woman in the room, I was hoping he wouldn't ask me to join in his dance. God knows I would have, as I wanted to show good courtesy.

As the fun frenzy continued, most of the guests forgot about their food. I proceeded to each little table and enjoyed a portion of marinated eel, *unagi*, my favorite.

Two months later we were on our way back. It wasn't easy to leave because I had fallen in love with my new family and the town of Yatsushiro. The only things I wouldn't miss were the mosquitoes.

There were tearful goodbyes with the promise of a return visit in the near future. I was even going to miss Ryohei's nephew Yujii who constantly did forward rollouts over my head while I was eating in his mom's home. I got even with him at judo practice one day—I think I choked him out. He also went on to be an extraordinary judo player.

We loaded ourselves, and our ton of gifts on the plane. We were going back to New York via Hawaii. All Japanese men at that time traveled with suits on. Ryohei had on casual shorts, a T-shirt and open sandals, looking more Hawaiian than Japanese. Everything had to be transferred onto our next flight, so I asked him to get the stroller. We were going to be at the airport for some time during our layover. He proceeded to climb over the bags looking for the stroller. I saw some guy in a pink shirt touch him and thought some gay guy was trying to pick him up.

"Hey, Fucko, he's taken," I said, jumping in, baby and all.

Turns out the man was an undercover cop who thought Ryohei was a beach bum trying to steal the luggage. *Ooops!* Most men had not been liberated yet and didn't wear pink.

Rusty & Ryohei front and center with their fellow judoka at the dojo in Japan.

46

AS I REFLECT ON THIS PART OF MY LIFE, IT SEEMED to be the calm before the storm. Both Ryohei and I were teaching every day, taking care of the children, and generally falling into the routine that we considered our normal life. Ryohei was still at Jerome Mackey's Judo School, and taught at the Hempstead Long Island branch on Saturdays. It was a very busy club because there wasn't too much going on in the area with legitimate instructors.

A big tournament was coming up at the Buddhist Academy in the city. Ryohei couldn't make it so he asked me to coach his student, Salima, whom I had never met. He said she was strong and that I should just tell her what to do since she was a beginner with a white belt.

Salima found me at the competition in this very crowded area. She was a young, black woman, about 23 years old. She had a severely crossed right eye and spoke with a heavy Southern accent. Salima looked like she had been plowing fields all her life. She was built like throwing bales of hay took little or no effort for her. She worked on Long Island as a housekeeper and nanny to a well-to-do family.

Salima was a solid heavy weight. I asked her to go into the bathroom with me after we introduced ourselves so I could sneak her a mini lesson against her opponents. I knew her most difficult match would most likely be in the finals with Maureen Braziel. Maureen was a strong fighter from Brooklyn, with tenacity and good judo skills. I didn't know Maureen personally, yet (we later became very close friends and have remained so ever since); but at that time her instructor more or less kept her away from me, just as most other instructors did with their female students. I was quickly developing a reputation as a bad influence in the judo community because each day I was becoming more and more vocal about the lack of women's rights in the sport. The teachers feared I would incite their female students to want equality, so they kept me out of the picture, at least as best as they could.

I took a good look at Maureen, sized her up and thought she had some Viking in her. She was taller than Salima but both were about the same weight. Maureen, being more advanced in her studies, had some good throws under her belt. Once I got a good line on her moves, I signaled Salima to meet back to the bathroom, where I showed her how to fight Maureen to win the match. I demonstrated how to lift Maureen when she attacked with her favorite throw, *uchi mata*, instructing Salima to jack her up and then throw her down on her back.

The game plan was ready. Both women bowed in for their match. It was almost comical watching Salima follow my instructions completely and do exactly what she was supposed to do. She launched Maureen on a counter technique. She had Maureen up in the air, ran halfway across the mat and proceeded to throw her. In the end, poor Salima threw Maureen into and onto the audience, and didn't get a score. The match was temporarily stopped while the referee brought them back to the center of the mat. When I looked at Maureen's eyes as she was walking back to the center, I could detect a crazed look and could feel it was the end for Salima, who didn't know the rules when she threw Maureen off the mat. She'd had her chance and now the incensed female Viking would dispose of her.

The referee said, "hajime," instructing the match to begin, and within moments Maureen scored a full point and just like that the match was over.

If looks could kill, I would have been dead. Despite coming out victorious, Maureen shot me her worst dirty look and she left the mat.

What a fantastic judo career Maureen would have in the years to follow. Eventually we became best friends, and I became her national and international coach. It would be several years more battling before women finally won the right to be included in the National Championships. Maureen would go on to become a three-time national grand champion and put the United States on the world map with her international record, which she carried with her through her work for women and judo for decades to come[11]. Maureen and athletes like her fed my deep desire to advocate for women in judo; their unwavering fight was my incentive to get women's judo equal to men's.

It was that time again—1971 and I was once again with a child. It was fine with me, as it never really stopped me from doing what I had to do. Dr. Bauersachs and his kids were still studying with us and, in fact, we had developed a friendship with the entire family outside of judo. His daughter, Heidi, was rapidly becoming a good competitor. The boys were good too, but Heidi was hungry to win.

This time there wasn't too much excitement in the labor room. There was quite a bit, however, when Ryohei came to the hospital to meet his new ten and a half-pound baby sumo. Ted Kanokogi was here and what a mark he would make! All the newborn baby clothes we owned had to be given away, as none of it would fit our big, adorable bundle of "feed me every hour" baby. We needed new clothes just to bring him home.

Rusty, throwing Dr. Bauersachs, at the Kyushu dojo in the 1970s.

Ryohei was thrilled. A boy to carry on the name was crucial, especially, coming from samurai stock. It was important to have a boy, since a girl would get married and change her name, or at least that was the assumption. Little did the world and its conventions know what would transpire in the future.

47

I KNOW THAT EDUCATION IS IMPORTANT AND money is really important; however, connections are everything. I learned this early on in life.

I began keeping a mental filing cabinet of people that I wanted to keep in my life for various reasons. First, I had to like them, and vice versa. I didn't have a significant rationale for this attitude, just a feeling—one which would later be proved correct.

As I moved each step forward on my path and in my career—and sometimes back a step—I would recruit a fellow believer to fight for equality for women in judo and in sports, and reach out to find a strong hand reaching back to pull me forward. Sometimes I wondered if it was my mother. She had passed away a few years before, about a month before Jean was born. Now I had two children, a job and passion, and a way of life she wouldn't have recognized. Still, I believed she was proud of me, wherever she was, and every so often I thought I felt her pushing the little Coney Island hustler in me to keep on selling my goods—it just wasn't bags of skimmed confetti anymore.

One of the greatest lessons I learned early on in my life in judo is that when you give, don't expect anything in return and you won't get hurt. On the other hand, if you give from your heart and do the best that you can for another person or organization, it often seems to come back to you—and it's even sweeter without the expectation. I'm often asked how I get all these people to help in so many projects for the promotion of judo. It's quite simple: I already gave my time, money and energy and they know they can always count on me. Is this a noble sacrifice?

Hell no!

It's just me being Rusty.

When the phone rang one day in 1972 or '73, did I know it would enhance my judo teaching career and bump me up to a whole new level?

Hell no!

The call was from *The Alan Burke Show*. I had watched his show before.

He would deliberately try to make a fool out of his guests, have them squirming in their chairs, and the audience would eat it up, both in the studio and at home.

What a nasty asshole this Burke guy is, I'd thought.

I considered him just as creepy as the bizarre dwarf clowns in Steeplechase Park.

When the call came in, the woman on the phone said that they had received several newspaper articles about me and would like me to come on the show. Knowing the sport of judo got hardly any attention, I figured why not. I asked how much they paid, and she said they didn't pay anything. I responded that I was a professional and should be paid, and to my amazement, she agreed. I couldn't believe it. I had only said it because I was trying to get off the hook from appearing with this Looney Tunes Burke.

I never asked how much. We just made a date for the show. I was to bring a student to toss around and any guests I wanted. I brought Kenny and Ryohei. Kenny was going to be my fall guy.

I wanted to give Alan a gift, as it was a nice Japanese custom, so I got him a judo belt. If this guy became obnoxious, my plan was to beat him up on his own show.

Surprise! Mr. Burke was super respectful. No one ever accused him of being dumb.

The show went well. There were questions from the audience.

"What would you do if you walked down a dark alley and were attacked?"

Well, duh, why the hell would I walk down a dark alley?

"What would you do if someone double your size attacked you?"

There is no one double my size. Have you ever seen a 400-pound mugger?

Alan loved it and laughed like crazy. Was I nasty? No, just honest.

Before the show was over, I made the presentation of the belt. It had his name on it in Japanese, along with an inscription, which I read aloud: "Alan Bug"—the "r" is not pronounced in Japanese. Alan's staff and audience roared.

The next day I received another call. It was from Steve "Mo" Spahn, the headmaster of the Franklin School[12] in Manhattan, a hoity-toity private school. Mo told me that he was formerly a basketball player and sportsman. His wife Ruth and he had seen the Burke show, liked my style and wanted to meet me to discuss teaching at Tripp Lake Camp, their girls' summer camp in Poland Springs, Maine. We arranged an appointment and ended the call.

I was so excited. When Ryohei came home, I told him the good news. I was finally going to camp, something I had never done as a child. My camp had been the streets of Coney Island. I was now moving up society's ladder and taking judo with me.

48

I ARRIVED IN PORTLAND, MAINE AND WAS picked up at the airport by a charming fellow who also doubled as a tennis coach. John was originally from England and sounded like he was from a good upper-class family.

The ride to Tripp Lake Camp in Poland Springs would take about an hour. I asked John so many questions we were lucky we didn't crash en route. When we arrived and I had a quick look around, I was taken by the beauty and freshness of TLC. It was a blend of stately trees and lush open fields. The hills sloped gently to a mile of the waterfront. I'd made it to the Promised Land!

TLC has been around since 1911.

Imagine my teaching judo here in those days!

After I got squared away, I met with Ruth, a.k.a. "Aunt Ruth" to the girls, and Dr. Spahn, a.k.a. "Mo." They were very cordial and pleased that I decided to join them at camp. Ruth had arranged for a little supper party at her house on campus, small but lovely. I knew I was dealing with society people, so I had brought a black cocktail dress for any special occasion.

When I showed up, people were already at the house. When I walked in there was a hush all over. *Wow!* I thought. *They must be impressed with this husky judo instructor from Brooklyn.*

Wrong. They all had casual clothes on and looked like an ad for Pendleton. I had on my lovely slinky black dress, chandelier rhinestone earrings, black pumps and lots of makeup. The only thing missing was my tiara.

After the introductions and some giggling here and there, we settled down for a glass of wine. I sat on the sofa. One of Ruth's friends was visiting from the City and she also sat on the same sofa, as far away from me as she could. We chatted about this and that, when the conversation turned to art. I casually mentioned that I was the niece of Lee Krasner and Jackson Pollock. Well, the woman moved so quickly to cozy up to me that she was almost on my lap. I guess even in high society there are equalizers.

I met with the girls the next morning for their first judo lesson. They were enthusiastic, cute as buttons, and all smelled like Ivory soap. I thought I better not do my usual heavy-handed class as they might faint. But, I can only repress for a short time—and much to my surprise, these little cherubs were ready to kick ass. They came from well-to-do families and their parents had a hard time even getting them to pick up a towel from the floor. But for me these babies would do push ups, falls, throws, and hold-downs. I was happily building Wonder Women! *Hooray!* One day my army and I would take over the world.

Wait until these girls go home after the summer. Their brothers will be surprised.

I taught six or seven classes a day. I loved my work so much that after thirty- eight years, I'm still there. Now I teach those girls' kids and, in some cases, their grandkids. It wouldn't be summer without my time at Tripp Lake Camp.

49

IT WAS 1974 AND OUR CHILDREN WERE growing up nicely and progressing well. Women's judo, on the other hand, was not. Fortunately, Maureen Braziel had the courage to venture out on her own to attend the British Open in 1971 where she took silver in the heavyweight division and bronze in the open weight class.

It was the US women's first participation internationally and the judo world was impressed. It also gave me insight into the tone of what was going on in Europe.

I had fought for years and finally gotten women into the National Championships, but the victory didn't satiate me for long; it wasn't long before I wanted more. We needed more! The next step would be to have an official team from the US compete at the British Open.

This wasn't received well. Most of the men were concerned about sharing any of the US judo budget with the women. Believe it or not, some women agreed with the men—they had been happy doing *kata* and didn't want to rock the boat or upset the status quo, namely the men who were comfortable with the women in their current place. Eventually, many of these women came around to the truth—that they were getting short changed out of competition and the short end of the stick in yet another facet of their lives—but the shift was slower than I expected and definitely than I would have liked. But as with all inequities, eventually they realized what I had known my whole life, that they both wanted and deserved more.

The first AAU National Championship in which women were included was held in conjunction with the men's competition at Phoenix, Arizona in 1974. Disaster lurked in every corner for me. First, I had a problem getting an AAU card that was needed in order to compete. I was told because I was a professional athlete, I was ineligible.

I asked how was that determined? The answer was that I got paid for teaching so that made me a pro.

What bullshit!

I really didn't earn that much at the time, and none of us got a money prize for winning. We were lucky to leave with our own teeth. I thought the cold shoulder from the AAU might be payback for constantly bugging them to include women's judo in the Nationals and threatening to start my own national championship for women if they didn't.

Turns out, getting my card was the simple part. Soon Maureen Braziel, Kenny Pollard, Frances (Skip) Watkins and I were on the flight to Arizona. The heavyweight divisions for the women at that time were 160 and under, and over 160 pounds. Maureen and I decided that I would go in the under 160 and she in the 160 and up. We didn't want to travel cross-country just to fight each other. Besides, I was Maureen's coach—this way we could both take home a gold medal. I was very careful on the flight not to eat anything. I just drank coffee and gave Kenny my meal. I was at weight and didn't want to blow it. You had to compete in the division you had registered in. I was a real pro at this weight business because within the last several months I had lost about eighty pounds. I had been way up there, but then I went to a doctor, took some I-don't-know-what shots and proceeded to lose the tonnage. Now I was a svelte 160.

When we arrived in the desert, it had to be at least a hundred degrees. We went to the hotel where weigh-in was moving quickly. We were running a little late so we quickly stripped down to underwear and stepped on the scale that was a combination scale and heart monitor. The dam needle was going all over the place. I had left Brooklyn at 160 and I now weighed in at 167.5. What the hell was going on?

"Get me a scale without all this crap on it," I said. "Get me a lawyer!"

Shit!

This was bad! I was told that I had two hours to make weight or not compete.

Maureen and I tried to switch weight categories, to no avail.

Okay, okay.

I would run it off. All my students were weighed in. They were fine, even Kenny who had eaten all my food. We went up to our room. I proceeded to put on all the available sweatsuits and wound as many towels around my head as I possibly could. Then I went into the bathroom, turned on the hot water faucets in the tub and sink to fill the room with steam. Meanwhile I began my jog in the bathroom, counting up to a zillion. Kenny made a mistake. He needed to pee and I went crazy when he came into the bathroom and let my steam out.

After about an hour Maureen took me back to the weigh-in. I had only dropped four pounds so it was back to the dungeon.

Do better, Rusty, and hurry up. There's no time left!

I did the routine again. They brought me down once again. There I was on the scale, punchy and naked. Kenny stuck his head in behind the screen. "Sensei, are you okay?" He asked, and like the proverbial bull in the china shop, he knocked the screen down. Coincidently, there was a coaches' meeting going on right behind me and with nothing separating them and me, I mooned the entire contingent.

I still had two more pounds to go. I was so mentally out of it that when I put my plastic sweat enhancer back on, I couldn't figure out why I was having trouble putting my legs back in the pants. I finally got my legs in but realized I had a gigantic hole between my pant legs. My support team of Maureen, Kenny and Frances lost it and started laughing so much they were crying. There I was with my legs in my shirt sleeves and the hole where my head should have gone swinging between my legs.

It was now my last shot to make weight. They took me back to the room for the last time. Some guy made a remark as we passed him telling me I looked like hell. Of course I did, but who was this jerk to tell me anything? I cursed him and vowed to get him later on.

I finally made weight. The troops put me in the shower and took me to eat and drink. Little did I know at the time that a few guys were placing bets on when I was going to die. At the restaurant I guzzled down several quarts of water and iced tea. I didn't eat much but I felt very bloated and lightheaded. We went back to the room and I had the worst case of throwing up and diarrhea. I must have lost another five pounds.

I had to compete the next day. It all seemed to be a dream. Everything was in slow motion. I heard my name called and I floated out to the mat. I bowed to my opponent, tried to take a grip on her judogi but my hands wouldn't close. I didn't feel aggressive or scared, just in la-la land. As it turned out, the medical team came on the mat when it became clear I needed to throw up again. This time there was a little blood. That was it. And just like that, I was out of the competition.

Someone put me outside and I sat under a tree for a long time. Maureen won the gold; Kenny played a few good rounds and Frances Watkins took third place even though she was only a yellow belt at the time.

I was advised to go in for testing when I got home. Back in Brooklyn, I went to the doctor right away. He was surprised that I didn't have a heart attack, or maybe I did, as my electrolytes were way down and I was potassium depleted and God knows what else. The doctor asked why I, a forty-year-old woman who had just lost lots of weight, would almost kill herself for a sporting competition? My answer was that I had to be in it as it was the first Nationals for women and it was a long time coming.

Though I wasn't able to compete, I didn't lose, because I won. I won the realization that my time was over. Now I had to put everything in the right perspective. I had to help other women excel in judo and never let anyone do anything as foolish as I did making weight.

Finally, in 1976, the national AAU judo organization agreed to the formation of a women's team. The team would be determined by whoever became the first- place winners of each weight division at the National Championship that year. We would not receive any funding or team uniforms emblazoned with the USA on them. We would receive only a travel permit to the British Open identifying us as the official USA-AAU Women's Judo Team. In other words, the establishment said, "Go away little girls. Here's a cookie, now just go play."

50

THE 1976 NATIONALS ATTRACTED AN ABUN-
dance of good judo women from all over the country. The competition was hard and fast. It produced a brilliant team.

The team almost typified the United States. There were four black women: Linda Richardson from Wisconsin, Delores Brodie from California, Christine Pennick from California, and Frances Watkins from New York and four white women: Diane Pierce from Minnesota, Maureen Braziel from New York, Lynn Lewis from Massachusetts, and Barbara Fest from Massachusetts. Elizabeth Lee from California, an Asian woman of Chinese descent, was selected as manager, and I, a Jewish warrior from Brooklyn, was the selected coach.

I believe Elizabeth was selected as manager for several reasons. The first was to keep an eye on me, since she wasn't pro women's competition. The other reason was that she did a great job with the paperwork. Although non-funded, we still had to be accountable and turn in our results.

The 1976 British Open was to be held in October at the Crystal Palace in the London suburb of Croydon. There was so much to do because we didn't have any funding and none of us were in a position to do any international globe-trotting. One of my students had a graphic artist father. I met with him and told him I had fifty dollars to invest in a fundraising pin for the team. We needed to raise at least $2,000 for the Open. He and I worked on the pin, which was really more like a large button. I wanted it to have a woman judo black belt who looked strong, yet sexy, on it, and I wanted the Stars and Stripes next to her.

The button was designed and manufactured. My student's father got us a big break on a thousand of these babies to pitch and earn our dough to represent the United States of America at the British Open.

The final black and white button looked quite bizarre. My designer put everything I requested on it, but the very long, flowing hair coupled with a shapeless judo body made it look like a scene from the Bride of Frankenstein. However, the black Stars and Stripes saved the button as the patriotism seemed to come through.

I distributed the buttons to the team and hit the go button on fundraising—I even enlisted the judo kids to sell them to anyone who was buying. People were beginning to hide when they saw me coming because I insisted they buy a button for every member of their family as well as all their friends. I even suggested that they would make wonderful Christmas gifts. I think I sold the bulk of our buttons. The team members who came from outside of the New York area were training with their coaches. We'd sold enough buttons to buy our plane tickets, but there was still something missing. We still didn't have warm up suits with the initials "USA" on them.

I contacted several companies with my tale of woe. Here we were the official USA AAU women's judo team going to the highest caliber international competition there was, and we didn't even have warm-up suits to wear at opening ceremonies. My pitch worked. I was invited to a few companies to get warm-ups. Before long I had warm-ups coming out of the kazoo. The team was thrilled. I took the suits and had "USA" embroidered on all the backs.

One of the warm-ups was a one-piece deal with a front zipper from the crotch to the neck. I got into it just as the phone rang. Maureen, on the other end, wanted to talk judo as we usually did even off the mat. I got stuck in the suit and was so tangled up that I dropped the phone and twisted down to the floor. I had to ask Mo to come over and help me get out of this thing because suddenly I had to pee and the situation was getting serious. I could hear the hysterical laughter coming through the other end of the receiver, and Maureen say something like "Call the police," and then *click*. I finally got out of the one piece and vowed never to wear it again.

I enclosed one of our fabulous buttons along with the thank you letters I sent to the companies that donated our warm-ups. I liked this marketing experience and knew anything was possible if you believed in it and if folks believed in you.

We arrived at Heathrow Airport at about 6 a.m. We took the latest flight out of New York because we were waiting for the women from the West Coast. None of us slept on the flight. We were too excited since this was the first international competition for most of the team.

We headed by train to Croydon where we were booked into the Queens Hotel not far from the sport center. Our rooms were in the basement of this not-very- large hotel. The rooms were neat but smelled of mildew. We were all as hungry as we were tired. I called a meeting with the team and demanded that no one eat until I was able to check weights.

We marched to Crystal Palace where the scales were available in preparation for the official weigh-in the next day. I put the first athlete on the strange looking scale and couldn't figure out her damn weight as the scale measured in stones, a British unit of measurement popularly used to calculate body weight, the modern equivalent of fourteen pounds.

Finally, I got a Brit to come in and help us. She converted the stones into kilos, which none of us knew either. We were in a pickle but did the best we could, and then went to a Chinese restaurant to eat. I still didn't know most of their weights, so I told them not to overindulge.

We went back to the mildew inn and tried to sleep. Maureen was so psyched mentally, preparing for the competition, that we began to grip fight as one does to get a good advantage for her throw. We really went at it until I gripped hard and fast, causing Mo to block just as hard and fast.

Suddenly there was pain shooting up my arm to my brain like lightning. I had a horrible jammed thumb on my left hand.

Of course, I'm left-handed!

I jumped around the room for a while suffering from a throbbing pain. I guess it bored Mo, because she went to sleep. I, on the other hand, didn't get much sleep as I was cursing both me and my thumb.

The next morning, we all had a British breakfast and went to weigh in and get some practice. The next day would be the test of the first American women's judo team.

51

THE VENUE FOR THE JUDO COMPETITION AT Crystal Palace was huge. There were three full mat areas of seventy-one-by-two-meter tatamis for each playing area, plus there were two more of the same on the very large balcony upstairs.

The locker room was typical, what it was handy for was not just to change into your judo uniform, but it gave you the opportunity to eyeball some of your opponents, checking out muscle versus fat. It was just a silly game, however our team was really fit, and it played right into their self-confidence. We parked ourselves on the bleachers, staking claim to an area that would give me quick access from mat-to-mat.

There was an abundance of nurses in their starched white uniforms along with nurse hats and the red cross emblem on them. They all had little yellow basins with an ammonia smelling liquid and sponge in it.

What the hell kind of tournament is this? I thought to myself. *Do they think we Yanks will get the vapors and need this?*

We all thought it was pretty funny looking at what seemed like a reserve of World War II nurses. Later that day we were so grateful to have that crew there as they were back and forth on the mats for any injury, giving exactly the same treatment for all temporary mishaps; they would simply squeeze the sponges, say something in "British," and the fighter would have a miraculous recovery.

Our team was having a fantastic day. It was really the beginning of international competition for women. We had so many of our women in the finals that one minute I would be on the main floor, the next up to the balcony, then back to the floor a moment later. It got to the point where I just stayed up on the balcony and bellowed my coach's commands down from on high. My voice is low-pitched and loud, so when I yelled, everyone from downstairs became attentive.

Linda Richardson was cleaning up her opponents with smooth throws, one after the other, Dolores Brodie won her division despite the fact that I had to run her up and down Hyde Park to get rid of some of the "I don't know how I put on these ten pounds," in order for her to make weight. She did in the end, and went on to win another gold with her fabulous hip throw. Chrisine Pennick was a tenacious competitor; she had good technique but was constantly on overkill. We wanted to win; however we didn't want them to hate us. More gold chalked up with Christine's first place.

Frances "Skip" Watkins was the low woman on the totem pole. She tried hard, but didn't have the experience to win a medal at this level. Diane Pierce had a one-track mind, and had a fixation on arms—when she got one, she would whip on an arm bar until they tapped out to give up, or yelled "Auntie!" I think when Diane was awarded her gold medal the presenter was reluctant to shake hands.

Maureen Braziel had done this drill before when she competed here two years prior. She did well in 1974, but she was going to be brilliant now, after the thumb pain I had all night, she would excel or die by my good hand. We weren't disappointed. Mo went out there like a steamroller and flattened all in her way. Lynn Lewis was a little speed demon; as soon as an opponent gripped her, it was over. She showed her best and fastest technique on the way to more gold.

Barbara Fest was our super heavyweight. Despite her size, she was fast and formidable, gave it her best shot, lost a round and had to settle for silver.

Our manager Elizabeth was stunned. For most of her judo career she practiced kata forms, not fighting, and now found herself in the middle of a band of aggressive women and a deranged coach, all of us barking orders at her. She tried to accommodate; however, her skills weren't up to the demands of such a high-caliber competition. Her written reports were meticulous and eloquent, but that hardly mattered in the heat of competition.

We had won the British Open and to us it was like sweeping the Olympics. This is how far we had come!

Besides our women, it was fairly easy to see how much potential all the other countries had. Still, even at that time, I knew I wanted more for women's judo. This opportunity gave me a chance to meet and speak with Charles Palmer, Officer of the Order of the British Empire (OBE), who was the head of the British Judo Association and the International Judo Federation. I also was able to speak with the coaches from a dozen other countries and a group in England that were major supporters of the sport. I took everyone's addresses, gave them mine, and let them know I would be in touch and we would continue to meet at the British Open in future years. That was the beginning of the powerhouse network, and the ongoing battles off of—as well as on—the mat.

We celebrated that night with dinner and dancing. It seemed all the aches and pains went away. We sure could have used some of those nurses on the way back to the airport. We looked like we went through a war and lost.

On the flight home all I kept thinking about was all the monumental steps still ahead of us. The US judo women won more medals at the British Open than any of our men in international competition had thus far—and yet we had to fund ourselves. We belonged in the World Championship.

The powers that be in US judo will never hear the end of this!

Rusty and the 1976 -77 AAU team.

52

I THOUGHT THAT RETURNING HOME WITH ALL
that gold would do it for women's judo in the States, but it only moved us up an inch. We received a few "atta girls," but still had to hustle to keep in the game. At least the formula for success was coming together for me: keep winning, keep networking, and keep nagging.

In the following years the team changed somewhat, as the US women were constantly competing for a spot in their weight classes and unseating each other at the National Championships, which was the qualifier for the British Open.

My efforts to elevate women's judo on the international stage were getting good results, and soon I was able to get some financial support and other goodies and swag for the team. We managed to change the team manager. Sandi Cornelius, an American Indian from the Oneida tribe, became the next manager. Sandi had been a champion in her own right and was practicing and enjoying judo in her part of the world, Wisconsin.

Sandi was an advocate for women's judo competition and we welcomed her aboard. Whether it be coach or manager, there is no glamour in the job. One had to be available one hundred percent of the time and give more than one hundred percent of oneself. The payback was success.

Each new member of our team gave her all. We continued to win quite a few medals all through the late '70s. A really young competitor, Monica Emerson from California, was with us at the British Open a few times. She was as incredible as she was young, at about fifteen or so. She was tall and lean, had very long blond hair and looked like Rapunzel. She was an excellent technician and really helped the team.

We also had Ann Maria Burns—now known as Dr. Ann Maria De Mars and mother to judo Olympic bronze medalist and famed MMA fighter Ronda Rousey— on our team. She was completely the opposite of Monica. Ann Maria was short with a brown, nondescript hairstyle, and was completely determined and thoroughly grounded. She didn't smile, laugh or become involved in any kind of cajoling. She was on a mission and walked and talked like it.

Later in the '80s, our one-track Ann Maria won our first gold medal at the Women's World Championships. Our manager, Sandi, went on to be a school teacher and worked for the President of the United States on Native American education. Dr. Ann Maria Burns earned her PhD and has a beautiful daughter climbing the judo ladder[13]. Monica became a federal agent.

Internationally I was making the right friends and contacts. Charles Palmer, the President of the International Judo Federation and international referee development guru befriended me. He gave me more direction for the uphill fight. Many of the British players felt he wasn't for women's judo, which I never understood. He had always been there for me.

Still, many judoka from across the pond had a different perspective, I later found out; full contact was illegal for women in the sport in many European and Pan-American countries, including Brazil, during the 1970s, a rule that was considered ridiculous and unacceptable in the eyes of any serious female competitor forced to compete under it.

I met the team from South Africa while at the British Open in 1978. This was one of the few events they were able to participate in because of all the apartheid problems. They pretty much stuck to themselves and weren't a big threat judo- wise to any of the participating teams.

I made it a point to speak with them. As women, we had the same problems in judo.

They were quite nice and thought our team was terrific. In passing, they extended us a loose invitation to visit them back home. I nodded my head and said it would be great to go to South Africa. I also mentioned it to my team, which was half black, with a possible Chinese or American Indian manager, and a Jew from Brooklyn coach who was married to a Japanese man.

The Empire State Games, which are held yearly, are an Olympic prototype of many sports with 5,000 athletes, coaches, and officials vying to be the best of New York State. While I was attending the 1978 games in Syracuse, I received a call from my husband that someone from South Africa was looking for me via an overseas call and that I should call him back. He gave me the number and I was about to use the phone in the Games office that they had so graciously allowed me to call home on when they asked me if I was calling home again. "No," I replied. "I'm returning a call to South Africa." I did, however, charge it to my number in Brooklyn.

I spoke to a gentleman in Sun City, South Africa, who turned out to be the president of the South African Judo Association. He informed me that the tickets to Sun City were already in the mail for me and an eight-woman judo team, plus coach and manager.

Seventeen thousand dollars' worth of airline tickets!

They would put us up in a plush hotel and we would compete for television.

Holy cow!

Here we were selling pins, almost begging to get any funds to represent the US internationally, and suddenly we were offered this Cinderella trip.

By the time I got home from the Empire State Games, the tickets were waiting for me. The names, with the exception of mine, were left blank, to be put in at a later date when the final team selection was made. I was so excited about the trip because we needed this kind of international competition to show the world and the powers that be that there was a great interest in women's judo growing both domestically and abroad.

By this time, I had a good relationship with Charles Palmer, President of the IJF and had called on him for advice, contacts, and in some instances, direction, on many occasions. He knew I wanted to keep taking women's judo higher. I remember calling him in London during the early part of 1979 to give him this great news about our invitation to South Africa. He also knew I was in a form of negotiation/agitation—soon to be litigation—with USA Judo to put forth a proposal to host the first Women's World Judo Championship (WWJC) in New York. If that moved forward, it would then have to go before the IJF.

Charles gave me a serious warning that if the USA women's team participated in a televised competition in South Africa, it would probably be used for propaganda. There would be grave consequences by the IJF voting board and they would not approve the first women's world championships. I made it very clear to all in US judo, especially the women and women's coaches, that participating in this event would jeopardize the support for the first WWJC, which was a prelude to the inclusion in the Olympics.

It didn't take me long to reject this trip to fairyland, nor did it have much negative effect on my team and staff of color, as some were somewhat reluctant from the onset as to how safe it would be in South Africa for them at that particular time.

I sent the tickets back with a nice letter that I'm sure they weren't thrilled with, but that was that. We needed the support of the IJF. The sorry part of the story is that several of the non-local white women on the team were contacted personally via their coach. The coach and four women accepted the deal, pretended to be the USA team and flew to South Africa under the guise of international sportsmanship.

I informed Charles Palmer of the situation so the IJF would know it wasn't the real deal. They were going to support the proposal for the first Women's World Judo Championship if USA Judo put it on their next meeting agenda.

I received a postcard, which I still have, from the selfish, arrogant group that went to South Africa. On it are two monkeys, with one picking bugs out of the other one's rear end. "We thought of you when we saw this card," was the only line written. It was a pity that their only growth in judo was physical, with zero-character development. They did not seem to care that the big picture was larger than a trip to South Africa.

The next major part of my huge plan was to put forth to USA Judo all the required finances, organizations and whatever it took to get that first championship done. I needed sponsors, a venue hotel, and a *damn* miracle.

Oy, vey!

53

THOUGH HOLDING THE FIRST WOMEN'S WORLD
Judo Championship in New York was still just a pipe dream—a reality only inside my head— the atmosphere around equality for both men and women in sports in the 1970s was beginning to change. There was major dissension in amateur sports. The AAU was under scrutiny by the US government because of so many complaints and injustices. US Senators Ted Stevens of Arkansas, John Culver of Iowa, Richard Stone of Florida, and Samuel Hayakawa of California would help develop a bi-partisan bill, known as the Amateur Sports Act[14] to promote and coordinate amateur athletic activity in the United States, provide for the resolution of disputes involving national governing bodies, and create rights and privileges for amateur athletes in the United States. It would give girls and women more opportunity and certainly more rights.

I was contacted by an aide from Senator Stevens office and gave testimony regarding the discrimination against women judo athletes. The bill was signed into law by President Jimmy Carter in 1978 and was an immediate blessing for women in sports. It would be very helpful to me when I was at war with the naysayers.

The Amateur Athletic Act was the law that the US Olympic Committee[15] would have to abide by. The AAU was later disbanded in 1980 and United States Judo, Inc. (USJI) was the national governing body for judo put in its place. USJI is now the direct connect to the USOC and the International Judo Federation. I was thrilled with new hope.

This important move in the history of sports didn't make my life any easier; because nothing really changed, women were still treated as second class citizens in judo. It did, however, give me a strong legal weapon that I could utilize in the upcoming complaints and lawsuits.

Another phenomenon was taking place in the name of Billie Jean King. I didn't know beans about the sport of tennis, but I certainly knew of BJK. I could only relate to tennis through my second favorite sport, handball, that I had played as a kid in Coney Island between street fights.

Billie Jean used a racquet. I used my hand. She beat guys. So did I. She was on TV. I wasn't. Her sport was for the middle class. At that time, mine wasn't. But all things considered, thank God for Billie Jean. My being able to bring women's judo to the limelight would never have happened without her.

Our beloved actor, entertainer and humanitarian, Bob Hope, took a fancy to BJK. He knew she was a fantastic athlete and wanted to support one of her causes. He gave her $5,000 to help her establish the Women's Sports Foundation in 1974. I remember going to a meeting in New York in the '70s where the new organization was being touted. I listened and agreed with everything that was said. We all knew we were treated as second-class citizens and were not allowed to play with the big boys.

Billie Jean not only proved them wrong, but beat Bobby Riggs in the most viewed match in tennis history at the time, and got more respect for women in one day than ever before in history. You see, when I competed with men in judo and even beat them, no one knew or cared. Tennis was the way to go.

What the hell?!

If I could have found a female boxer to beat Rocky Graziano, I don't know that I could have achieved the same results.

Billie Jean was still a busy athlete with Wimbledon and had many other great tennis fetes to conquer, so she hired a fantastic, extraordinarily intelligent woman from San Francisco to begin and bring the Women's Sports Foundation forward— Eva S. Auchincloss, the new executive director. Eva brought Holly Turner aboard. Now there was a dynamic duo to continue the growth of women in sports, to research, advocate, fund raise, and gather up the huge following of supporters and allies.

Billie Jean King should receive damehood, sainthood or any other great accolade because she is truly a pioneer, committed advocate and humanitarian of women's sport. We have become very good friends over the years. My family and I adore her and her partner of many years, Ilana Kloss, also a great tennis player, hall of famer, and remarkable person. They remind me of my husband and I: the maniac and the peacemaker. That's what it is all about—great teamwork.

54

THE CHAIN OF EVENTS TO MOVE WOMEN'S JUDO out of the national arena and place it on the world map would take a toll on my family and me. I became more obsessed with this challenge as it wasn't only wheeling and dealing, organizing and getting a world championship accomplished, it would mean dealing and pursuing the International Olympic Committee, the US Olympic Committee, and USA Judo.

I sometimes wondered what was going on with my family; the guilt would bother me later on in my life. I asked my daughter, Jean, how she felt when all this was going on. She said that she knew, as a 12-year-old, that if she wanted to see me, she would have to get involved. She felt that something very powerful was going on and she also felt that she had to grow up faster than her peers because so many times she was the only female in the household—and Mommy's replacement.

Jean went on to be a formidable judo competitor for the United States and was one of the signers of the lawsuit against the USOC and USA Judo that we initiated through the NY State Division of Human Rights. Even though she is now a federal agent and a major asset to the human race, according to her, her potential has not yet been met. She will always understand that women have to continue to push up the glass ceiling. She is a beautiful and compassionate person. That certainly relieves some of my feelings of guilt regarding neglecting her over judo during our heydays.

On the other hand, our son Ted put us through the wringer. He was rambunctious, even as a little kid. He was large for his age and unusually strong. Ryohei tried to be as helpful as possible; however, so many things went awry. First, being Japanese and Ted being his first son, he basically was too lenient. He rarely told him no. It put me in the position of major disciplinarian, thereby making me the bad guy.

Did I care? Sure I did. Although I was very pissed off many times, I just had to keep going.

As a result of all this turmoil, Ted started downhill on a banana peel. One of his main problems was that he had my personality and aggression, two dangerous factors when pointed in the wrong direction. I survived my youth in hell, and prayed to God he would also.

Today Ted is a strong, caring man who, like his sister, is an asset to the US and the world. He has had a successful military career. His mission in life is to help all others except the bad guy and he is willing to pay the price. His take on judo is, "all they do is talk judo from morning to night, teach judo for a living, volunteer as referees or coaches on their day of rest. They would trade me off for a good judo competition."

Hell of a way for a kid to grow up!

With his ability, had he been born into another family, he could have been a world-class athlete in any sport.

My husband of forty-plus years has been my strongest supporter. Are there things missing in the marriage? If you compare it with the old movie and television shows, the answer is yes. We don't show affection publicly, many times not even privately. That's something that I learned to live with all my life, as it never happened from my mother, father, or brother. I always had a dog that loved me unconditionally and was very affectionate.

I remember reminding my husband about February 14, Valentine's Day. "We don't celebrate that in Japan," he'd said.

I decided early on whether I wanted a storybook type of marriage or a kind, sweet, supportive man to be my partner forever. I made the right choice.

Under the AAU in 1977 we were allowed to have a women's judo subcommittee. This served us well as we had a place to air our ideas and moan and groan. For the most part it was okay, but I unintentionally made most of the women members nervous with my attitude that was, "we are entitled and want it now!"

I was so fed up with the bull that I didn't have any patience for the judo women that were afraid of their own shadow or so controlled by men. Or maybe they were afraid that they wouldn't get their next rank or cookie. I tried but could not play that game. I had paid my dues in judo as a competitor, local organizer and coach and I wanted no part of the waiting, whining and ass kissing game. I knew we had rights. I just had to find them. There were productive women on the committee. My friend Sandi that I spoke about earlier, Phyllis Harper, the shaker and mover from Chicago, and my friend Maureen who, when she didn't have her mind on her upcoming matches, would support whatever I proposed.

Faye Allen was the chairperson of our committee. She was diversified in her judo ability and had a friendly disposition. She was not a threat to our male leadership and therefore was considered by them to be a good person to have in that position. Sometimes she put our requests forward. Other times she may have been under too much pressure to push our proposals forward. I knew I could cultivate her. She was an intelligent woman with a teaching background. It was not long before she saw the light.

One of the prerequisites before the IJF would even consider awarding any country a world championship was for that country to host an international championship with member countries of their union participating. We are in the Pan American Union so we were to have the first women's Pan American Judo Championships.

Faye brought the proposal forward. The male dominated board of directors beat the hell out of it with a no money, no time, no venue set of excuses. She pursued, at our urging, and we finally came to a compromise. The first Pan Am Championships for women would be held the day following our annual Senior National Championships in St. Louis. I would be the coach. There would be three US women in each division—first-, second- and third-place winners of the National Championship.

The Pan American countries were invited. They were poorer than us so only a few countries showed up: Ecuador, Puerto Rico and Mexico. The US cleaned up. We had a team of twenty-four. We were number one. I thought to myself, "Girls, don't let this go to your head." Basically, this competition was smoke and mirrors. Yes, it did happen and looked good on paper, but best of all it fulfilled the prerequisite.

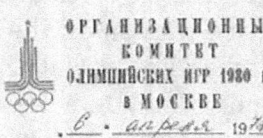

In 1977 I received a telegram from Charles Palmer, President of the International Judo Federation. He was at an international sports meeting in Monte Carlo. In my meetings and communications with him, he had promised to bring up the inclusion of women's judo in any international event. His telegram stated that during the meeting when women's judo was brought up for the 1977 Pan Am Games, it was denied. The excuse this time was that there was not enough room in the athletes' village. However, they would consider it for the future.

Hell, we would have camped out in tents if we could have gotten on the schedule!

It didn't diminish my hopes and dreams as I had reached out in many world directions. I had already set up an international base of advocacy within several countries. I wrote a letter to Vladimir Sergeevich Rodichenko, head of the sports program department for the IOC and a big shot with the Soviet Union government. Since they were hosting the 1980 Olympics, I thought, "Hey, they are communists and believe in all things being shared. How about sharing the mat with us?"

> Unofficial translation
>
> Mrs. Rusty Kanokogi,
> Coach USA - AAU Women's
> Judo Team
>
> Dear Mrs. R. Kanokogi,
>
> The Sports Programme Department entrusted by the authority of the Olympiad-80 Organizing Committee have considered your proposals to include the women's judo event into the programme of the Games of the XXII Olympiad.
>
> In this connection we inform you that the programme of the 1980 Olympic Games in Moscow was approved by the 79th session of the IOC in June 1977 and judo competitions for women have not been entered into the programme. Furthermore, the Organizing Committee at this stage cannot support proposals for changes in the programme of the Games of the XXII Olympiad.
>
> Very truly yours,
>
> V. S. Rodichenko,
> Head of Sports
> Programme Department

I did receive a reply—that in itself was amazing. Unfortunately, however, the reply informed me that the program of the XXII Olympiad was already done, approved, and could not include women's judo. That was the year that President Carter ordered the United States to boycott the Moscow Olympic Games. Can you imagine if my proposal had been accepted and we had gotten in? There would not have been enough Secret Service or Feds to protect Carter from me. He and I would have had a fierce judo match at the White House.

At least I was stirring up the pot. 1977 was also the year that I took a team to the Maccabiah Games in Israel. I was told we needed more international events listed on our future Olympic proposals, so off we went. The NY Maccabiah group had to be threatened and cajoled to enter us. We paid our own way. And yes, it did help us in the future.

These women had more than earned their rights to be in the Olympics by their sweat and their fight—as did their male counterparts—except for the fact that the rules excluded them.

Hell yes. No, no!

Women's judo belonged in the Olympics, and I was determined to get it there if it was the very last thing I ever did. Growing up on the streets of Coney Island, I developed my own philosophy: you don't mess with your parents, cops or teachers. Anyone else who bugs you, *kick their ass!*

The International Olympic Committee was messing with me. It was going to be another uphill fight.

Here we go again...

Rusty and the team at the Maccabiah Games, Israel 1977.

55

IT WAS THE 1979 FALL MEETING OF AAU JUDO, which was the last time all of the Olympic sports had the AAU title in their name. The Amateur Athletic Act had passed in the United States Congress, submitted by Senator Ted Stevens of Alaska. It was supposed to mean no more discrimination. *HA!* For me it was the same good old boys, just under a different flag now.

As the AAU representative from New York, I put a proposition in order to the effect that, USA Judo had to propose to the International Judo Federation that the USA will host the first Women's World Judo Championships. I knew that in order to be considered for the Olympics, which was my next and ultimate goal, we first had to have a world championship.

If only I could pull off this major feat!

Of course, I had done my homework and somewhat knew what I would need— lots of money, tons of help and the willingness to go insane.

The power people of USA Judo at the time were the organization's President Wey Seng Kim, a Korean national with dual citizenship who allegedly worked for the Korean KGB, and Vice President Frank Fullerton, born and raised down south and still pissed off about losing the Civil War. He was an attorney by trade whose job was to represent the water works in El Paso, Texas. He resembled the Looney Tunes character Foghorn Leghorn, the cantankerous old rooster that would drawl throughout all his boring speeches, "Ah say, Ah say, Ah say."

Another person I would go to battle with was Thomas Dalton, a.k.a. Tim, but by no means tiny. He was a large man and a former Marine, and he never let anyone forget it, including many of the national judo constituents at the meeting who were of Japanese descent. Tim had a decent side to him, but it was hard to come by with his very gruff exterior. The worst part was that he didn't have a great deal of respect for women, especially judo women.

When I put the proposal forth, it was seconded by one of my pals and was open for discussion, or I should say interrogation. It was a hell of a fight. I held up the paper that was the phony letter my good buddy and ally George Spitz had helped me get from his friend Ed Kayat, publisher of a small New York newspaper—one you could pick up free from the boxes in the street.

I knew that I had to have a sponsor with a commitment of $30,000. I also knew no one in their right mind would give me that kind of money. All I needed was a letter with a pledge of that amount to get me to the next step.

George was as crazy as I so he convinced Ed to write the letter on the newspaper's fancy stationary with "Manhattan's #1 Newspaper, Our Town" scrolled across the top.

Now I had to convince this skeptical, misogynist executive committee that this was the real deal. I also made the commitment to have the first Women's World Judo Championships at Madison Square Garden in the heart of New York City.

Dalton asked to see the money. "I don't carry it around," I said. "Here is the damn letter. Read it!"

The debate went on for hours. I was definitely winning over the board of directors because I had agitated the executive board so badly, they were getting downright nasty. Fullerton was against most everything anyway so I blew him away quickly with my noble speech indicating that if he and the others stood in the way of women's judo progressing, I would hold them responsible for the rest of their lives and haunt them in the thereafter.

Wey Seng Kim began to be supportive even though I believed he could see through it all. He knew that if it passed, no matter what, I would get it done. The USA Judo meeting was going to be held in December of 1979 and if it passed, Mr. Kim would take it before the International Judo Federation.

It finally came to a vote and it passed.

What a relief!

Now all we needed was the IJF's approval for the US to host the championship. And why wouldn't they? No one else really wanted it except maybe communist Yugoslavia. They had even less money than I did, and I had none!

As good luck would have it, the people that represented the best mat company in the world had attended the USA Judo meeting. We made friends and they offered to help me with one of the most important items, the tatami mats that were compulsory to have at a World Championship. I needed hundreds of them, and they were pretty expensive. The Judogi Company of France would be the official sponsor of the mat.

Whew, one problem solved, and just 860 more to go.

In December, I received a call from Mr. Kim. He was at JFK Airport and wanted me to meet him there so we could talk.

At the airport, he had only one question for me. "Can *you* do it?"

I said that I could, to which he responded that he didn't like women's judo but he was going to support the proposal because of me. He told me that he believed I would do it and do it well because I was a powerful force that couldn't be stopped. I told him that he was a very clever man, and that he should have a good trip.

56

I RECEIVED A CALL IN MID-JANUARY, 1980, FROM Wey Seng Kim after he returned from the International Judo Federation meeting in Japan. There had been an election of officers for the next quadrennial, as well as other business. Our bid for the first Women's World Judo Championships was in that category.

The newly elected president was Dr. Shigeyoshi Matsumae.

How ironic for me.

I was so afraid that if Charles Palmer of Great Britain was not re-elected as president, my bid would go in the toilet no matter who proposed it for our country. I believed that if Dr. Matsumae got elected, he would not support anything for women's judo. I thought he was from the old school and believed women should stay home, don their lovely kimonos, and nurse babies.

I was never so wrong about anything in my life—except, well, maybe my first marriage and for not walking the one hundred miles on the highway to collect my wedding gift from Jackson Pollock.

In any case, this was my most recent misjudgment.

The tournament was approved and later on Dr. Matsumae would become one of my best advocates, a total supporter and best friend. I feel it was a privilege to know and work with such an amazing man. There are volumes of books on his life and accomplishments. It would be an injustice to try and summarize his life story, so, I will only mention some of the enormity of his successes.

As an engineer, Dr. Matsumae invented the underwater cable. As a result of this and good business sense, he became a millionaire. Another of his ambitions was to educate young people. To that end, he began the Tokai University Educational System (TES), opened universities, high schools and grade schools from Hokkaido to Kyushu in

Japan, and later throughout the world. His main objective was peace and friendship through education and sports.

Now I could develop, organize, and conduct the first Women's World Judo Championships in New York. But how the hell was I going to do all that?

As luck would have it, the United States of America Amateur Boxing Federation was going to conduct a World Cup of sorts here in the city. Since I was the AAU chairperson for judo, the local boxing group invited me and any volunteers I could bring in to help them with their World Cup.

It was being held in Madison Square Garden and I jumped at the chance it would give me to work on a world-class event. Making more connections was also a definite plus.

The boxing event would be held in the early spring and the Women's World Judo Championships was scheduled for November 29 and 30 of the same year: 1980.

57

MY LIST OF TO-DO ITEMS CONTINUED TO ESCA-
late by the minute. The list went something like this:

1. Open an account for the first WWJC. – One problem—no money.

2. Get a list of things needed to host a world championship from the director of the IJF, Henri Courtine. I got the one-hundred-page list with about 1,000 items, from pool sheets to paper clips. I swore to follow it religiously.

3. Get the official hotel. I decided on the famous Penta Hotel, formerly the Statler. This hotel was once the home of the big band king Glenn Miller. It was right across the street from Madison Square Garden and that's where I decided we had to hold our tournament, no matter what!

The IJF requested a check for a $5,000 hosting fee immediately. I couldn't go to Ed Kayat of the *Our Town NY* newspaper since that was make-believe money. So again, I went to my buddy George Spitz.

George was connected to a good guy by the name of Percy Sutton, the former borough president of Manhattan. At the time he was the CEO of Inner City Broadcasting. George told Percy about my plight. He loved George like a brother, lucky for me, and agreed to come in as a sponsor even though he really didn't have a clue what judo was.

I met Percy. He was a charming, intellectual gentleman and I thanked him over and over again. I even offered him judo lessons for the rest of his life.

He gave me the check and I opened the bank account, raised a little more money and sent the check to the IJF as though the money had just been lying there in my huge account waiting for them to ask for it all along.

> - 2 -
>
> 2. On the proposal of the Sports Director, Mr. Courtine, the Directing Committee considers it necessary to make an intesive referees' instruction on the occasion of the 1st Women's World Championships.
> The Directing Committee requests the Organizer to consider if the referees could arrive one day earlier than fixed in the time-table and if the Organizer can make available the rooms for the instruction.
>
> 3. In order to solve a great number of outstanding problems within the Directing Committee, the D.C. asks you to think over the possibility if the Directing Committee members can arrive one day earlier than scheduled so that the meeting could be held on two days.
>
> The Sports Director, Mr. Courtine, will pay a visit to you at the end of september in New York. This will be a good opportunity to discuss all details.
>
> Please send me soonest your reply.
> I wish you much success in preparing the important 1st Women's World Championships and look forward to meeting you in November.
> Best regards.
>
>   Yours sincerely,
>
>   Heinz Kempa
>   IJF General Secretary
>
> Enclosure: - Invitation to the 1st Women's World Championships.
>   - Address list of officials, jury members and referees.
>
> cc. Dr. Matsumae, IJF President
>   Mr. Courtine, Sports Director of IJF

Time was moving too rapidly for me. It seemed twenty-four hours in the day were just not enough with the tremendous amount of things I had to get done.

Aside from my daily teaching of judo, home, and family, I also had the assignment of national coach for the first Pacific Rim Championships to be held in Hawaii around Valentine's Day.

As usual, we had a team but no funding.

At last, a miracle!

It was announced that each of us would receive a travel stipend from US Judo in the amount of fifty dollars.

Big WHOOP.

On one hand it was a joke, but on the other it was finally, at least, something. Two full teams of women were selected from the past Nationals. The women,

in many cases young girls, had to raise their own money from parents and/or take out loans.

Several other major phenomenal revelations were also taking place at this time. The first one was the discovery that Mr. Iso Inokuma, a worldwide and Olympic judo champion from Japan, had absolutely no discrimination against women in in the sport. He was the competitor back in 1962 who had given me flying lessons when I practiced with him. He really didn't care whose ass he kicked.

Mr. Inokuma was now the assistant to Dr. Matsumae and he made the introductions. Dr. Matsumae and I looked at each other for a very long time. I saw a strong-looking, elderly gentleman with a mane of snow-white hair and the wisdom of the world in his eyes. I didn't know his take on me, but it didn't matter at the time. I thanked him for supporting the award of the tournament to the US. He smiled and said he would continue his support of me as he admired my courage and tenacity—in other words, my *chutzpah*.

I spoke with Mr. Inokuma after Dr. Matsumae left the room. He read me The Riot Act. Why hadn't I supported the election of Dr. Matsumae? Why had I supported Mr. Palmer?

Of course, I didn't get a vote, but I guess I was a good lobbyist and had rocked the boat. I explained that I hadn't had any information on Dr. Matsumae and I was concerned he would not support women's judo. I believed Mr. Palmer would. Mr. Inokuma must have been able to see I was telling the truth, because he forgave me. He indicated I would be hearing from him and the IJF soon. This news put me in a good mood.

The next day was competition for the Pacific Rim Championships. Our teams were fantastic. We took most of the medals, coming in first place.

The men's team, which had been totally funded, didn't do so well and had to settle for a few bronze metals, or in many cases, nothing at all. It was celebration time.

The team was really up over their victory after we beat Japan. Our judo president, Mr. Wey Seng Kim, was at the hotel when we returned and welcomed us back with congratulations and a huge heart-shaped Valentine's Day cake.

We had most of the next day free since our flight was in the evening. All eighteen of us rented motorbikes and zoomed like the Hell's Angels up to Diamond Head. We were on top now.

Hooray!

On the other hand, how long could this last?

It was back to Brooklyn for me, as I needed to form my army to ensure that the first Women's World Judo Championships in New York would happen and happen successfully.

58

THE RECRUITMENT POOL FOR THE ORGANIZING committee for the first Women's World Judo Championships consisted of the following combination of people: believers, followers, and people who didn't have a clue how or why they were going to help.

So far, we had only the date and location: November 29 and 30 at Madison Square Garden in New York City, USA.

The cast of characters began with the executive board. President? *Me*—Rusty Kanokogi—whose background was a love of the sport of judo, hate of injustice and discrimination, and a desire for equality for women in judo. A graduate of the streets of Brooklyn, I acknowledged no boundaries and had the ability to bounce back from pain quickly.

Vice President was Mel Applebaum, PhD. At the time, Mel was president of Pepsico, a fellow judo player with executive abilities and connections. He supported me to the death, once again—as always. He was my ride-or-die guy in the fight for equality in judo.

Vice President Pat Earle was a woman I had met at one of the committee meetings in the '70s, which was organized to bring the 1980 Olympics to New York. I was impressed with her talents as a speaker. She seemed savvy and I liked the way she handled herself around men. She seemed to get what she wanted. She had political and media connections; she was known about

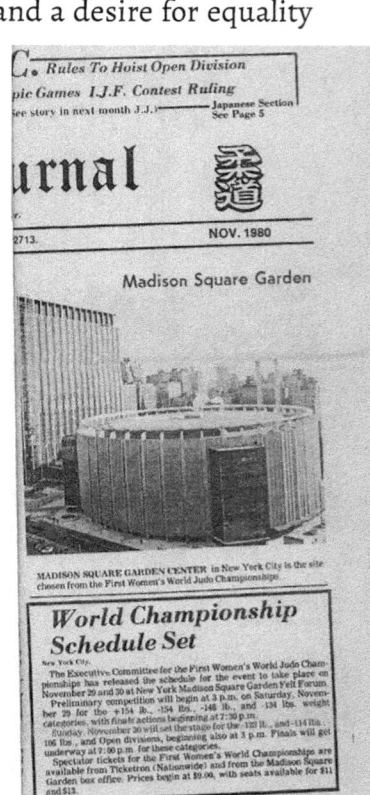

town. It didn't hurt that she liked me, believed in the cause, and had TV connections.

Secretary Peter Perazio was my twenty-four-year-old student of many years who had been helping me with paperwork on all fronts since he was very young. He was diligent, intelligent, and could almost read my mind. Plus he could spell. Peter was my left-hand man. I'm a southpaw.

Treasurer Mary Potanas, a.k.a. the judo bean counter extraordinaire. I found Mary at my student Anita Mathius' health club where we practiced judo. Mary was not involved in the sport but was a good-hearted accountant who came to our rescue. She did the books for Anita and came highly recommended. Poor Mary didn't know what she was getting into.

Our legal counsel was Edward Serrapede, Esq., whose sport of choice was team handball—another sport that people hardly knew about. I met Ed when minor sports were invited to do a demonstration for the New York state legislators in Albany. We hung out and had fun. We were both involved in contact sports and could relate in several areas. When the time came, I was fortunate enough to get this super bright, gutsy attorney to go all the way for us. He saved us so many times.

Let me share a few anecdotes about the above-mentioned people. Mel Applebaum entered into my project as a man of ideals and a mover and shaker in the corporate world. I knew that it was important to have that kind of support. Much to my amazement, Mel couldn't raise any major bucks. He did, however, manage to get tons of M&M's candy donated to us, as well as other candy bars from PepsiCo. We added the treats to the goodie bags handed out to the registering athletes.

> **MADISON SQUARE GARDEN CENTER, INC.**
> TWO PENNSYLVANIA PLAZA
> NEW YORK, NEW YORK 10001
>
> GEORGIA A. MC ENROE
> SENIOR LEGAL ASSISTANT
>
> November 19, 1980
>
> Mrs. Rusty Kanokogi
> Tournament Director
> First Women's World Judo
>   Championships
> Brooklyn, New York 11229
>
> Re: "1st World Women's Judo
>   Championships" -
>   November 29-30, 1980
>
> Dear Rusty:
>
>   Enclosed herewith is a fully-executed Agreement between Madison Square Garden Center, Inc. and First Women's World Judo Championship Organizing Committee, Inc. relating to the above Event, for your files.
>
>   Thank you for your cooperation.
>
>   Best regards.
>
>   Sincerely,
>
>   *Georgia*
>   Georgia A. McEnroe
>
> Enclosure

    These gifts were met with mixed reactions since the athletes compete in weight categories and many were on strict diets to stay within their weight limits. Since we were all working around the clock, the candy did help me, as well as the rest of the crew, with a source of instant energy. My daughter, Jean, is still paying the dentist for all those hours helping us in the office. As a fourteen-year-old at the time with a mother not cooking, her meals consisted of handfuls of multi-colored M&M's. Even though he was a high-level executive at PepsiCo, Mel often did the chicken run when we ran out of food for our officials at the Championships.

    Somewhere along the way things went awry. I was preoccupied with so many facets of the operation that I'm sure I neglected people and did not give the adequate attention or recognition. In retrospect, I believed someone sabotaged the award I was to receive during opening ceremonies from the organizing committee. I was standing at center stage when the announcement of the award was made to the audience. Co-Vice President Mel Applebaum walked over where I was standing holding the award in his hand. He made a lovely speech honoring me and then under his breath said, "Smile. Accept the box but don't open it. Someone stole the fucking plaque!" I still have the empty box as a memory and a reminder not to expect awards for service.

I probably worked Peter Perazio harder than anyone on our organizing committee. It was his fault for being so capable! There wasn't a job I didn't lay on him, and for the most part he became a co-conspirator. He wasn't afraid of any legal ramifications, just judo ramifications. We had to look the IJF officials straight in the eyes and repeat the same little white lie: "Of course we will have the money to do this event." Had they known the truth, our project would have been dead in less than thirty seconds.

I remember Peter and I going over the budget in my humble house in Brooklyn in August of 1979. Peter reminded me that we had only $116 in the account. I screamed at him that I would get the money. He never brought it up again.

I managed to get my hands on a rickety old typewriter, and Peter spent many evenings in my kitchen doing the paperwork. My ideas were good but I needed his college education to help with spelling and grammar. I fed him enough coffee to improve the economy of Colombia, but poor Peter would still fall asleep with his head pressed onto the keys. At the actual world championship, he was so sleep-deprived that Mr. Courtine, the IJF director, referred to him as "the zombie."

Peter was a true hero to the cause and supported me unconditionally. He now lives in France with his lovely wife and daughter. He is an artist and photographer and is well on his way to becoming a recognized leader in his field with a bright future. I've often wondered if Peter moved to France in an attempt to get some distance between us just in case I came up with another mega project.

Mary Potanas got things done but if I needed something done financially and called her, I got pissed off when she could not get me the cash I needed at three o'clock in the morning. Thank goodness she was an easy-going person and could tolerate my craziness. All said and done, she did a great job, as all our bills were paid and none of us went to jail.

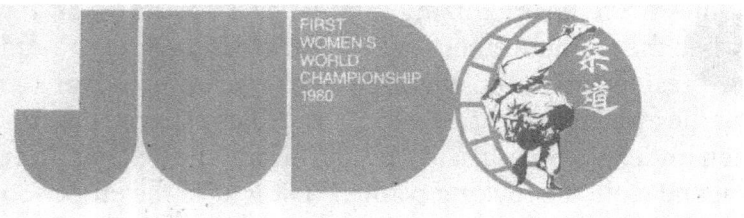

Edward Serrapede, our legal counsel extraordinaire, incorporated the organization as a non-profit organization in the state of New York, and obtained tax-exempt status for us from the IRS. He also obtained copyright and trademark protection from the federal government. But more importantly, he obtained and forced through provisions in the

1978 Amateur Sports Act for USA Judo to give our organization a sanction to hold the necessary competitions here in the States. On top of that, all of this critical and necessary paperwork was done in record time, because in New York the average time can be several years.

Ed also persuaded me not to choke the President of the USA Judo organization, Frank Fullerton, into unconsciousness on the judo mats in Madison Square Garden in front of all the spectators that came to the world championships. Fullerton had denied and resisted giving the sanction for the event. Rather than thanking Ed for all his pro bono work on our behalf, Frank referred to Ed as an "arrogant, punk lawyer from New York."

Ed also did the chicken run for our officials, who we were required to feed— along with the staff—during the championship. We had a budget of zero dollars. When we ran out of food, those who "ran for chicken" not only had to run and buy, but also understood they would not be reimbursed. Ed is another true hero of the cause and justice. Thank God that Ed and his wife survived the 9/11 tragedy, as their apartment was very close to Ground Zero. It took over a year of reconstruction and cleanup, but they were finally able to go back home again. I know Ed wouldn't blink an eye if I called him for any kind of help in the future. He has been through it all.

I spoke about Percy Sutton before but want to continue with his accolades as he was one of the folks who was on this team and probably still doesn't know why. My friend and fellow conspirator, George Spitz, was responsible for hooking me up with Percy.

What a man!

Percy was born in 1920, the youngest of fifteen siblings, of African American descent. He was in the Army Air Corps, and served with the famous Tuskegee Airmen. He was well-decorated for his valor. He put himself through law school and went on to become Manhattan borough president from 1966 to 1977.

Besides helping me with the world project for women's judo, Percy was a pioneering political trailblazer and an extremely active civil rights advocate, representing figures like Malcolm X, alongside hundreds of other protestors arrested for speaking out in the South.

In 1971 Percy co-founded Inner City Broadcasting, the first black-owned station in New York. He was also solely responsible for the refurbishing and reopening of the historic Apollo Theater in 1981[16].

Percy couldn't attend all of our board meetings, so he often had one of his top aides, Mr. Wallace Ford, come along. All they wanted from me and the organizing committee in return was to approve their request to have the Harlem Boys Choir sing at our opening ceremony. I was thrilled to have that group of talented kids aboard, and would have settled for far less. Believe me, if they wanted a group of ducks quacking, "The Star-Spangled Banner," I would have made it happen.

59

GEORGE SPITZ, MY MAN OF LA MANCHA, WAS quite an incredible guy. I was so very lucky to have our paths cross. George gave me the gift of both guidance and his great connections. He knew everybody. He either sued them, wrote about them, or supported them.

There was no halfway with George. In political circles, he drove people nuts by running for everything. And believe it or not, he did get support. He and I differed big time politically; however, I found myself on street corners in New York City touting him for whatever he was running for just because I loved him. The mayor at the time, Ed Koch, called George a "City Hall gadfly." He was politically astute and an excellent writer who scared the shit out of a lot of bad guys.

George had Mayor Koch proclaim November 29 and 30, 1980 as the First Women's World Judo Championships Days in New York. I still have the proclamation. He also got me the blue room in City Hall for a major kick off reception. There will be more on that funny story and George later.

Margaret Grossberger was the New York State Athletic Commissioner who was pleased to be involved with the event. I remember she picked up the tab for one of our big lunch meetings, was always available to make a toast to almost anything, and was just a good old gal. She had good credentials, good looks, and was a welcome addition to the committee.

Michael Abernethy was a sports genius and a man of courage. As the Executive Director of the Empire State Games, he was able to bring more athletes and officials together than the Olympic Games. He could remember almost everyone's name.

Mike became one of my major consultants. He gave me tremendous guidance and use of his staff. He supported the inclusion of women's judo into the Empire State Games from day one when many were against it, wanting to stick with sports included in the Olympics only. He refused them all and allowed us in.

Mike and I also put our heads together when the US Olympic Committee and the national governing bodies of sports were having the major national event known as the Olympic Sports Festival. Women's judo was not invited since we were not yet on the Olympic schedule.

The Olympic Sports Festival was to be in Syracuse in 1981. Mike reminded me that the judo event at the 1981 Sports Festival in Syracuse was in a state-owned school. New York state has a law[17] on the books that one cannot host or contract with any entity that discriminates against race, religion, color, or gender.

I made my case to the Department of Human Rights, filed charges against the US Olympic Committee and US Judo for discrimination against women and won. The greater victory, even more sweet than the USOC conceding, was the knowledge that we won the right to be in the Sports Festival. Now I had to round up our fifty best women athletes to compete in the event.

Everyone in boxing knew John Condon's name. He was the main man for Madison Square Garden's boxing events. He was well connected and loved by folks from both sides of the tracks.

I met John at a few dinners. He wasn't against women's judo but he was a little skeptical about women fighting. John passed away in 1989, and would have been knocked for a loop to see how women in full contact sports have evolved. John loaned me the famous old scale I used to do the weigh-ins for the US women's judo trials to see who would make our team. The scale was the same one that weighed in Joe Louis, Rocky Graziano and many of the big names from boxing.

John was supportive, connected me with the right people at the Garden and let me use his name all over the place, as it carried clout, especially at the New York Athletic Club. When I booked a major welcome party for the Championships, I said it was for the World Judo Championships. They assumed it was for men and I didn't tell them otherwise.

Ryohei, did any job I requested. He moved quietly but thoroughly and was the extended part of my backbone. He comforted me when all things seemed impossible, stayed out of my way when I went ballistic, and cleaned up after me when I didn't handle someone correctly. He was the complete opposite of me, thank goodness, as we are still together and will be to the end. He is my best friend, husband, and the love of my life.

I met Doreen McLoughlin when I was soliciting sneakers for the Polish women's basketball team that was coming to New York for a competition with the men's judo team. I contacted PONY, the sneaker hotshot of the year. Their CEO, Paul Landau, was charming, handsome, and a real sweetie pie. He gave me sneakers for the women and big PONY bags for the judo team. His number one girl, Doreen, helped me with what I needed in the future. Little did Paul know how helpful he would become thanks to darling Doreen.

Shelly Nangle, Mike Abernethy's right arm, was always there for me. No request was too crazy or great. Shelly was with the New York State Parks and Recreation Department, and helped me do anything for judo—from stuffing mass mailer envelopes to securing me a workspace to conduct business, or getting a major venue and TV cameras to the Empire State Games judo event.

Jack Prenderville was very close to Governor Hugh Cary. Jack was a Deputy Commissioner with the New York State Office of Parks, Recreation and Historic Preservation. He would get anything I needed from the state done. He also later served under Governor Andrew Cuomo.

Stephen Spahn was from the Dwight School, the Franklin School and Tripp Lake Camp. Stephen was the headmaster of several prep schools and would help me every time I got in a jam, which was quite often. He had an abundance of connections and he pulled them out of his magical hat whenever I needed the help. So many kids from affluent families went to the prep school. Spahn became part of our board.

Gary Catarina was a judo player from our club who I put in charge of protocol. He was tall, dark, and handsome. As you will find out later, Gary came through with an incredible job for the cause—he may have also lost his real job as a result. He was selfless and dedicated to the cause.

There are so many heroes in this story. Their stories are next. Some have had to wait thirty years for my heartfelt gratitude.

60

THE UNSUNG HEROES OF WOMEN'S JUDO ARE about to be recognized and thanked, whether they still like me or not. Several of the shell-shocked may not even remember participating. This chapter should not only remind them but return them to reality. Grab the Prozac as this is going to be a bumpy ride! The order has not been prioritized; it is just a series of reminiscences. Margie Brown was from Saugerties, New York, about three hours north of the city. Margie had an outgoing personality and a big heart. Visually, she could have doubled for Marjorie Main, playing Ma Kettle in that great old film. We became friends via the judo world. Our families hit it off and it was like going to visit relatives when we dropped in on them upstate or vise versa. Margie and her husband Bob had three sons, all in judo. They worked out with us whenever they could and we enjoyed these strong, young, pleasant fellows.

I had recruited Margie several years before as my typist, envelope stuffer, babysitter, and confidant, so it was natural to invite her to help me with all the upcoming first Women's World Judo Championships. Margie was one of my army that worked with me until the end, helping me see everything through for the first Women's World Judo Championships. When it was over, Margie dragged herself back to Saugerties and landed in the hospital with a breakdown. If I could choose one person from my crew to receive the Medal of Honor, she would be it.

It was so hectic during our preparations for the "Worlds" at our tournament headquarters at the Statler- Penta-Pennsylvania Hotel that we each ended up doing ten jobs or more. One of the jobs that I gave Margie was to work with Mrs. Emerson, the mother of one of the USA's youngest competitors, Monica Emerson, to sew on the competition numbers. These numbers had to be sewn on the back of each competitor's judogi.

The judogis are made of a very thick cotton to withstand physical abuse. I was able to convince a company in New Jersey to lend us a few industrial sewing machines and in turn I would give them credit on our program book.

Unfortunately, the judo gi's were stronger than the machines, which promptly broke. I cursed the damned company; meanwhile, Margie and Mrs. Emerson worked around the clock and managed to sew all one hundred and fifty patches on the uniforms by hand. The patches were fifteen-by-fifteen inches. I think Mrs. Emerson eventually snuck away, but good old Marge worked until she could barely move her fingers.

Part of our agreement with the International Judo Federation was to give the referees a daily allowance. I thought it was to be thirty dollars but it turned out to be fifty—each. We hardly had enough money to pay the lesser amount, so I had to think fast. I sent Margie and a few more down to the lobby of the hotel and throughout the building to sell our souvenir world championships T-shirts. It worked. Hawking our shirts brought in the additional money I needed to pay the referees. They all stood around waiting for their gelt, especially the guy from Cuba; to him, it was a year's salary.

Margie had moved into the hotel headquarters with me. On any given night, several of my staff stayed over. We had one bed and as many as four people trying to catch a catnap. Gender was not a factor. When Margie's hubby, Bob, came down to visit during the turmoil, I was so rude to him I accused him of getting in the way. He was a rather large man and I needed all of my office space. I wasn't in the mood to entertain. He didn't expect my rudeness but it was my lack of sanity that put me in such a state. By this time I was working on about four hours of sleep in three days. To Bob, you have my apologies all the way from Brooklyn to Saugerties, three hours' worth.

I was probably closest to Paul Brown, one of Bob and Margie's sons. He had moved to Brooklyn for college and judo training with us. He met his future wife, Ruth, at our judo club, Kyushu. I had met Ruth before, at the British Open. She was a world-class judo woman and champ from Switzerland.

Ruth came to New York to continue her education. They met, fell in love and eventually got married. They also worked hard for the championships initiative. They gave me time and energy without asking for a dime. They gave with all their hearts. The Browns have been rewarded. Margie and Bob have several grandchildren who are without exaggeration in the genius category. All are healthy and thriving—a family of true unsung heroes.

61

ALL OF THE PEOPLE THAT WERE INVOLVED WITH this pull-together project were from out of town and either stayed with friends, at our house, or in a hotel on their own dime. They were lucky to get a bag of M&M's from time to time as tribute. I was completely driven and obsessed with delivering a successful world championships—eating and sleeping were irrelevant needs to me. I thought they should be irrelevant for everyone else also. I imagined some of the staff and volunteers snuck away to refuel from time to time, because every once in a while I got a whiff of Chinese food on their breaths.

Although the crews' hearts were in the right place, some of them unintentionally added to my insanity, as I was trying to host the world's largest judo event for women; others kept me sane.

Kenny Pollard, my protégé: I gave Kenny several simple jobs to do, one of which was to go down to our rented van and bring up the special event T-shirts I had ordered to help raise some of our much-needed revenue. Kenny went down and brought up a load of shirts, leaving the van door open. Thieves took the rest. We had lost our income generating stock, and now had competition; the thieves hawked the shirts on the street, while my people ran around the hotel selling them to anyone that would buy one. Oy!

Richard Kennedy, my student from York Prep: It was so impressive to me that he was allowed by the headmaster, to practice judo with me throughout all the six classes I taught at the school every Wednesday. He was a good student and a big kid, so I could really use him to demonstrate all the techniques that I was teaching. I later found out the reason he was allowed to stay with me all day was to give all of his other teachers a break.

I had him on the hospitality committee at the hotel. *BIG mistake!* He showed up on roller skates, gliding through the hotel on their rugs.

Richard's idea of hospitality was to try and get the competitors to run off with him. Fortunately, sanity prevailed and no one took him up on his offer.

Another mistake I made was to put him in charge of supplying the audio guy at Madison Square Garden with the national anthems of the first-place winners in each weight division. He messed this up big time. Only the first few bars of "La Marseillaise," the French national anthem, played over the speakers and then total silence. After what seemed like hours, but was only a few seconds, someone began to whistle the remainder of the song and everyone who knew the tune joined in. But the French, being the French, were insulted and have never failed to mention it to me at every opportunity. A British judo magazine referred to Kennedy as "an American oddity" when they reported on the World Championships.

Gigi Gonzales: Gigi was a good light-weight judo player, originally from Long Island. Her only downfall was not being able to read the signs that said, "Tow Away Zone." Every time I sent her out with a van on a chore, the van disappeared. She worked her butt off as a volunteer, was willing to help me every step of the way but goodness, nearly each time she took that van on an errand, it just about landed in the NYC tow-pound. We just kept retrieving the impounded vans and I should add, in her defense, NYC street signs are as easy to read as hyroglifics. Nonetheless, I am grateful to her for her hard work and selfless dedication.

George Pasiuk, a guy who would help most anybody in judo: George had a big heart. Unfortunately, his mouth was just as big. His job was to handle the airport run, along with tow-away Gigi. George didn't get towed away, he just returned from the airport on several occasions without the officials he was supposed to pick up. Was he at the wrong airport? Did he hold the sign too low? Or was he focused on the stewardess walking out? Who knows the truth? I reimbursed the irate officials from the IJF for their taxi rides. Until this day, George still blames them: "Damned foreigners. They can't read."

Jim McKay, from the New York City Public School Athletic League: Jim was kind enough to supply us with the podium where the athletes would receive their awards. Aside from being free, that ridiculous orange-crate-looking podium would continue to push me toward the edge. First, it was a terrible beige color and really shabby looking. I had it painted white and kept my fingers crossed that when the awards were presented to the heavy weights, they wouldn't fall through the stupid, rickety thing. The numbers one, two and three were painted on by one of our students. I had just run him through the ringer for messing other tasks up, the numbers were clear but shaky looking.

Carmen Mussomeli, nothing could get her down. She was pretty and cheerful. Aside from some basic administrative chores, she did an outstanding hospitality job by welcoming the international officials and really rolling out the red carpet for them. I knew I could always depend on her diplomacy. A true professional all around.

Mindy Douglas, Leslie Conte, and Heidi Bauersachs, three outstanding judo players from our Kyushu Judo Club: Mindy—short, cute, smart and built like a Playboy magazine cover model—was a fierce competitor. She was very good at choking people out and she managed to do it several times at the Empire State Games in the open division, where her opponents were literally twice her weight. When not competing, Mindy was in our headquarters office most of the time. Some days she worked so late that I found her sleeping under the table the next morning.

Leslie was tall, wiry, witty, smart and very attractive. She was going to be in the opening ceremony of the World Championships as the reader of Dr. Matsumae's speech to the athletes, officials and spectators. Nothing phased her, so I knew she would do a good job. Leslie won the Empire State Games gold medal in her division seven years in a row. That's still the record in judo.

Heidi was a big, wholesome, sweet and beautiful young woman with a lot of heart. It took her a long time to build up her self-confidence, as she didn't realize how strong she was. We always had faith in her and she proved us right. We trained her nonstop, she never gave up, and she won a gold in the Pan American Games and was number one in the United States for several years. She was a tremendous help with the opening ceremonies and so many other random tasks. Mindy and Leslie were the judo models for our logo.

Heidi's dad, Dr. Rudolph Bauersachs, was an obstetrician/gynecologist and one of our official team doctors. He also delivered two of my kids, Jean and Ted.

Dr. Joseph Fetto, is an orthopedic surgeon and a more appropriate type of doctor to have at a judo competition served as another one of our medical staff.

He donated his time and energy to the World's and has gone on to be a world-renowned physician excelling in his field. Everyone in my family has his surgery mark on them.

Bill Chisolm, the head of the Brooklyn College athletic trainers program. Bill volunteered to be our head trainer. We were happy to get him. His work as an athletic trainer is legendary, he put more people together than humpty dumpty's caretakers.

Jean, Rusty & Maureen Braziel at the 1983 Empire State Games.

Sandi Cornelius, my faithful Indian companion: Sandi was an Oneida Indian by birth, and we had known each other for a long time. She had an attractive poker face with the look of someone you don't want to mess with, topped off by a cheerful personality and an easy laugh. We weren't intimate friends at that time, both being somewhat cautious for who knows what reason. Still, Sandi was recruited, came in from Milwaukee on her own dime, just like the rest and did an outstanding job. She covered anything and everything, and always worked quietly and diligently, and got the job done. This bond lent us to trust each other and become and remain good friends.

Rusty, Jean & Bruce at the Empire State Games opening ceremonies.

Jean Kanokogi, my daughter: Jean was fourteen at the time. Even at that age, she was already a competitor moving into the women's division a year early because of her ability. Jean had heard the word judo while still in the womb, as I taught throughout my full pregnancy and was teaching the doctor almost up to delivery. You had to think she would have had enough by her teens, but she never did.

As a savvy, gutsy girl I knew I could depend on Jean. She has her father's personality for the most part: easy-going. She was always taking care of herself and her kid brother while I was preoccupied. It even went as far as her covering a press conference for me while I had another urgent appointment. She handled it magnificently. Jean went on to be a world-class athlete in judo, member of the US judo team and won numerous medals for the United States. After her competition career, she went on to enjoy life as a special agent for the US government, and eventually went back to graduate school to earn her PhD in psychology.

Ted Kanokogi, my son: Ted was a nine-year-old kid at the time, who could easily get in trouble. He had an abundance of energy and many of my personality traits. The best way he could help was to listen to

Jean and Margie Brown, who stayed at our house during this time, and try not to get in any trouble that would take me away from the big job.

He really tried his best, but being nine isn't easy. One funny incident that will stay with me forever is the time that Ted was home alone with our huge, all white German shepherd, Yuki, which means snow in Japanese. Ted got home from school first and was told to stick around the house until Jean joined him. If anyone bothered him, he was to run down the driveway to the backyard where Yuki was. Ted was told not to let anyone in under any circumstances. Of course, a fellow came from the program printers' office to pick up the last of our ads for the program. Ted happened to be playing samurai in the backyard at the time, and had a large metal type of samurai sword and a hachimaki (Japanese scarf) on his head, looking like a kamikaze.

The messenger rang the bell. No answer. He looked down the driveway and saw Ted and proceeded down the driveway to speak to him when the dog ran out of the garage like a bat out of hell to bite him and Ted chased him with the sword. The poor guy ran away as fast as his legs could move. At that moment Jean was coming down the block and, not knowing about the messenger, suspected foul play and jumped on the poor guy. He eventually managed to get his story out but refused to go back to the house where the white beast and the crazed midget samurai were. Jean took care of the paperwork and the messenger left. I'm guessing he was never the same again. Maybe this is where they got that whole *Home Alone* movie idea from!

Then there were the midshipmen from the United States Merchant Marine Academy out in Long Island. Ryohei was the chief self-defense instructor there and asked several of them to volunteer. They served well—God, their country, and me.

PHOTO CREDIT: PETER PERAZIO.

Ryohei Kanokogi, circa 1984.

62

MY HUSBAND'S STUDENTS FROM THE US

Merchant Marine Academy at Kings Point, New York, were originally asked if they would be honor guards for the World Championships, dealing with the flag and escorting the VIPs. Once I got them involved and in the city to help, I soon took advantage of a good resource with disciplined, strong and loyal midshipmen.

Several deserve extra credit, including Sparky Lyle, a happy-go-lucky fellow, and Ken Rusterholtz, the straight as an arrow intellect of the group. Ken was so fast, he would get things done before the last word was out of my mouth.

The gem of the crew was Tom Raile. Like me, he didn't have any boundaries; he totally committed himself to the championships and the hell with everything else. He was incredible. There wasn't a job that Tom couldn't do.

Before the world championships, we had a press party at city hall with Mayor Koch. I was told to invite some of the athletes and officials to the Blue Room at City Hall. The only drawback was our frugal mayor would not provide any of the refreshments. We had to provide the goodies ourselves.

I invited one athlete from each country, the coach of each country, several of our international referees, and several VIPs. We were able to solicit cheese from a famous French cheese company, wine from Sylvia Sichel of the Schenley Liquor Company whom I'd met earlier in the year, and I sprung for the crackers.

We got all the attendees to City Hall alright, but the food and drinks were a little late. I had asked my redheaded dynamo, Tom, to get everything delivered prior to the noon conference. We just happened to have a hand delivery cart that we had "borrowed" from the company that delivered our awards, so Tom loaded everything onto the cart and hailed a cab. Being from New Mexico, how would a young man in college at the Merchant Marine Academy know that a New York taxi would not take him, his cart and all the boxes of booze and cheese downtown to City Hall from 34th Street in Midtown? Tom did the next best thing, pushing the overloaded cart the five miles to City Hall. When he showed up, the real festivities began.

During the official photo shoot for the event, one of the press people asked Margie Castro, a member of the US team, who was six foot three and 225 pounds, to pick up Carole Bellamy on her hip for a judo photo. Carole was a New York City official at the time. Margie easily picked up Carole, but Carole's feet got caught under a table. Margie carried on and picked up both Carole and the table. I hoped she would be able to do it again at the competition, where she ended up taking home a bronze medal.

Mayor Koch was called away on an emergency, so his deputy mayor, Herb Rickman, subbed in for him. All the foreign athletes and officials thought Herb was Mayor Koch and I didn't bother to tell them he wasn't. Herb immediately fell in love with my big, handsome referee from Tunisia. I had to grab the slightly built Herb as he swooned all over the place. "The Tunisian" didn't have a clue what was going on, thank God.

When the party ended, we headed back to the hotel. It was pouring rain and we were on a zero-dollar budget. I gave my hero, Tom, some plastic to keep the crackers dry and told him to take all the leftover food and drink back to the hotel for our next reception. He did, walking all the way back to 34th Street. I think this was an omen of what was in store for us. The actual World Championships were in two days...

...*Oh, God.*

63

WITH THE UPCOMING CHAMPIONSHIPS JUST A breath away, I wanted to review my checklist. I reread all the telexes that I had sent and received to make sure I had all the correct information on the teams, officials, delivery of the mats, scoreboards, scales, sewing machines, etc. The 140 feet of telexes I had accumulated were courtesy of Doreen McLauglin who utilized the machine of our good friends at Pony Enterprises. They will now be able to figure out why their stock went down that year. Don't worry, Doreen, we have passed the statute of limitations for telex pilfering.

I had contacted the Japanese Ambassador in New York to let him know about the upcoming championships and to ask him for a special award to give a chosen athlete at the competition. He allowed me to select the trophy and figure out what the award should be for. The only reason I even got a response was I had mentioned Dr. Matsumae's name and connection, as well as his planned participation. Dr. Matsumae's name would be the magic that continued to do wonders for the cause before, during and after the tournament.

Sandi, Gigi and I took a trek to Tiffany's on Fifty-Seventh Street and Fifth Avenue to pick out the ambassador's gift. It was quite a scene in the exclusive shop.

We made our way up to the silver department: Sandi in her typical Milwaukee everyday clothes, Gigi in jeans and a judo T-shirt, and me in shorts and a judo T-shirt, despite the November weather.

After the sales personnel caught their breaths, I told them I wanted a silver apple, the same size as a real apple with the following engraving: "The Japanese Ambassador's award for best technique." Sandi was standing near the counter with her arms folded in an Indian pre-war stance with her strongest poker face. I guessed she didn't like the way we were received by the sales staff. Gigi, who had a clear head, was in awe of all the shiny stuff and oohing all over the place, shouting, "Hey, Rusty, check this shit out! Ain't it gorgeous?"

All the attention was on me now as they totaled it up, wrote the pertinent information on the sales slip, and then asked me how I chose to pay, cash or credit card? I told them to charge it to the Japanese Ambassador.

I thought I saw the sales woman's hand move to the alarm button. I told her to call him to confirm. She was all a dither and didn't know what to do. I could see the beads of perspiration on her forehead. She called for the manager. Slim Jim came over, took a look at the three of us and almost keeled over. He did finally call and confirm the purchase, and gave me a date to pick it up, then took another look at us, the unusual trio, and on second thought offered to gladly deliver it. I thanked him and told him I would happily pick it up myself.

There were so many details that still needed to be resolved. Believe me there is no college education in the world that would have simplified my upcoming challenges. I had to rely on my Brooklyn ingenuity and *chutzpah*.

The advance people for Dr. Matsumae's visit and his attendance at the championships informed me that they needed a private, comfortable room for him at the Garden. He needed a place to relax as well as entertain some of the local Japanese dignitaries who would also be in attendance. I found a nice-sized room just off the main lobby that we could use under the radar. If the Madison Square Garden people knew about us using that room, there would have been an additional charge. They charged for every little thing, plus they wouldn't let us carry anything in or out of the Garden. It had to be official union people only. *Right!*

My tall, dark and handsome student Gary, was the manager of a furniture store on Flatbush Avenue, a few doors down the block from our Kyushu Judo Club. I immediately called Gary and told him that he was on the Organizing Committee and put him in charge of decorating. There was a lovely living room set, including carpet, sofa, chairs, coffee tables, and lamps showcased in the front window of the furniture store. I told him we needed to borrow it. He agreed and he and some students snuck the whole ensemble into our special room at the Garden with no one the wiser. I did have to give the security people a song and dance about the why-fors and where-does of the furniture, but in the end the room looked fabulous. The store window, on the other hand, had newspapers covering the entire length of glass along with a sign saying they were in the process of changing window design.

Our logo was marvelous. The figures were created from a reduced photograph of Leslie Conte and Mindy Douglas, taken by Peter Perazio. The calligraphy for the kanji word for judo from the artist Kentaro Oshima was inserted. My other contributions to the design were to select the throw that Leslie and Mindy did and approve our colors of magenta and orange. The selections were bold and beautiful, just like our judo models. We slapped the logo on everything.

PHOTO CREDIT: PETER PERAZIO.

Logo for the first Women's World Judo Championships, designed after judo models Leslie Conte and Mindy Douglas, who threw each other uncountable times to get this perfect moment caught on camera.

EXECUTIVE COMMITTEE
President
  Rena Rusty Kanokogi
Vice President
  Mei Appelbaum
Vice President
  Pat Earle
Secretary
  Peter Perazio
Treasurer
  Mary Potanas
Percy Sutton
Wallace Ford
George Spitz
Margaret Grossberger

BOARD OF DIRECTORS
Michael Abernethy
John Condon
Marty Frechtman
Ryohei Kanokogi
Doreen McLoughlin
Bill Miller
Mary Michelle Nangle
John M. Prenderville
George Spitz
Ed Silverglade
Steve Spano
Legal Counsel
  Edward Serrapede

FIRST WOMEN'S WORLD JUDO CHAMPIONSHIP 1980

September 29, 1980

President Jimmy Carter
The White House
Washington, D.C.

Dear President Carter:

Thank you very much for the message of greeting from Alfred J. McGuire, Chairman of the President's Council on Physical Fitness and Sports, written on your behalf. While we in the United States are well aware of Al McGuire's reputation and fame and value the message of greeting from him, the foreign teams may not be as knowledgeable. I am sure, however, that no one in the world is unaware of who Jimmy Carter is.

I would respectfully request, again, that you send us a message of welcome to the more than thirty foreign nations that will be participating in this First Women's World Judo Championship.

Thank you.

Respectfully,

Rusty Kanokogi
President

FIRST WOMAN'S WORLD JUDO CHAMPIONSHIP ORGANIZING COMMITTEE INC.
2126 East 17th St., Brooklyn, New York 11229, (212) 339-0322

64

ABOUT TWO MONTHS BEFORE THE BIG EVENT, the International Judo Federation informed me that I had to purchase and supply jackets for the referees; they would bring their own trousers, shirts and ties. The jackets had to be Kelly green, as that was the IJF referees' color that year. My first thought was where the hell would I get these bizarre jackets? And even if I did get them, they would only be able to wear them on St. Patrick's Day. If they wore them any other time on the streets of New York, judo or not, they would probably get beat up.

The IJF supplied me with the names and addresses of the referees selected to work at the first WWJC. I designed a letter with a man's figure on it, requesting sizes, weight, and height for each. Aside from police and firemen garb, the only stupid-looking uniform I could possibly relate to was the meter checker. I approached one on the street and asked where he got his. With an attitude and a very dirty look, the answer was, "Why? You want one?"

"No," I said. "I need a dozen."

I thought he was going to write me a ticket, however, being I was on foot and not driving, he was stuck with me. Finally, I got through to him, and he gave me the address of the manufacturer.

When I received the information forms back, I went up to the uniform company and ordered the bright green jackets. Most of the sizes were fairly average, with the exception of the referee from Germany. The company asked me if I was sure that he had a fifty-two inch chest and a fifty-two inch waist?

"Yup, he sure does," I assured them.

Of course, I had nightmares about the damn jacket, hoping I didn't make a mistake and the German referee was some skinny guy. It turned out fine; Mr. Lind needed every inch of that jacket.

I was on a roll with my designing ability now, or so I thought. I was asked by USA Judo to get warm-up suits for our team, the coach and the manager. *Why not?* I was doing everything else. Heaven forbid they lift a finger to help. They must have thought I was a miracle worker.

Rusty & Paul Guez of Sasson Jeans, 1980.

I got Paul Guez, the President of Sasson Jeans involved, thanks to Howard Albert, the company sports coordinator. Paul was a very kind, wealthy guy. He was kind of young, and nice looking, but with some bad habits. Howard was a boxing promoter who helped Paul secure the well-known boxer and World Heavyweight Champion Larry Holmes as the point man for Sasson products.

Paul indicated from the outset that he wasn't going to give me any money, but would help with any garments we needed. Unfortunately, he didn't have any green jackets, so I had to pay for them. My list to Paul was for all the jeans, shirts, and socks for the twenty-seven kids that were going to be the carriers of the placards with each country's name, blue jackets and shirts for my executive committee, gold

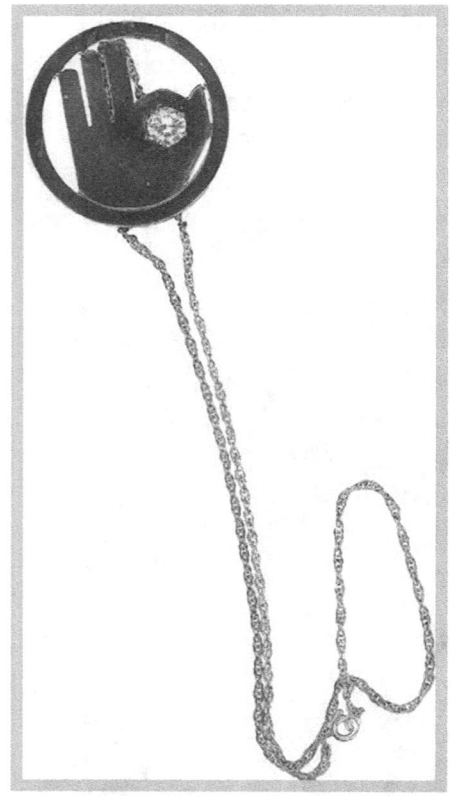

Gold medalist necklaces for the 1WWJC courtesy of sponsor, Sasson Jeans.

ooh-la-la Sasson pendants for the eight first-place winners, warm-up suits for the US team, and an ad in the program. He agreed.

Wow!

All I had to do was ask.

Paul wanted his girlfriend of the day, some dizzy blonde who thought she was a fashion designer, to create the warm-up suits. I didn't know any better at the time, so I agreed. When I went to pick them up, I nearly had a heart attack. They were the ugliest "darling suits" I had ever seen! She took a basic gray sweatsuit, had red and blue sateen ribbons sewn up the side, and handed them off. Even the poor team from Yugoslavia had better garments than this crap.

I told Paul that they were unacceptable. It was too late to try and make new ones. He asked what we should do.

"Just give me $1000. And I will go to Macy's and buy some appropriate gear," I said.

He gave me the money and I flew to Macy's. I bought beautiful Adidas warm-ups, which just happened to be Sasson's biggest rival. They had the biggest damn logo on the chest I had ever seen, a no-go for Paul and the folks at Sasson. I called Paul and promised I would change the logo. I took the suits back to our headquarters and hatched a plan. I grabbed a bunch of our logo patches, and had Ryohei pick me up and drive me to Brooklyn. We went to a Hassidic neighborhood, found a rabbi in a basement apartment that doubled for his sewing business, and hired him to sew the patches over the Adidas marijuana leaf looking logo. He also embroidered around it in big orange letters, "Sasson, Sasson, Sasson." The ploy worked. The warm-ups were lovely for our team, and we had our sponsor right over our hearts.

Another problem to be solved was food for my officials and VIPs for two days at Madison Square Garden during the tournament. I thought that the most appropriate fare would be Japanese food. The Garden was going to have one measly concession with hot dogs, soda and the like, but I wanted sushi and green tea.

A few months before, our friend Bill Otto had invited Ryohei and me to a lovely Japanese dinner at the Sagano Restaurant that was located in a building he owned. He introduced us to the owner and I mentioned the upcoming championships to him. He seemed interested, as the sport from his homeland was going to be highlighted at one of the most well-known venues in the world. It was only natural for me to approach him with my deal.

I suggested he could make history by being the first and only Japanese restaurant in Madison Square Garden's history. He was overjoyed. He and some of his staff would set up a sushi concession at the Garden on November 29 and 30, sell all they could and not give me a dime, aside from feeding my officials and VIPs and buying an ad in our program. I guess he was seeing many yen signs in his head as he welcomed and accepted my proposal. Of course, nothing was in writing.

The big day came and the Sagano folks brought in their barrel of rice for sushi and wonderful fresh fish, wasabi and all the other ingredients they needed for the day. I gave out a special ticket to all who would be privy to our Japanese restaurant, along with instructions on how to find it in the Garden. When the food was brought in, I gave security a song and dance on how this was going to be food for the Japanese delegation as they had allergies to American food and would die if we didn't keep them supplied. Security scratched their heads, but bought it.

I placed the concession on the far side of the entry area, near where all the cleaning supplies were kept in an open but seemingly abandoned concession space. It worked like a charm, at least for me. However, after two days at the Garden, Sagano had not turned a profit. In fact, they had a major loss. You see, I couldn't announce the concession, as I had snuck them in, so all the food went to my officials and VIPs.

A girl's gotta do what a girl's gotta do.

I thanked the owner, apologized for the lack of profits, gave him a lovely plaque in appreciation to the Sagano Restaurant for their contribution to the first Women's World Judo Championships at Madison Square Garden and recognized them as the first Japanese restaurant in the venue in its one-hundred-year history. As we were a not-for-profit organization, they were able to write off most of their loss as a donation.

For the next several days I worked around the clock. So many of the plans were back-to-back. I had television shows to do, interviews with the press, parties to throw, registration of athletes, mats to be laid, and a parade to promote and attend all before the actual competition began. I also had to have meetings with Dr. Matsumae, the IJF President.

Somehow I managed to get a couple of major advertising companies interested in the event. I really shouldn't take the credit as Francesca Lack, who handled the "Ooh La La" Sasson Company account, helped us out. She was classy and didn't have any idea what judo was, but she did have great connections. She schlepped me from one show to another, and paired me up with the ball player Bucky Dent of the Yankees as the guest stars of a party at the Garden. I guess they thought I was the bat girl.

I was on *The Joe Franklin Show*, that must be two hundred years old by now and still going. God bless him anyway. I was going to do a judo demonstration so I dragged my student Kenny with me, as he loved to showboat. We took a cab with our judo uniforms on, got to the studio and started to warm up.

The show began and Joe asked the right questions about our upcoming event in order to promote it. Kenny and I bowed in. I was getting ready to throw him around when I noticed that they didn't have a mat.

Now what?

Kenny's tough, but I would have killed him on live TV. I asked Joe if he had something a little softer than the hard wood floor for Kenny to land on. He motioned to a stagehand, who proceeded to bring out a large orange beach towel. The show must go on, so I threw Kenny a few times and figured I could always wrap him in the towel for the burial. He lived. People were in awe of him smacking the towel and floor to fall and still surviving. We left during the commercial break but instead of following me, Kenny walked towards the camera. The show came right back on and there was Kenny's big head smack dab in the middle of the shot, with Joe Franklyn yelling at him to get out.

So much for promotion!

Another amazing promoter was Suzanne Kramer who worked for John Scanlon, a nifty PR firm. I don't remember how we got hooked up. Suzane was a buxom blond and reminded me of a younger Mae West. She got many magazines and newspapers interested in us. Of course, I ended up being interviewed up the wazoo. I mentioned to Francesca that we needed to hold a cocktail party to welcome our big shots, sponsors and the like, and she had Paul Guez pay for the party.

We held it at the New York Athletic Club. Dr. Matsumae was the guest of honor. My friend Rusty Staub, the ball player, was in attendance. There were movie stars, models, all invited by Suzane and Francesca.

I was there physically, but at this time of my insanity, I was in a controlled coma. I think the party went well. The Japanese were surprised at all the glamorous people in attendance. Little did they know that they were partying with us because their agents thought it the right place to be that evening.

Rusty Staub and I had known each other for several years. We met at his restaurant on the Upper East Side. After judo practice, we would often go there to have a bite and a beer. Rusty and I kidded around with each other, both being Rustys with red hair. Every time there was a call and the bartender called, "Rusty," we both reached for the phone!

He would sit with us and shoot the bull as sports people do. We always said we would go bar hopping one New Year's Eve and kick everyone's ass just for fun. Not quite the philosophy of judo teachings, but it was all talk.

Rusty was a good cook. I wanted some of my VIPs to experience Thanksgiving in New York. His restaurant was closed for Thanksgiving, but he was a sweetheart and cooked a private dinner for some of the judo kingpins: Mr. Inokuma from Japan, Mr. Courtine from France, and Rusty and Ryohei from Brooklyn. He dined with us and gave me a huge doggie bag for Ryohei to take home to the kids, who were completely neglected. I knew I would make it up to them.

Earlier that day was the fabulous Macy's Thanksgiving Day Parade. All the athletes and officials were told they were my guests. All they had to do was walk the one block to Thirty-Fourth Street and watch the largest, most colorful parade that they would ever see in their lives. They still talk about the wonderful parade I threw for them for the First Women's World Judo Championships. We were the only country celebrating the holiday. What's the difference? I didn't have the patience to explain Thanksgiving in New York City to them, so the myth still lives on.

Rusty sure knows how to throw a parade!

65

THE HEADQUARTERS WAS A SIGHT TO BEHOLD IN the days leading up to the first Women's Worlds. The very large main room had several desks in it with cork boards on the walls that were so covered with messages and notes that it was difficult to see any actual cork. I was handling two telephones at a time with the load of incoming calls.

Many of the calls were from NY-based Japanese companies trying to get a line on Dr. Matsumae's schedule in hopes of getting an appointment with "the great man from Japan." Slick Rusty thought this would be a good way of selling blocks of tickets. My answer would be something like this:

"Yes, I'm working with Dr. Matsumae's scheduling secretary and I will see what I can do. By the way, Dr. Matsumae would like it very much if your company bought tickets for the championship."

Soon after that the messengers were flying up to my office with juicy checks for their reserved seats at the Garden. They then dispersed the tickets to their employees, many of whom were Americans and going away for Thanksgiving weekend.

Oh well, not my problem.

I sold the seats. With a $47,000 rental fee for the weekend—and that was with a connection—I didn't care if I sold them to the dead. And thank goodness I had that connection in order to get in the door in the first place—with all our months of planning and the blood, sweat and tears of my ranks of volunteers, we were almost locked out of the space at the eleventh hour.

I had stalled the bean counters at the Garden until my bankroll came in from Japan. Chris Hanson, who was in negotiations with me from the onset, gave me until November 28 to pay the $20,000 balance for the space. I kept telling him the check was in the mail, except this time it was.

"The money man is on his way from Japan."

"No deal," he'd said. "We're not opening the doors."

I called Stephen Spahn, my longtime friend, headmaster of the Dwight School. He had mentioned to me that the father of one of his students was Dave Judleson, the head of Madison Square Garden. Stephen reached out on my behalf and the word went immediately to Chris: "Open the doors."

Whew! Another close one.

On occasion, I would get phone calls from cuckoos that had a thing for strong women. They always sounded legit at first, until we moved on to what you learn in judo. The first clue was when they would ask how hard they had to be squeezed when they were being pinned and could I put my legs around their neck and keep them there? At that time, it was these ones I hoped would call again soon, so I could sell them tickets to the main event to be with lots of strong women. Though I did look around at the championships to see if there was any pocket pool going on.

Some of the local judo community had their noses out of joint as I made everyone buy a ticket; there were no freebies, not with a pending $47,000 rent payment coming due.

I was selling ads to our journal like crazy, as that was another important part of our revenue. In fact, I even asked Dr. Matsumae if he wanted to buy an ad. He just smiled at me, especially when I added that I would even give him a discount. Believe me, I would not leave any stone unturned.

I arranged for a silver stretch limo to pick up Dr. Matsumae and his delegation at JFK. About eight Japanese companies found out his arrival time and arranged additional limos so that there were nine limos to pick up the boss. Mine was rented from Vinnie, "the Hook" (he had a twisted nose). Thank goodness Dr. Matsumae got in that one.

He entered, sat in the middle of the seat and requested the

door be closed. He had on his kimono and his large walking stick in hand, so if you didn't hear what he had said, you heard the stick. The staff all followed nicely in some of the additional limos.

Dr. Matsumae's favorite place to stay was in my office. I think he was mesmerized by the intensity, commitment and non-stop determination to get everything done. He was well aware that United States Judo, under the control of President Frank Fullerton, would not give me any funds for this event. To the credit of the judo community, several members chipped in eighty dollars each for an ad that netted us about $500.

I remember Mr. Hashimoto, one of Dr. Matsumae's executive staff people, coming into my office and asking me to go to a smaller back room to discuss a private matter. We went to the back, which was really the bedroom, and he handed me over $40,000 in cold cash. I shoved it into the pocket of my slacks like it was an undercover deal, thanked him profusely, and as my thoughts raced largely with excitement from the support, I knew I had to get this money safely from Manhattan to our bank in Brooklyn tomorrow morning and put it in the World Championships' bank account ASAP!

I called Ryohei and asked him to pick me up at about eleven o'clock that night so I could sleep in my own bed for a change and then wake up, put the money in the bank, and return to headquarters. I was too busy to leave when he showed up, so he put the car in the lot a few blocks away and waited. By 1:00 a.m. I was ready to go.

We walked along seedy Eighth Avenue to the garage. Everyone looked like a mugger to me. It would have been a fight to the death if there had been a robbery attempt.

Their death!

I returned to the office bright and early, woke up my staff that were sleeping under their desks and on tables, and felt guilty as hell for sleeping in a bed for a few hours. Then we opened the doors, as the athletes were pounding away outside, trying to get to the scales we kept in the office. They had to make weight, so they often checked it ten times a day before the official weigh-in. I had lots of naked women floating around the office. The Europeans didn't think anything of it as they bared all, checked the scale, and moved out of the way to give someone else a turn. My male staff were so punchy by this point that they didn't even notice, or if they did—*what the hell?* It was considered a perk.

While I was registering the athletes as they arrived, I noticed this tall drink of water from Belgium, with a nerdy face and glasses. She was registering for the heavyweight and open divisions. Naturally, also being a heavyweight, I checked her out. I never knew when I might make a comeback.

There was something about her. I felt it. It certainly wasn't her appearance.

"You will become a famous world class competitor," I told her. She thanked me and went on her way.

Ms. Ingrid Berghmans—slightly less famous, but far more badass, than the actress—won the heavyweight division of the first WWJC and went on to win the next several World Championships, as well as Olympic gold. She became a gorgeous model, fitness instructor, and a good friend.

Ingrid still resides in Belgium, has two children and is a member of the Belgium Olympic Committee now.

Ingrid Berghmans & her fellow gold medal winners from the first World Women's Judo Championships, New York City, 1980.

66

THE DAY WAS HERE! I GOT DRESSED AT OUR headquarters in the outfit from Sasson: winter white trousers, red shirt, and a navy jacket. I thought it would be a nice gift to the Sasson people if I wore their gold logo on the right side chest of the jacket while I did the color commentary. Everyone knew the four finger logo, with thumb and index finger touching in the "everything is OK" sign. If I really had my way I would have had a logo with the middle finger sticking up to give all the non-supporters and non-believers their due.

The walk from the hotel to Madison Square Garden was less than five minutes. I decided that I wanted to do it alone. You cannot imagine what transpired in that short five-minute stroll.

First, I saw Dr. Matsumae and his entourage getting into taxis to go to the Garden, which was right across the street. As I was in half a fog to begin with, I didn't try to stop them. The cab drivers went around the block and then let them out.

As I crossed the street at Seventh Avenue and Thirty-second Street to get to the side entrance, I heard fire engine sirens roaring down the block. They slowed down near the entrance as I was approaching and ran in with full gear and hoses. I could not believe my eyes. My World Championships were on fire!

My high anxiety attack was short-lived, however. The fire was in the athletes' dressing room and was quickly extinguished with little damage. All that was left was a smoky smell. But, the show must—and did—go on.

Everything was in place and it was magnificent to view. The green tatami mats with the red danger zone, the referees in their gray slacks and green jackets (ugh), the athletes in their white judo uniforms and respective numbers on their backs along with their country's name. My officials were spiffy.

The children sign-carriers were excited, shiny and clean. The special dignitaries and our medical staff were seated in the proper places. The midshipmen from the US Merchant Marine Academy were at attention and ready to go. The TV cameras were rolling to film the whole thing. All we needed now was to get through the opening ceremony and the actual competition. All I could think was: *just one more day, then I can die and, hopefully, rest in peace.*

The opening ceremony went well. The Boys Choir of Harlem did a great job. Don't ask me what they sang; I shut my brain to anything that was not pertinent to the competition. Plus, I still had to figure out how to be a sports commentator, and what the hell did I know about that?

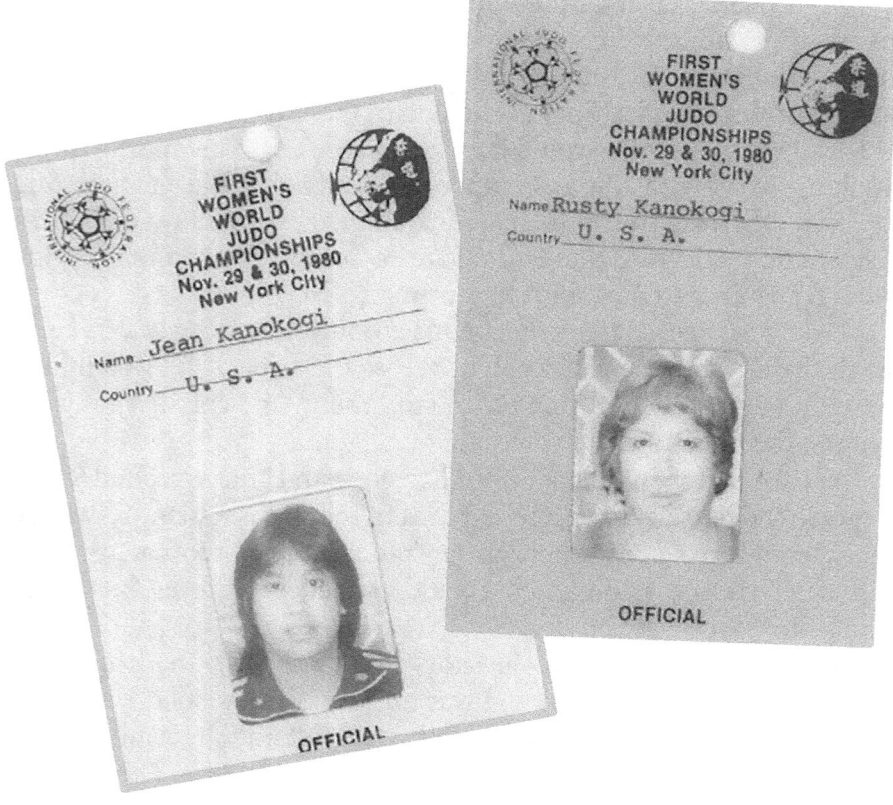

67

THE ATHLETES WERE LINED UP ALPHABETICALLY by country. There was a darling young boy or girl, most of them local judo players, carrying a sign with each country's name. They looked so cool in their Sasson jeans, shirts and socks. The athletes wore their colorful national warm-up suits. As the United States didn't spring a penny for our athletes' and coaches' warm-ups; we were happy to have the converted Adidas for our folks. I selected a good-paced Sousa marching song for the athletes' entrance. It was upbeat and steady. After all twenty-seven countries entered and were lined up on the mats facing the dignitaries, we had our opening bow.

Dr. Matsumae, Jack Prenderville, Chairman of the New York State Athletic Commission, Paul Guez, and I were already standing at the official staging area, ready to make our speeches and greetings to all. Dr. Matsumae looked brilliant in his beautiful samurai-type kimono along with his famous walking stick. He spoke first, giving his opening remarks in Japanese. His speech had been translated into English, and our student, Leslie Conte, read from the English script each time Dr. Matsumae paused.

He gave the organizing committee and me great praise as he noted this was history in the making—not as an event sponsored by a country, but rather by an individual, her family, dojo and colleagues. It almost brought me to tears.

Almost.

Jack and Paul gave nice congratulations and kudos to all. I read several of the telegrams from political leaders from the US and abroad, including the White House, then went on to thank everyone I could remember for their support and help with making this historic event a reality.

I tried to keep the opening ceremony short, not wanting it to drag on because the athletes who were competing had to get their brains and bodies ready for their upcoming fights. Four divisions were set to compete that day, November 29, 1980, and four the following day. All 125 competitors were raring to go. Some already had great results from smaller international competition. I was hoping for the United States to do well, as I was so familiar with the team who had consistently produced gold medals for me at competitions when I was coaching. I knew they had the right stuff.

The results of two days of grueling competition, with some heavy-duty upsets, were as follows:

48 kg

1st	Jane Bridge	Great Britain
2nd	Anna De Novellis	Italy
3rd	Marie-France Colignon	France
3rd	Mary Lewis	USA

Jane was awarded the Japanese Ambassador's silver cup (from Tiffany's) for best technique. Mary kept us on the map.

52 kg

1st	Edith Hrovat	Austria
2nd	Kaoru Yamaguchi	Japan
3rd	Bridget McCarthy	Great Britain
3rd	Pascale Doger	France

Kaoru Yamauchi was the youngest competitor of the event, at just fifteen years old.

56 kg

1st	Gerta Winklbauer	Austria
2nd	Marie Paule Panza	France
3rd	Loretta Doyle	Great Britain
3rd	Janine Meulemans	Belgium

61 kg	1st	Anita Staps	Netherland
	2nd	Laura DiToma	Italy
	3rd	Inge Berg	Germany
	3rd	Martine Rottier	France

66 kg	1st	Edith Simon	Austria
	2nd	Dawn Netherwood	Great Britain
	3rd	Catherine Pierre	France
	3rd	Christine Pennick	USA

Under 72 kg	1st	Jocelyne Triadou	France
	2nd	Barbara Classen	Germany
	3rd	Avral Malley	Great Britain
	3rd	Jolanda Van Maggelen	Netherland

Plus 72 kg	1st	Margarita De Cal	Italy
	2nd	Paulette Fouillet	France
	3rd	Ingrid Berghmans	Belgium
	3rd	Christina Kieburg	Germany

To me, the last division—the heavyweight—was the most exciting. Of course, it was also my weight category.

Margarita was sweet and jolly, and the heaviest of the competitors, way over the 158-pound mark. She was apologetic when she pinned Paulette in a holding technique that would have kept any man I know in place. When the athletes were to shake hands at the end of the match, Paulette gave the big one the dirtiest look I have ever seen in my life. If looks could kill...

Beautiful Ingrid gave it her best shot, but seemed to be outweighed and out-classed. Christina was my German twin, similar in body and looks; only the hair was different. "Big, strong, hard verker, good to make babies also." Any good farmer would have hired us in a heartbeat.

The open division was next. Anyone could enter. It was an open weight class. Usually the larger competitors would enter this division, but it was not impossible for a light-weight with big balls to enter and win. The results were fascinating:

OP			
	1st	Ingrid Bergman	Belgium
	2nd	Paulette Fouillet	France
	3rd	Barbara Classen	Germany
	3rd	Barbara Fest	USA

Ingrid was determined to go home with gold. Not only did she win it here but, as I predicted, she would do it many more times at future World Championships and Olympic Games.

The final match between Ingrid and Fouillet was one of the best I had ever seen. Fouillet had Ingrid going with a fast clean technique, when suddenly Ingrid reversed in midair and turned it into her win. The raw emotion on her face when she flipped it into her victory was a sight to behold.

Hooray!

Another medal. We didn't leave naked, but we realized the rest of the world was ahead of us. And that meant more work, work, work was to come. Though Barbara didn't win the top spot, her efforts still placed her.

I adored all the champs and my heart went out to all the women who didn't fare as well. They had all worked their guts out. They were all spectacular and would go on to have remarkable lives, and fabulous careers in judo. They had each helped me and women's judo progress just by being there.

International officials, sit with Rusty, at the first Women's World Judo Championships.

Judoka from the Dutch, British, Belgian, and Italian teams at the first World Women's Judo Championships, New York City, 1980.

68

FOR THE NEXT TWO DAYS I HAD A MICROPHONE attached to me for the ongoing color commentary. I could recite most everyone's record offhand, because I had coached against most of the foreign competitors in the recent past. I certainly knew all the techniques that were involved, and I could easily understand most of the referees' calls, as I was also a referee. The difficult part was trying to tone down my Brooklyn accent and speak real, clean English,—never my strong suit. I also had to learn to breathe between words. After all, I was going to replace Howard Cosell in the future. I wanted to sound good.

The fact that I was somewhat braindead from all the nonstop problems going on that most people didn't know about, didn't matter—I still had to take off the mic and run like hell to remedy whatever situation was currently in chaos. My co-anchor was a stylish, polished sportscaster. He was not a major player, and seemed very stuck on himself. He didn't know jack about judo and seemed to resent women whose bodies were covered up with a T-shirt and judogi. Still, I had to work with him so I added "actress" to the growing list of my credentials. At the end of the tournament, presentations were made. Time is money at the Garden. We had finished the event and now we had to get out. I had pulled some fast ones on them, so I didn't feel insulted. Wrapping up was almost as difficult as setting up. Aside from the physical breakdown of mats and equipment, there were schedules to attend to, and the transportation of athletes, officials, and VIPs out of the Big Apple. I was constantly running back and forth to the checkout desk at the hotel dealing with mistakes, language barriers and other similar problems. I was extra short staffed by now, as almost every one of my helpers had run away from me at full speed. Given how hard I'd worked them thus far, I didn't blame them.

At about eleven thirty at night on the first day of competition, I was catching my breath at the headquarters office. Two cops came walking in with one of our VIPs, Charles Palmer, OBE. I asked what the problem was. Knowing Charlie, he may have made an off the cuff remark and upset someone.

The big burly cop said that Charles hadn't paid for his room. He was arguing with the women at the hotel desk and had threatened to kill them all, which he was certainly capable of. The cop went on to say that Charles kept claiming that he was an OBE that didn't mean a thing to anyone in New York. They just wanted him to shut up and pay up.

What had happened was that a notice was hung on Charlie's door that the amount he had paid for the room had expired. Would he please come to the desk and pay for the next night? All rooms had to be prepaid with the exception of the tab I had to pick up for the officials and certain individuals. Charlie never saw the note. He was tired and not used to being treated like this, so he went bananas.

I paid for the night as a peace offering and then took my new friend and the two cops into the back room where we had a drink and saluted OBE, knighthood and England.

In order to handle the score tables during the matches, you had to be a certified national referee. All of them came to help, bless them—they are part of this history as well.

Our announcer, Gail Stolzenberg from Texas, had a nice calming drawl. Our additional announcer Phyllis Koiwai could speak several languages. She had a unique voice that if you weren't used to it, could run chills up and down your spine.

Is it time for me to rest in peace yet?

69

DECEMBER 1, 1980.
It's done! It's all over! Or is it?

The first Women's World Judo Championships was successfully completed. It was a prerequisite for the International Olympic Committee to install women's judo into the Olympics. I thought I was done, but as tremendous as this undertaking had been, it was only the beginning of another major uphill fight.

I had received congratulations from all over the world. There were numerous pre- and post-tournament articles. I earned the highest respect from world judo leaders. Now there was hope for women's participation in many other Olympic sports; after all, this was the first full-contact sport to have an official World Championship. Many of the countries that didn't participate because of lack of funds or just plain skepticism, were waiting to see if the competition would be successful.

They also waited to see what the IOC would do next.

I'm sure there were groups who wanted to see both me, as well as the event, fail.

Why?

Who knows? Maybe they thought we women would now be satisfied, having had our world championship.

Well, think again!

We wouldn't settle for mere crumbs when we deserved the whole damn cookie, just like the men got. Now, my sights settled on the next rung up in our climb to equality: the Olympic Games. We had to be included in the Olympics, and that was that.

While the event itself was behind us, all the paperwork, bills and other obligations still had to be completed. Our good lawyer friend, Ed Serrapede, said we had to keep our non-profit organization open for a period of time in case we didn't conclude all these responsibilities or in the event someone wanted to sue us.

All business had been taken care of when I received an additional bill from a printing company that completely overcharged us. I had, however, signed off on the incorrect invoice in all the craziness leading up to the event, so we were obligated to pay the additional $6,000, wrong as it was. There was about $7.60 left in our checking account, so I appealed to our national governing body to bail us out.

Hell, they hadn't given us anything to begin with—the least they could do is use their organizational strings to help us out of a jam after the fact.

I'm a Jewish mother, so I knew how to instill guilt.

My proposal passed and we were saved. The final bill was paid. The total cost of the championship was $180,000 cash and in-kind.

DONE!

It was a huge step forward for women in judo, and one step closer to our destiny: Olympic glory.

PART 3
THE LAST BATTLE

70

THE YEAR 1980 WAS SOON OVER. NOW IT WAS time to get reunited with my family. Even though we were with each other a lot, I had been emotionally disconnected from everyone around me for at least a year while working on the event. Would there be a price to pay? You bet! But it wouldn't raise its ugly head until many years later.

Dr. Matsumae and I kept our newfound mutual admiration and friendship going. This remarkable man not only gave me praise in his IJF report, but continued to use me as an example at all the Tokai University graduation exercises until his eventual demise in 1991, having lived a long and good life. He spoke about the spirit of Bushidō[18]—an unwritten code of conduct or principles the samurai lived by—and never giving up when all the odds are against you.

Needless to say, I was extremely flattered. He said in one of his books, when talking about his life story that he highly admired and respected several women he had met. Mrs. Gandhi, a brilliant woman from India and the wife of Mahatma Gandhi, Madam Boulou France, a former member of the IOC who was rather outspoken about women's rights, and me from Brooklyn, New York, USA.

Dr. Matsumae did admit to me at a party once that he was a feminist.

Bravo!

In early 1981 my husband and I received an invitation from Dr. Matsumae via the IJF to attend the first coach and referee seminar at Tokai University during the spring of that year. It would be international, instructive, and a good start to unification of the different countries. As much as I liked Charles Palmer, OBE, the former president of the IJF from Great Britain, his flaw was exclusion of the eastern European countries. He never forgave the communists.

Dr. Matsumae, as the new president of the IJF, believed in peace and harmony through sports, and in our case, judo. I believed the same and didn't hold the athletes responsible for the ideologies of their governments. Look how our own former leader, President Carter, screwed us up that same year, forcing the non-participation of US athletes at the 1980 Summer Olympic Games in Moscow. What the hell did it accomplish? How hard had he ever trained his mind and body for a sport?

We gladly accepted the invite. We were the only two Americans to be invited, so you can imagine the animosity of the USA Judo president and his cronies. They weren't thrilled with me to begin with. I had two words for them and it wasn't Merry Christmas.

Fullerton, the organization's president at the time, wrote a letter of protest to Dr. Matsumae and the IJF. They couldn't have cared less, as there was little respect for Mr. Fullerton in the international judo community or at least in the part of the community that believed in fairness and gender equality. Through the years, he used his position in USA Judo to pull some low-down shenanigans and because of this, most of the world knew he was simply a self-server.

We arrived in Kanagawa, Japan, and got to the hotel. There we were briefed on our schedule. It was fascinating and certainly would give me an opportunity to work on the inclusion of women's judo in the Olympics. There were delegates in attendance whom I had never met before—the mysterious Soviet Union, Madagascar, Poland, Iraq, and many others.

This was a big box of candy for me. I would convince countries that didn't have women practicing judo to do so, and the ones that had teams to participate in international competition. Too bad this seminar hadn't happened before the first Women's Worlds. I would have had at least fifty countries there.

Damn!

In any case, the IOC only required that we have the minimum amount of countries necessary for consideration for inclusion into the Olympic Games, which at the time was twenty-five. I had twenty-seven.

The IJF seminar was going very well. We spent several hours a day working on judo techniques from both the coaching aspect and how the referee interprets them. Most of the time was serious, however, we also had some fun. Some of the questions from several countries where judo programs were not greatly developed were pretty funny. As an example, in judo, you always have to start from a standing position. You only get to the mat if your standing throws are not completely effective or if you both land on the mat during the fight without a winning score being made. When the opponent is immobilized on the mat, in order to get a score for the pin, the opponent must have some part of his or her back touching the mat and be controlled by the attacker so the opponent cannot turn out or get away.

My dear friend Alex Ifidon, president of the African Judo Union, had a technical follow-up question.

"Why can't we pin them when they are lying on their stomachs?" he asked. "It may be okay for men," I replied, "but we women have extended chests."

After it was interpreted in a multilingual game of telephone, the participants roared.

One of the interpreters, and certainly the most colorful, was a huge six-foot-eight, 300-pound Yugoslavian by the name of Radomir Kovacevic. He was the only non-Japanese on the Tokai judo team and he was the training partner of Yasuhiro Yamashita, who would go on to be one of the world's greatest judo competitors in history. Radomir could speak five languages: English, Japanese, Yugoslavian, Russian and Polish. He was definitely an asset to Tokai. We made friends immediately since we both have a sense of humor and are pretty fast with the tongue.

After practice one day as we were going back to the hotel, we saw Radomir heading back to the dorm. His mode of transportation caused me to laugh hysterically. He was wearing his judo uniform and riding what looked like a child's bicycle. As he pedaled, his knees seemed to come up to his shoulders.

Evenings were for social affairs and they were wonderful. Arrangements were made for us to be wined and dined at famous Japanese restaurants. As we traveled en masse, many of the foreign coaches and referees depended on me when it came to food because I had visited

Japan three or four times previously. Ryohei was able to help with the language when necessary.

One evening we were in a large, exclusive Japanese restaurant for a big party. This was a special celebration, so several of us were asked to go on the stage. We were given big wooden hammers about twelve inches in diameter and took turns beating some mushy rice into a gluey concoction called mochi that we would all later eat. It was an honor to be selected.

The hard part was getting it right and hitting the rice glob in the large decorative wooden bowl after downing twenty sakis that had been drunk one after the other. So, with five of us up there bashing away, I considered myself lucky that I didn't kill anyone or get hit by any mushy rice shrapnel.

When we sat down, the appetizer was served. There were little hibachis in front of each one of us. In Japan, the more they like and respect you, the more alive the fresh fish is going to be when served. The staff proceeded to serve this special fish that was skewered all the way through with a stick running in from its mouth and out through its tail. When I picked mine up to barbecue it, its eyes were open and its lips moving so that it seemed to be blowing me kisses.

The poor thing!

How could I eat it? I gave it away. The rest of the dinner was fine.

The Russian delegation was somewhat standoffish. They stayed to themselves and didn't mingle too much. I pursued them and finally not only got a smile out of them, but a gift as well. I made sure it wasn't ticking.

When I had the opportunity, which I made as often as possible, I discussed women's judo with the different delegates. Some had to be encouraged quite a bit. Some wanted me to stay in touch with them to help with their girls' and women's judo development. In all cases I seemed to win them over when I told them my mission was to get women's judo included in the Olympic Games. When I spoke, they listened—now that I had a good track record.

71

SELF-CONFIDENCE IS NOT SOMETHING I FELL short in as I moved through life. Bolstering this self-confidence was the knowledge that I had just pulled off a modern-day miracle by getting the first Women's Worlds done. I knew overcoming the obstacles I had faced to accomplish this would open many doors. Sadly, some of these obstacles in my way were placed there on purpose for whatever reason—clearly the placers didn't want women to have equality in judo. With underlying obstructors still lurking about, I knew, even after the Worlds win, that I was once again beginning an uphill battle to get equality for women and I would have to take on more of these challenges with full force to accomplish my goal. Nothing would stand in my way to pave both my own future and the future of women's judo.

While I was in Japan, Dr. Matsumae suggested that he and I meet with Ken Kizuka, President of RKB Mainichi television. This meeting would continue the growth of women's judo and the rapid development of the Japanese female competitor. Ryohei accompanied me, as I wanted to make sure nothing was lost in translation.

Ken Kizuka was a very charming man with a lot to offer. He wanted my opinion and assistance for the forthcoming Fukuoka International Women's Judo Championships. The championship would be televised for approximately one hour each day of the two-day tournament. The event highlights and interviews with the top foreign competitors would then be shown on the RKB Mainichi network in Fukuoka and other parts of Japan.

I'm sure that part of the strategy was to make a good TV show, but what it would do was bring the crème de la crème of women's judo players to Japan and allow the Japanese judo women to get lots of competition experience. Additionally, there would be tons of judo footage to study before the next World Championships— or if I succeeded, got lucky, and did it right, before the first Olympic games to include women's judo.

As far as I was concerned, we needed additional international competitions, promotion of the sport and public relations. The IOC would scrutinize the participation of all judo events leading towards Olympic inclusion, so everyone agreed it was a good plan. It was very costly but RKB agreed to pick up the tab.

The first Fukuoka International was held in December 1982. They put together a fantastic event. It was colorful with flowing banners draped from the ceiling. They had two adorable cartoon female squirrels in their judo uniforms with flowing pony tails as the logo. They also had marching music to inspire all, and lovely young Japanese women dressed in colorful, expensive, full kimonos standing on stage in front of every team. There were about twenty countries at the first Fukuoka International. There were judo demonstrations with little kids from the local clubs and drummers beating the traditional taiko drums. It was like a pro-sport event in the USA. I was so proud to be part of it. I was the guest of RKB Mainichi TV many times throughout the years, I think as a way of paying me back for assisting them, as I wouldn't accept any money.

Through the years I would attend the Fukuoka tournament either as a VIP coach or referee. In any case, it was always a blast. It was a ritual that after the competition, there was a huge party for all the athletes and officials at the hotel. We would be asked to get on the stage and sing and dance. Some of our US athletes were really talented. Our Lynn Rothke didn't win a medal, but she did knock our socks off with her great voice and songfest. Another tradition was that I would organize the troops of US and foreign athletes, and we would go to a cool disco in town and have some fun.

On one occasion there were about thirty of us, including Ingrid Berghmans from Belgium, a perpetual tournament winner, and many of the women who placed in the tournament. Some of our US group included Eve Aronoff-Trivella, Margie Castro, Lynn Roethke and my daughter Jean.

The disco was quite crowded. We took over the floor and, of course, soon became the show. We were gyrating all over the place when I felt my butt being grabbed. When I turned to see who, or what, it was, there was a benign looking Japanese college boy looking at me.

I glanced at him and his pathetic imitation of Elvis and kept right on dancing.

When it happened again, I looked around again. He looked at me and smiled. I thought okay, the next time I will retaliate.

Do it. I dare you.

The butt was fondled again.

Bingo.

That was it! When his back was turned to me, I grabbed his whole ass cheek and twisted it around severely. He screamed and ran for his life. I thought, "that would teach him." As I turned, I noticed Margie, Ingrid, Eve and several more of my co-conspirators falling down on the floor laughing. It turned out that it was big Margie touching my butt, kidding around and trying to bait me into doing something stupid. I didn't disappoint them. The poor guy is probably still in counseling and more than likely won't go within a hundred yards of an American woman.

The Japanese women's teams improved very quickly and some of the European teams became reluctant to participate, as they felt they were being studied too much.

Hello! Any country in the world could have done the same thing. After all, this is competition.

The tournament still flourishes and there are four Japanese women allowed in each weight division, so if you placed in this competition you were certainly ranked world class and would most likely have a good shot in the next World Championships.

72

I MET A NEW FRIEND AND PARTNER IN CRIME, Leopold Correa (Leo) from Venezuela. Leo was an attorney and the Secretary General of the Pan American Judo Union[19]. We first met in New York at the first Women's World Judo Championships, then again in Japan at the IJF seminar in 1981. Because of his help, women's judo was brought to yet another pivotal point in history.

We worked together and he shared all the information from the Pan Am judo meetings, as I would only get significantly filtered information as Fullerton shared only what he wanted us to know. When I received the letter from Leo it informed me that women's judo was included in the official Pan American Games for 1983, and that it was passed in 1978 at the Pan Am Judo Congress in Puerto Rico that women would be able to participate at the Pan American Judo Championships in 1981. The Pan Am Championships are different from the Pan Am Games. The Championships include just one sport, while the Games include most of the Olympic sports and sports that may be under consideration for the Games in the future, plus a sport from the host country that was not already included on the Olympic roster.

To me this revelation was like the bible had arrived. The US representatives had been present at all these meetings. How come we were *never* told of the upcoming event? Was this discrimination in not wanting to share the funds, or just plain old neglect?

This knowledge was a major step. In order to be considered for the Olympic Games, the sport had to first be in the Pan Am Games. It would make us. The US women in judo would be privy to a major world event. The US Olympic Committee's own rules stipulated that a sport can receive funding if it is on the Pan Am or Olympic schedule. Additionally, it can be in the US Olympic Festival, a nationally prestigious event for the crème de la crème. This would showcase our athletes

Despite Defeat, Women Press for Judo in '88

From Times Wire Services

A number of U.S. women judo competitors accused the International Olympic Committee Wednesday of sex discrimination for refusing to admit women's judo for the first time into the 1988 Games at Seoul, South Korea.

Attorneys for the American Civil Liberties Union, who joined the athletes at a news conference in Los Angeles, vowed to take the matter before international legal bodies—including, perhaps, the United Nations Commission on the Status of Women—in an effort to force the IOC to introduce the event at Seoul.

However, an IOC aide said later that the body's program commission, which met here just before the Los Angeles Games, refused to add women's judo in 1988 due to a "lack of international experience in this area, not enough world championships (have been held) in women's judo."

Rusty Kanokogi, coach of the U.S. women's judo team, said the sport's third World Championships will be held in November in Austria. But the IOC aide, who insisted on anonymity, said: "Maybe seven or eight" world championships must precede an event's entry in the Olympics.

Susan McGreivy, chief attorney for the Southern California ACLU on women's rights cases, said that because the IOC in 1982 "provisionally accepted" women's judo as an Olympic sport, "to some extent, I think the IOC is guilty of reneging on a promise."

The IOC aide noted that the committee added the provision that there had to be a substantial number of world championships in a sport before it would gain Olympic status, some time after it granted provisional acceptence to women's judo. The new provision changes the picture entirely, he said.

The half-dozen or so athletes at the press conference said the change of direction by the IOC had ruined their hopes of competing in the Olympics, a goal for which they said they have been preparing for years.

"If I don't go (to the Olympics) in 1988, that'll make me 32 (when the next opportunity comes in 1992)", said Tina Harris, a judo competitor from Dallas.

and allow women to train at the US Olympic Training Center in Colorado Springs. I was thrilled, spinning around the room, jumping up and down like a person who had just won a hundred million dollars in the lottery.

Hooray!

We were on our way.

Wrong!

Everything on the above happy list had to go to litigation, one way or the other. Rules were in place, but the bodies of power were not following them. Instead, they constantly lied and made excuses and told me more times than I care to count of events *after* the fact deliberately so women in the sport would miss out. So many times, at the last minute, I would be told to "pack a bag, we're going…" or "next week you're competing…" This was how it was, and for this reason, I trained our competitors to always be ready to compete at a moment's notice, because sometimes we just had to.

Here we go again…

Sue. Sue. Sue.

73

I WAS READING AND STUDYING ANY DOCU-
ment I could get my hands on, including: *Robert's Rules of Order*, the Constitution of the United States, and general information pamphlets put out by USA Judo, the US Olympic Committee, the International Olympic Committee, and, of course, the Amateur Athletic Act, just as soon as it was published. This was pretty heavy duty for me—I had read classic comics in school to get me through history. Now I would have a part in making history.

One of my greatest allies from the onset was the press. There is nothing like juicy controversy and discrimination to get them on board. The plus side of being in a full contact sport for women was that it was still a novelty. Seeing women fight always got us coverage, and I knew how to milk it. Being an underdog was not new to me.

The United States has always been a cheerleader of the little guy and that helped my cause. Sandy Deetz from NBC-TV filmed one of our workouts which included her participating in an on-camera judo lesson. She then threw the biggest guy in the class. It worked well and as part of that or any interview I was privy to, I would get on my soapbox and cry foul.

Letters, memos, and telexes were circulating to all the countries in the Pan American Sports Organization (PASO) and the Pan American Judo Union, including US Judo and the USOC regarding what was happening at various meetings. Radames A. Torruella, the president of the Pan AM Judo Union, kept me informed. He was a friend of mine and a great friend of women's judo.

One letter sent to US Judo President Fullerton basically indicated that all judo federations contact their respective national Olympic committees and insist emphatically that they should vote in favor of including women's judo in the eighth Pan American Games. Fullerton didn't make a move on it. I approached him at a meeting and asked him about the lack of interest in supporting our inclusion in the Pan Am Games. His response was that he didn't believe anything in the correspondence he received from any of the Pan Am Union people as they never knew what they were doing. Ironically, he was and had been the sports director for the Pan Am Union for several years. One of the downfalls of life, I guess, is a short memory. This, however, was not my affliction.

I still cannot figure out why Fullerton kept his position in judo. Could it have been his wealth? It certainly wasn't his disposition or his integrity, in my opinion. I dug deeper and asked Leo Correa to send Fullerton proof when PASO passed the proposal and had scheduled women's judo in the Pan Am Games for 1983. We needed to start receiving training funds and be privy to the same perks as our male counterparts. It didn't work because Fullerton had no regard for official documents that came from the Pan Am Union. There seemed to be a definite lack of respect. He said it had to come from the US Olympic Committee before he would believe it. After contacting the USOC President Don Miller with the information, he said that the Olympic committee could not make a move on it until US Judo formally notified them.

I think Miller just got caught up in this mess because he was basically a nice guy. It was a perfect example of passing the buck. With all my reading of the documents on laws, entitlements and rights, I didn't know where to turn. But not for long. I had already been to Los Angles to give testimony to the American Civil Liberties Union regarding discrimination of women's judo and would, at a later date, join several other sport groups who were organizing against the International Olympic Committee.

I contacted my friend George Spitz whom I kept in the loop since we had first met. He was totally involved with discrimination of any sort. He had just sued the state of New York for age discrimination and won. He was just the kind of guy I needed at my side.

George was politically savvy, and opened doors for me. First he contacted the NY State Division of Human Rights with all the documents and proof that I had gathered up to find out if we had a case. We sure did!

We filed a complaint with them, #5-P-S-81-77306, against USA Judo and the USOC[20]. The complainants were my daughter Jean, my students Heidi Bauersachs and Eve Aronoff, and a judo player from Columbia University, Terry Hyman, as well as myself. There would be interviews, press conferences and proof to put forward.

```
STATE OF NEW YORK : EXECUTIVE DEPARTMENT
STATE DIVISION OF HUMAN RIGHTS
- - - - - - - - - - - - - - - - - - - - - - - - - -x
                                                   :
     STATE DIVISION OF HUMAN RIGHTS                :
                                                   :
        on the complaint of                        :
                                                   :
     HEIDI BAUERSACHS; MAUREEN BRAZIEL; TERRY S. HYMAN, :
     JEAN KANOKOGI and RENA KANOKOGI,              :      CONSOLIDATED
                        Complainant,               :      NOTICE OF HEARING
                                                   :
               -agsinst-                           :      CASE NO. P-S-77291-81
                                                   :               P-S-77297-81
                                                   :               P-S-77309-81
                                                   :               P-S-77294-81
                                                   :               P-S-77306-81
     UNITED STATES OLYMPIC COMMITTEE,              :
                        Respondent(s).             :
- - - - - - - - - - - - - - - - - - - - - - - - - -x
```

PLEASE TAKE NOTICE that pursuant to Section 297 of the Human Rights Law, a hearing to determine the charges of unlawful discriminatory practices alleged in the annexed verified complaint, as the same may have been amended, and all relevant issues in connection therewith, will be held before an Administrative Law Judge of the State Division of Human Rights as follows:

DATE	TIME	PLACE	
		Room No.	5427
APRIL 2, 1984	10:00 A.M.	Address	TWO WORLD TRADE CENTER
		City	New York, New York 10047

The happy day came on June 30, 1981. The NY State Division of Human Rights determined, after investigation, that it had jurisdiction in this matter and that there was probable cause to believe that the respondents had or were engaged in, or were engaging in, the unlawful discriminatory practice complained of.

Bingo.

This was a full point for women's judo. The next match was coming up soon.

All the signers of the complaint went on to win gold, silver, or bronze medals for the US at the Pan Am Games or other championships. I would continue as a coach assisting them.

NEW YORK STATE : EXECUTIVE DEPARTMENT
DIVISION OF HUMAN RIGHTS

COMPLAINANT

      RENA KANOKOGI

    VS   Case Nos. 5-P-S-81-77306

RESPONDENT   UNITED STATES OLYMPIC COMMITTEE

NOTICE OF DETERMINATION

On June 30, 1981, Rena Kanokogi, who is a female, filed a verified complaint with the State Division of Human Rights charging the above-named respondent(s) with an unlawful discriminatory practice relating to public accommodations, because of her sex, in violation of the Human Rights Law of the State of New York.

After investigation, the Division of Human Rights has determined that it has jurisdiction in this matter and that there is PROBABLE CAUSE to believe that the respondent(s) has (have) engaged in or is (are) engaging in the unlawful discriminatory practice complained of.

The Division will now proceed with endeavors to conciliate. Any inquiries regarding this process should be directed to .

Dated:

    March 30, 1983   STATE DIVISION OF HUMAN RIGHTS

                                      By *Ethel P. Titchener*
                                            Ethel P. Titchener, Regional Director

TO: Rena Kanokogi
      Brooklyn, NY   11229

      Don Miller, Executive Director
      United States Olympic Committee
      1750 E. Boulder St.
      Colorado Springs, CO   80909

74

I FELT WHAT IT MUST BE LIKE TO BE STEAMROLLED— knocked down and flattened. I was plenty busy with the pending litigation with the sports bodies, communicating with interested writers on lots of articles, writing for our USA Judo magazine, and always covering our women's teams and their great performances bringing medals home all the time regardless of our inadequate, or in many cases entire lack of funding.

Don't whine, Rusty, I told myself. *Get up and fight!*

I would call IJF President Charlie Palmer from time to time, getting his take on our evolution onto the world stage. As a typical Brooklynite, I would always start off a call with a little schmoozing.

"How's your family?" I asked Charlie on one occasion. "Dead," he replied.

I'm not usually dumbfounded, but I sure was here. Passing over the remark, I noted to forget the small talk the next time I talked with him and launched into the reason I had called—a series of questions, specifically, regarding Olympic inclusion. He thought it would be a good idea for me to speak with the President of the IOC, Lord Killanin of Ireland. The Lord and Charlie were friends and, I suspected, drinking buddies. He actually gave me the number in New York where the Lord was staying for a week while on business for the Bank of Ireland. I called the number several times but it was busy.

When my phone rang, I answered and spoke to my friend Maureen Braziel. We spoke several times a day, especially before a tournament. I was really good at making her a psycho prior to entering a tournament, revving her up so she would fight like a maniac, which I usually did. Because my priority was to reach the Lord seeking his advice, I brushed off Maureen by telling her I couldn't talk to her right now because I was trying to reach the Lord for advice. I neglected to indicate that I meant Lord Killanin. She immediately assumed I had flipped out.

I told Maureen to get off the phone because the Lord was waiting for my call. I dialed again and this time I got through. I thought I would reach an aide or secretary of some sort, so I asked the male voice if I might speak to Lord Killanin.

"This is he," the voice answered.

After I picked up my jaw from the floor, I gave him the Palmer-told-me-to- call spiel quickly so he wouldn't brush me off. He was kind, understanding and did give me some good advice that reaffirmed what I already knew—I must stay the course, discouragement be damned. I was grateful, and yes, Maureen, I *did* speak to the Lord.

75

THE VICTORIES WERE BEGINNING. THE PRESS was with us every inch of the way. One article's headline read: "Girls Shut Out of the Celebration." They were referring to the Olympic Sports Festival in Syracuse, NY, in 1981. This showcase event was for all the Olympic and Pan American sports that were coming up in the next Games. I had proven discrimination and the NY State Division of Human Rights found the USOC and USA Judo guilty, yet we were still being excluded from the festivities. As usual, I was not going to accept rejection.

I contacted my friend Mike Abernethy, who was very sport savvy—in and outside of his role as Executive Director for the Empire State Games—and a standup guy. He knew of all the battles going on with the various sports bodies and, in particular, about my case with the Division of Human Rights. He knew and reconfirmed the New York State law that states NY cannot go into contract with any organization that has been found guilty of discriminating against a person's race, religion or gender.

Bingo!

We had them!

The Sports Festival was in the process of setting up. All equipment had been moved to Syracuse. All the advertising and sponsors were in place. All the athletes and officials in all of the sports were set to travel. The contracts between the City of Syracuse and the USOC had been signed. Then I dropped the bombshell: the USOC had been found guilty of discrimination and New York State would have to nullify everything and not allow the Sports Festival to take place in the state. The irony was that the venue judo was to be held in was owned by the state of New York.

Double whammy!

The USOC conceded and informed USA Judo that women's judo would be included in the Sports Festival. The burden then was on me to contact fifty of the top American women to go to Syracuse for the event.

Our women were not training very hard, as they believed they were off for the summer and had no competitions to attend. I checked the past National Championships and invited the top six in each weight category. They were thrilled as this was major recognition and certainly would help open more doors. I was not invited to be the coach or even the janitor. The powers that be were very pissed off at me.

So, what else was new?

I needed to get up to Syracuse because several members of my club were on the team. One of my students, a young man named Rudy Tsai from one of the private schools I taught at, had just got his driver's license and a brand new car. He was seventeen or eighteen years old at the time. Rudy came from a very wealthy Chinese family.

I called him and said, "Hey, Rudy. You want to practice your driving in your new car?"

"You betcha," he replied.

No one else would get in his car and go anywhere with him. I told him we were going to Syracuse. He asked me where that was. I told him not to worry, because I knew the way and it wouldn't take too long.

We had the ride of death going up. Rudy, although doing his best, was a poor driver. I didn't want to drive because I was too emotional with my victory and I couldn't settle down. A higher power, however, watched over us.

When we arrived, I immediately went to a judo meeting that was being held. The kiss-ass coach and manager were telling the women athletes at this meeting to make sure they all write thank you notes to the US Olympic Committee for inviting them to the Sports Festival and to President Fullerton for making sure this happened. My blood pressure must have gone off the charts at hearing this. Some of the athletes really didn't have any idea of the legal wrangling, complaints filed and pending lawsuit, or my involvement. I interrupted the meeting and bellowed the truth. Then I informed those officials that they were a disgrace.

Rudy and I went back to Brooklyn. The trip took about six hours one way. He was so supportive, even though he didn't quite know what was going on. When I told Rudy to get gas because we were going back up the next day to watch the competition, he agreed. We got together real early and made the trek again.

When we went into the venue that I had been ready to put an injunction on a few days earlier, I was asked to pay for entry. I was totally ignored by the US Judo Committee. I knew what it felt like to be a leper. What was most important was that our women were there officially; a major victory, even if my own presence was actively and aggressively discouraged.

My next challenges were the Olympic Training Center and funding. I was raring to go and would have a wonderful new weapon: the discrimination laws of the great state of New York.

76

THE NEW YORK STATE DIVISION OF HUMAN

Rights knew I had spent lots of my own money for phone calls, mailings, and attending meetings in and out of state in order to pursue and continue with the fight for women's judo. At one point they asked me if I wanted to add to the complaint for reimbursement. It was so important to me not to fall into self-serving that I thanked them but refused. What I did want was for the women who had attended the World Championship trials in New York in February of 1980 to be fully reimbursed for their travel, hotel, and out-of-pocket expenses.

After more work, letter writing, and threats, that finally did happen. While they did not get fully reimbursed and received only a percentage, it did cover some of the expenses of going overseas to win more medals for the United States.

I also wanted equality of funding for women's teams as compared to the men's teams. Believe me, I still watchdog it to this very day. Women cannot take anything for granted!

The Division of Human Rights asked me what else they could do for us. I demanded a letter from Fullerton attesting to the fact that I had gotten women's judo into the Olympic Sports Festival and not him as he publicly claimed. How shameful of him since he was the actual obstructor. Was I looking to be a hero?

Hell, no!

I just wanted to keep the record straight.

I had a big chuckle when I received the letter in the mail. Fullerton thanked me for getting women's judo into the Festival, as requested, but what made me laugh was the document number of our case stamped at the bottom of the letter. He was the President of USA Judo, and the Division of Human Rights basically put a gun to his head. It was one of the demands Fullerton had to comply with in the complaint from us. He didn't do it from the goodness of his nasty heart.

OFFICE OF THE VICE PRESIDENT
WASHINGTON

June 18, 1981

Ms. Rusty Kanokogi
2126 East 17th Street
Brooklyn, New York 11229

Dear Ms. Kanokogi:

    Thank you very much for your recent letter to Vice President Bush expressing your concern over equal athletic and educational opportunities for all.

    The Vice President will be informed of your thoughts on this important issue and appreciates your taking the time to write him.

Sincerely yours,

THADDEUS GARRETT, JR.
Assistant to the
  Vice President

TG:mjg

77

I KEPT THE AMERICAN CIVIL LIBERTIES UNION (ACLU) in Los Angeles informed. They were a proactive group that I had been working with as a result of their interest in women's rights in sports and inclusion in the Olympics. Women's marathon and women's judo were to be proposed again to the IOC at their next scheduled meeting to decide whether they would be included in the next games, which were to be held in Seoul, Korea in 1988. That meeting would be held in conjunction with the 1984 Olympic Games in Los Angeles.

I remember many of the USA Judo women had already been wearing T-shirts that said, "Women's Judo, 1980 Olympics," for years. We didn't know then that you had to have a world championship first. And then, of course, the USA had not attended the 1980 Olympics because of the Carter boycott. We were hot to trot and screw the rules.

Our circle was growing larger every day. I was hoping to grow that circle into five circles: the Olympic rings for the women in judo.

I had major correspondence going on with judo athletes, coaches, and presidents of judo organizations in many countries who were pro women's judo. Part of the strategy was for all to contact their respective Olympic committees and persuade them to support the inclusion of women's judo in the Olympic Games. If there was an IOC member from their country, they would contact him as well. I recommended they keep the press in their country aware of every letter or memo that went out, and to keep their politicians in the loop as well. I pushed for the letter writing campaign of the century! Hopefully they would generate favorable press and sympathy for our cause. It was no longer a sports issue for me. This was discrimination against all women, whether they knew it or not.

I felt pretty good about our tentative inclusion, as now we had fulfilled all the prerequisites, plus we were not trying to insert a new sport, but merely open up an existing sport to include the other half of the human race.

The IOC was beginning to be concerned about the abundance of Olympic sports and worried that future candidate nations might not be able to handle the financial and space burden.

Madame Monique Berlioux, became an IOC member and General Director in 1969, also working with his successor Lord Killanin then with Juan Antonio Samaranch who was elected president in 1980. She was removed from office in 1985 and replaced by the Swiss lawyer Francois Carrard. She was in favor of the inclusion of women's judo for the next games in Korea. She was an outspoken advocate of women's sports, and had a short-lived career as a member of the IOC. She was one of the women named in Dr. Matsumae's book regarding the most memorable women he had met. With airline tickets in my pocket to Los Angeles, the telephone numbers of the ACLU and several friends who resided in the vicinity, I left home, leaving survival instructions for the family while I was away—or possibly in jail. Being in LA at the Games would allow me to hear the results sooner regarding the inclusion of women's judo in 1988, watch the men's judo competition, visit with old friends, and see my good friend Dr. Matsumae. I thought we would be able to celebrate our great victory together.

Prior to leaving for the West Coast, I called Jackie Ortiz, a young woman who I affectionately called Jackie Mañana, because anytime you ever asked her to do anything, her reply was always *mañana*, a.k.a. tomorrow. I had coached Jackie at several competitions, and felt comfortable asking her if I could stay with her and her family. I received a very fast "Yes!" which was good, as the airline ticket had eaten up most of my funds.

When I landed, I found my way to Jackie's house, which was basically in the Mexican ghetto area. It didn't bother me—I was grateful to have somewhere to flop. Later this home would become the headquarters for World War III.

The house was fairly small. My sleeping area would be in the living room on a pullout sofa that took up the entire space when opened. At night the family of about ten or so would have to climb over me to get to the bathroom. It was okay as long as they kept moving. The family hobby appeared to be fighting pit bulls. They owned five and kept them downstairs several feet from the entrance to the house. The fighting dogs were ugly and vicious and only had a weak looking fence to keep them out of the house. Now I had a little more concern about who or what would be passing over me at night.

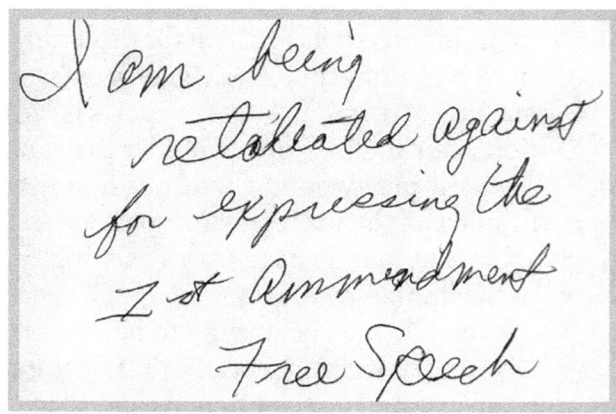

Rusty's handwritten notes from her many years fighting for women's rights in judo, sports and life.

Breakfast consisted of a burrito and coffee, not too different from Brooklyn's bagel and coffee. I brought with me a gift for my host family, plus all the paperwork I had collected so far, including progress reports by different countries, as well as national and foreign press regarding our plight. In all, it was about twenty-five pages that I would give to my friends at ACLU to keep them informed.

A judo colleague of mine bought my tickets to the judo event. Before I left to watch the competition, the most important thing on my mind was to contact Dr. Matsumae at the hotel, hoping to get good news that we were in for 1988. His secretary Ms. Miyagi answered the phone.

After cordial greetings she gave me the grim news that women's judo had been rejected. The women's marathon had been accepted for the next games, but not us. Although I was happy for them, my heart dropped to the floor.

Ms. Miyagi told me that Dr. Matsumae was extremely disappointed and that he would like to meet with me as soon as possible. My initial response was similar to that of losing a loved one—it felt like a sucker punch to the stomach. I told Jackie and we both had tears in our eyes. Did this mean that all the work, including the first Women's World Judo Championships, was in vain? Was all the hard training of the athletes all over the world for nothing? Was it all over?

Hell no!

The sadness quickly turned to anger and the urge to kill. I hate to say it, but I had intense and wild rage flowing through my veins. I wanted to get to the IOC members who voted against us and strangle them one by one. But I knew that to be effective, I had to calm down and get back to planning.

I called the ACLU immediately to speak with Ramona Ripston, the Executive Director, and Susan McGreivy, the lawyer with whom I had worked regarding women's judo. The office was not open yet but there was an emergency number to call. The man who picked up turned out to be the janitor, who spoke little English. I was on fire. I called Ms. Miyagi back to tell her I would meet with Dr. Matsumae at the judo venue, but first I had to go to the ACLU office and wait until it opened.

Rusty speaking at the ACLU press conference.

Jackie managed to drive me to the office. I couldn't care less that she didn't have a license. She said she would apply "mañana."

When we arrived, I almost flew through the door without opening it and didn't even say hello to Susan. I just blurted out the story.

Ramona was due in shortly. Susan calmed me down, not with soothing words, but with a possible alternative strategy.

Ramona arrived and Susan filled her in. After a few hours' worth of discussions and reading all the paperwork and international press clippings, it was decided that we would have a huge press conference within a couple of days publicizing the rejection and the discrimination against women's judo. There were lots of foreign press at the Games, as one would expect, and that would be to our benefit. Ramona and Susan gave me my immediate assignment: Get to the judo venue and invite several members of the IJF to the upcoming press conference, along with any American female athletes and national and foreign officials who could be interviewed.

78

JACKIE GOT ME TO THE VENUE, BUT TOLD ME that she had to give the car back to her dad and would not have access to it again. It seems he was pissed off at her for taking it because she didn't have a driver's license. I told her not to worry, that I would find wheels somehow.

The competition was going on as I found my seat. I scoped out the room looking for the people I needed for the press conference and the wheels. There were approximately 5,000 people at the event, so I really had to move around to kickstart my roundup.

I found several women athletes who would come aboard and got their information on how to reach them for the conference. I found the IJF people and US supporters that I was looking for and filled them in on the plan. Several would make themselves available for the press conference. Then I spotted my old friend Bernie Semal from Brooklyn judo who now resided in San Diego.

Wheels!

I told him the whole story. I told him I needed his help. I needed him to drive me all over the place every single day. Would he help me?

I must have looked crazed because Bernie, who usually debates what time it is, agreed immediately. Thank goodness or I would have had to borrow a car and I didn't know if my hot-wiring skills would work on these new models.

Rusty, Connie Halporn & the ACLU legal team.

I only got to see a little of the competition as I was far too busy working the room. Bernie and I then went back to Jackie's house to get my phone calls and messages in his fire red Porsche.

A fellow judoka speaking in support of women's inclusion.

How appropriate for me!

Fire and speed was exactly what I needed. One of the messages waiting for me when we arrived was from the ACLU office requesting I call them to get all the details they'd set for the press conference and to update them on my mission. It all jelled and a huge press conference was set up at the ACLU main assembly room. Our athletes, several official US supporters, and judo representatives from a dozen countries were in attendance. As the president of USA Judo, Frank Fullerton was invited but declined. The press person and the program committee for the IOC were invited but also declined. I was not surprised. It didn't matter; the seats were completely filled.

Ramona Ripson opened the conference with a brief history of women's judo and what had transpired in women's sports in general. She made a good presentation of the case on our behalf that clearly pointed at the IOC for discrimination. One by one we testified to the press and were asked questions which were answered from the heart. Lots of photos were taken. The conference lasted two hours.

The next day the *Los Angeles Times* published the story favoring our inclusion. The paper also included an interview with the IOC that gave some lame reasons for exclusion—the medical field had not yet concluded their findings of what could happen to a woman's body in a contact sport. They were worried about reproductive organs, supposedly. I didn't understand that excuse, as our organs are well protected and do not stick out, as with men in judo. Another rumor was that they did not want us in the Games as a contact sport because women in contact sports could encourage lesbianism. Another myth.

How can you possibly fall in love with somebody simply because they're smashing you down, trying to choke you, or putting an arm lock on you?

They really didn't get it.

I felt that the real reasons they voted nay were: first, hey could not relate to women in judo because they showed too much strength, independence, and were capable of handling themselves; second, women's bodies were covered up pretty well with the judo uniform so there was no wiggly jiggly to be ogled at; and lastly, we didn't have any commercial value or major sponsors providing a money- making opportunity that could be associated with us.

Who knows what their actual rationale was? In any case, it didn't matter. The issue was far from over. Dr. Matsumae and I would continue the fight and get more people on our side.

His statement at the conference was excellent. He asked, why would the organization intentionally deprive young women from the enjoyment and benefits of our sport and the lifestyle of judo?

I was feeling much better because I knew this was certainly not the end, just another new beginning.

An idea was forming in my already over-taxed brain. I would make copies of every piece of information and press that I had with me, add on the recent press conference articles, and write a personal letter from me that would include a complete update of our plight and where people could write to help our cause. I managed to get the names and addresses of several of the IOC program commission members, as well as the president of the IOC and would add this information to the entire package, which was now about thirty-five pages and growing.

My letter would have to be typed up so Bernie drove me around to find one of Jackie's cousins who had a typewriter. We finally found her. It took two hours for one letter, as she didn't have a good handle on English, and both Bernie and I could not type.

Now I had my packet.

The next problem was how to make 5,000 copies, correlated and stapled, for absolutely no money.

I brought the booklet with me to the judo venue the next day. I located Dr. Matsumae and told him what I had and needed to do. I wanted to distribute the booklet to every judo spectator as they were leaving the venue after the matches. He called over to the secretary of the IJF, Heinz Kempa from the German Democratic Republic, known as DDR in German (formerly East Germany).

Kempa and I had become good friends over the past several years, never discussing anything besides judo, our common bond. He was a good guy, on the ball and would proceed to get me into the no-pass zone at the Games where official credentials were required. As we marched through at a speedy pace, there were many attempts to stop me, however Kempa would whip out his Olympic credentials and some official identification from the DDR and wave them off. After all, no one wanted to be accused of adding coal to the already cold war. We were going to the copy machines.

Kempa and others helped me. I don't know exactly how many full booklets we made, but the machines had smoke coming out of them before we were through.

We made it close to my goal of 5,000.

I left the venue through the back door with help carrying the huge amount of positive women's judo propaganda. Bernie met me outside. When the folks vacated the judo venue, they received a booklet. Some stopped to chat and said they didn't know about this discrimination. "Now you do," I replied. "Please help us."

Then it was back to the Bernie-mobile and continuation of another adventure.

Rusty practicing her throwing technique, mid-1980s.

August 10, 1984

Dear Judo Enthusist:

The recent decision of the International Olympic Committee regarding the rejection of the Women's Judo Entry for the 1988 Olympic schedule is a terrible injustice which we must work diligently to change. Not only does this apparent discriminatory decision affect the elite women judo athletes throughout the world who have already changed their lifestyles to gear up for the 1988 Olympics, but also it affects the future participants and encouragement of the entire Women's Judo Program.

It is also an insult to the entire world of judo as it means only the male athletes may compete in our sport for the Olympic medal. In so many other Olympic sports, both men and women have the chance to win medals for their country with this, the highest level of competition.

Women's judo has fulfilled all the requirements to qualify as a sport of the Olympic schedule. In fact, we have more than met our prerequisites especially compared to other sports that have recently been added to the Olympic Program. Besides the competition on the Women's Development Survey Report the following International Open Competitions are held throughout the year that are enthusiastically participated in by the women judo athletes: Austria, Belgium, Britain, Canada, Dutch, Japan (Fukuoka Cup), France, W. Germany, United States, Poland, and Scandanavia.

On behalf of all the World Women Judo Athletes and in the name of International peace, friendship, and understanding, I am appealing to you to help the Women Judo Athletes, their families, and managers to reach the ultimate goal in sports, THE OLYMPICS.

There are several ways that you can help us. (Noted below are the names of the President, the Director, and the Chairman of the International Olympic Committee.)

1. You can contact your national olympic committee and encourage them to appeal this decision.
2. You can write letters and send telegrams to the IOC officials listed below indicating your protest of this decision and encouraging them to reconsider their decision and encourage further negotiations on our behalf with the International Judo Federation.
3. You can contact the media to enlighten them of this situation and have them encourage people to help us.
4. You can initiate a petition and pass them on to your local regional and national government agencies to encourage their participation to recify this injustice.

President of the International Olympic Committee
SEM Juan Samaranch
Member of International Olympic Committee
Avenida Pau Casals 24
Barcelone 6, Espagne

M. Vitaly Smirnov
Member of International Olympic Committee
RSFSR Sports Committee
Furmanova Street
121019 Moscou, URSS
Director of International Olympic Committee
Mme Monique Berlioux
Member of International Olympic Committee
Chateau Vidy
Lausanne, Switzerland

Please take a few moments from your life to support this
very important cause.

Sincerely,

Rusty Kanokogi
2126 East 17th St.
Brooklyn, NY 11229
USA

79

GARY SMITH, ACE WRITER FOR *SPORTS Illustrated*, and I had become friends over the past year and he wanted to do a major piece on judo for their upcoming Olympics issue.

Wow! What an opportunity!

When I first spoke with Gary, his question to me was, "Rusty, in your opinion, who is the best male judo competitor in the world?" It took me exactly one blink before I answered Yasuhiro Yamashita from Japan and Tokai University.

Gary wanted to highlight Yamashita in the 1984 Olympics edition of the magazine. Many athletes from many sports were recommended for the issue, so Gary had to wait to see who would be selected. I had some acquaintances from *Sports Illustrated* because I always took the time to do a story on someone from judo and would always send them results from competitions, which they mostly didn't use.

Mr. Yamashita was selected. I was so happy because I knew the word judo would be mentioned so many times in the most important sports magazine in the world.

It wasn't easy for me to convince Mr. Yamashita's teachers, Inokuma Sensei and Sato Sensei, to allow Gary to go to Japan to interview Yamashita prior to the 1984 Games. I believe Dr. Matsumae, who was then the president of Tokai University and the number one man, gave the nod.

I contacted my big Yugoslavian friend Radomir, who was still at Tokai and would be competing in LA, to help with the project. Gary went to Japan, met with the big boys and went out to lunch that *Sports Illustrated* sprang for at a cost of approximately $3,000. They ate, talked, and drank for seven hours. Yamashita was competing on the last day of the judo event. I did not want to miss that match. From time to time, I watched some of our Americans place in their categories and gave them a good old-fashioned American cheer. Gary and Radomir had become good friends. I guess we all have borderline insanity/genius syndrome to find and like one another.

Radomir was competing for Yugoslavia. He had lived in Japan for so long and had many differing ideas from most Yugoslavian citizens back in the old country. He was always getting into trouble for speaking his mind on national TV back home. During one interview he accused the government of filling their pockets and home with luxury and crapola for the athletes. It was just a matter of time before they would put him in jail or kill him.

Gary knew what was going on but couldn't help. I, on the other hand, could. I decided right then and there that I would assist him with his great escape.

Bernie and I managed to get near the Olympic Village. I had been in touch with Radomir. We set up a time and date to meet. Despite Radomir's six-foot-eight stature and hefty build, believe it or not, we folded him right in half and smuggled him in the back of the Porsche. We could have sent a photo to *Ripley's Believe it or Not* for their book.

We drove to Marina del Rey in Los Angeles and met with Gary. We didn't really have a plan, but we were going to make one. Radomir indicated that if he didn't return to Yugoslavia, the government would punish his family, coach, and teammates. We had a dinner that Gary took care of, and then returned to the Olympic Village. Radomir had eaten a lot so it was more difficult to fold him up for the trip back.

We ditched the immediate defection plan, but I promised Radomir that I would take care of him in the future and get him out of Yugoslavia. That was good enough for him; he knew that my word was my bond.

I had been pretty sleep deprived with all the running around, tension and the like, so Bernie suggested that I crash at his apartment one night so I could get a decent night's sleep. We drove to San Diego to Bernie's place. I took a long wonderful shower, had some dinner and wine and went to bed without anyone climbing over me.

I was almost in slumberland when the phone rang. It was Bernie's girlfriend. He told her his old friend from Brooklyn was staying with him. He tried to explain the situation but this chick would not listen. I was a female and that was all she needed to know. Poor Bernie. She almost broke up with him.

What a dip!

Refreshed and raring to go, I got some more lobbying in and spoke to more people to enroll them in the crusade.

It was the last day of judo and the famous Yamashita would fight for the gold medal. He didn't have any problems throughout the day with any of his opponents, however he did sustain a major ankle injury during one match. He entered the finals to compete for the gold against Mohamed Ali Rashwan from Egypt, a fast judo athlete who weighed almost four hundred pounds.

Rashwan and Yamashita had trained together in Japan at Tokai and really respected each other.

They bowed in. The room was silent except for the Egyptian coach who was yelling something over and over. We later found out that it was instructions to sweep Yamashita's leg hard by his injury. Rashwan did not listen. He just tried to do other techniques to throw his opponent. The painful match was almost over when Yamashita pulled out his big throw with all the fight and spirit he had left in his body and tossed Rashwan for a full point, winning the match. There was a standing ovation for both of them.

Radomir lost in the finals for third place to Mark Berger, a Canadian who had recently defected from the USSR.

Back in Brooklyn more progress had been made, but there was no light at the end of the tunnel, yet.

80

OUR UNIQUE JUDO CLUB ON FLATBUSH AVENUE in Brooklyn, NY, was almost oblivious to my efforts regarding women's judo with the exception of a handful of female judoka in the club and the guys that I had already recruited for my crusade.

We named the Kyushu Judo Club after the part of Japan that Ryohei is from, home of some of the world's finest and most famous judo players. The people in Kyushu are similar to our Brooklynites—straightforward, not fancy or too puffed up with themselves.

Kyushu dojo seemed to be the extension of Ellis Island. Every immigrant judo player ended up finding and joining us. It was amazing to have all that diversity on our mats. We embraced all. At any given time there were at least twenty different nationalities on the mat working out. Thank goodness my husband and I had other incomes to help subsidize the lack of money Kyushu had. We already had a following of judo players from schools that we taught at. Some were still with us from many years ago. They had started as kids, went on to college and then returned. Others came from the YMCA and still others from the neighborhood. The children at Kyushu were primarily from Caribbean backgrounds. They lived not too far from the dojo. Some came from East Flatbush, Bedford-Stuyvesant, and Bushwick. Some were from one-parent homes. They were from all walks of life and incomes. Occasionally, we would get some white kids in class. It was a healthy melting pot.

We had rented a storefront, put up a sign, got the mats, had showers installed in the basement with some locker rooms, ordered a payphone to hang on the back wall and were set to open. We had an abundance of students and charged a menial monthly fee to cover expenses. However, it seemed we were always in hock because some couldn't pay—they had lost their job or had an unexpected emergency—or they would keep postponing their dues and so on. We were not very good at record keeping, because as soon as we got to the dojo, we had to teach. The students were long gone by the time we remembered the dues. We also didn't have the heart to let a kid go because of money.

The students trained hard and Ryohei and I put all our expertise and energy into them. Your dojo and your students are an extension of your family, and just like any family, there would be good and bad times. We had excellent results in competition as we stayed true to our traditional judo teaching philosophy, rather than the knock them down any way you can strategy. We taught techniques on which we could build good basic judo. Winning was important, but the development of the entire personality and character was essential. When teaching judo, if you are sincere and technically astute, there is great satisfaction because you are passing on your knowledge to another, new generation.

It was interesting when we took a group of our minority youngsters to a tournament out of town in those days. The public would stare as Big Red (me), the Asian (my husband) and a half dozen or so black and Spanish kids walked into a restaurant in upstate New York or some other suburban area. You could almost hear their wheels spinning, "Hmm. Is that what you get when you have a mixed marriage?" We would all have many a good laugh about it.

The kids and adults in our dojo became pretty good competitors, as well as good students in school and a credit to their communities, because they were required to do volunteer work in an area of their interest. If they didn't, I volunteered them for some good cause.

Besides our serious part of teaching judo, we probably had more fun than any other club in the world because of our constant cast of characters. I have already mentioned some of them earlier, but now I can go on to some of our superstars of mirth.

Rusty & Ryohei's Kyushu dojo on Flatbush Avenue in Brooklyn, New York.

Ryohei usually opened earlier so the kids that needed help with their homework or just needed to wind down before class always had a place to come to. The senior class never ended on time. We would get out about 10 o'clock. In the winter the windows would get so fogged up and the body heat was so intense that it looked like a steam room from the street.

There was a constant energy being dispelled throughout the space. The judo uniforms were so heavy that you could drop lots of weight in one workout. When it got too overbearingly hot, even in the freezing winter, we would keep the front door open while gusts of steam would shoot out. Some passersby thought we were a Chinese laundry.

PHOTO CREDIT PETER PERAZIO

Summer had its own unique effect. Although we had a small air conditioner, it didn't cool off very much. We wanted the students to become strong mentally and physically so many times the practice was done with the doors closed and the AC off. It paid off when our daughter, Jean, and our student, Eve Aronoff, competed at the 1985 US Olympic Sports Festival in Baton Rouge, Louisiana on a very hot and humid day in July. Not only did they win, but they were two of the few that didn't pass out because of the lack of air.

There wasn't much space for sitting spectators so on many occasions a player would land up on the laps of the few people who were seated in the room. It became a ritual. Only the strongest parent or spectator sat to watch; others peeked through the window when it wasn't steamed up. More than once a throw continued through the door and onto Flatbush Avenue. We all screamed and managed to stop the pending fatality.

Sitting in front of the Kyushu dojo storefront on an old, strong milk box was Tony Campbell, a huge man, over three-hundred pounds, a correctional officer, father of several students, uncle to some and brother to the world. Tony had a voice that bellowed. I kept him outside as much as possible, as he fancied himself a judo coach and usually yelled the wrong instruction to the kids and to anyone else, he took on for the evening.

Rusty & Ryohei with a group of students at their Kyushu Judo Club.

Tony sat outside chatting with the curious pedestrians, and gave them information on the club. Some folks were a little reluctant to get close to him, as his gun was always on his hip. Having him was a plus and a minus but, in any case, he was a part of our crew.

Parnel Legros, a.k.a. "the Haitian creation," was my gem. Parnel hooked up with me at New York City Community College when he was a freshman, then joined us at Kyushu. His family had recently emigrated from Haiti. He had lots of siblings, several of whom would join us in the future.

Parnel trained hard. He won everything with good technique and had enough energy to compete in two divisions many times. He competed at the Nationals several times but just couldn't place in the top three. I knew it wasn't his skill holding him back. It was some kind of psychological thing. Case in point: Parnel got married the first time when he was very young and had fathered two children with his wife. Many Haitians have deep roots into voodoo. Parnel's wife became very jealous of his other love, judo, and said she was going to have voodoo curses put on him if he went to the National Championship. The problem was Parnel believed it and was scared of the power of voodoo. Every time he sustained an injury, though minor, he believed her voodoo did it. Now I had to pull in the forces of my grandmother, the Russian soothsayer. I convinced Parnel that her force was working to remove the Haitian curses. Most times it worked. Moreover, I never wanted to hear another coach bitch about how hard the job is—removing voodoo spells is not easy!

Parnel pursued his education. He was like family to us and we would do all and anything for his success in judo and life. I was pretty well connected to the IJF even though I didn't have any official position. When I found out Haiti had not paid their IJF dues and the Haitians would be excluded from the World Championships and not have an opportunity to qualify a team for the upcoming Olympics, I got on the stick. I communicated with the president of the Haitian Judo Federation and got their dues paid.

Haiti didn't really have anyone to go to the World Championships in Barcelona and no money to send them if they did. Parnel had dual citizenship, so he could compete for them. The president of the Haitian Judo Federation gave us a letter and permission for Parnel to represent Haiti. I raised the money for the trip and expenses.

Parnel would be at the World Championships later that year. I was asked to be his coach and I agreed, except that I would not march in the opening ceremony under another nation's flag. Some of our New York judo friends were present at the world event. I gave the Haitian fellow, Wisler Jacques, my jacket and he marched with Parnel, carrying the Haitian flag.

Parnel was in awe of all his judo heroes who were in line with him. He was in a semi-trance from seeing all the athletes that he had admired for so many years, and following their competitive records. Maybe a voodoo curse did manage to sneak in on him because he didn't go far in the meet. He did, however, have one nice throw against a Romanian who later pinned him.

Parnel got his degree in physical education. I connected him up for his teaching jobs and am proud to say that after thirty years with us, he is one of the best instructors around. His students have excelled to the highest level on the national and international judo scene. He was very strict with his students, requiring them to maintain good grades in school and demonstrate good social behavior. The Mayor of New York and the United States Olympic Committee recognized Parnel as an outstanding coach.

Going to the dojo would always hold a sense of excitement because I never knew who would show up. Occasionally, I would first receive a call at home with a request from a judo acquaintance to accommodate a personal friend of theirs in the judo community. This latest call would send me Petra Motsof, a Romanian judo player, who was in his early thirties and had an abundant amount of judo knowledge. This was good for us because we practiced traditional judo. The commie countries were moving up the ladder very quickly in international competition and this would give us an opportunity to discover their secrets.

Petra was also the former national coach of the Romanian junior judo team. He had befriended a young girl at the Romanian Olympic training camp who would cry a lot because of hunger pangs. He would sneak her little pieces of meat from his dinner. Feeding a judo person is certainly different than feeding a tiny gymnast. When I speak to Petra's friend, and now my friend also, Nadia Comaneci, she still thanks Petra for his kindness.

Petra had gone to Austria, stayed for a good while and became the boyfriend of Bridgette Kucera, who was the daughter of the president of the European Judo Union. Kurt Kucera was also a vice president to the IJF and a major supporter of women's judo. He was also a good friend of mine.

Kurt called me to tell me that Petra was going to the USA for some job and asked if I would help him. I gave my typical fast "Yes!" answer. It turned out that Petra would be living in Brooklyn, not too far from my house, and his job consisted of helping a writer whom he had met in Transylvania with her book on Dracula.

Famed judoka Yasuhiro Yamashita, who Rusty often named "the best judo player in the world," with Ryohei at the Kyushu Judo Club.

Oh, Ollie, what have I gotten myself into this time?

The writer and her husband gave Petra room and board, and the way I heard it, Mrs. Writer would be giving Petra a little bonus on the side. When I met her, I looked for teeth marks on her neck.

For us, it worked out really well at the dojo. The students enjoyed Petra and some of his training techniques. We couldn't afford to pay him, but we took him to dinner many times. He connected with Radomir at our club, who worked part time as a bouncer, and in turn got a job as a clean-up man at some bars in the city. Petra asked for political asylum in the United States and in due time, it was granted. He started pursuing the American dream. He continued to work out with us, went to Columbia University full time, did his bar jobs, and studied his ass off. He got accepted to the medical school and did brilliantly there. He became a resident at a major Chicago hospital and married an American girl. Dr. Petra Motsof now lives in the Midwest with his family and has, as most doctors, a lucrative business.

But believe me, he paid the price for it. After the writer's husband thought Petra was getting too close to his wife, in every sense of the word, he told him to leave. Petra wanted to stay with us. We told him no can do; we had Big Radomir living with us at the time, and the kids objected, as they were getting somewhat squeezed out of their room.

After Petra cleaned up the bar he would study for the rest of the night, sleep on the bar, then get up and go to school. He did this until he finally moved into the dorm at Columbia. He did most of his studying on scholarship money.

Rusty & her students preparing to start class at the Kyushu dojo.

Rusty throwing student during class at the Kyushu dojo, while Ryohei and students watch.

Everything turned out well for Petra, but I was still haunted by befriending him. I was a referee at some major tournament in Eastern Europe. When I was checking into the hotel, two guys approached me. They were typical KGB types, especially the one with a big scar running across his face.

"Where is Petra?" they asked in a demanding voice. "Give us all information about him."

Luckily, I'm from Brooklyn and don't get intimidated too quickly. I denied knowing him and told them to fuck off. I was brazen but not too bright, as I was in their communist territory. I guess they took one look at me and said, "Forget about keeping her here. We couldn't afford the food."

The next day at the competition, I was sitting in the referee area in front of a table with a white cloth covering it down to the floor. I heard a psssst and looked down. There was a man crawling under the table.

"I'm Petra's friend," he said in very broken English. "Please give him this message."

I took it and he crawled away. What the hell was going on here?

When the tournament was over, the host held a reception for athletes and officials. I could feel lots of eyes on me. I didn't know what was going to happen next. Thank goodness, nothing happened. I left for the good old USA the next day. When I saw Petra I gave him the note. He smiled and thanked me. By his demeanor, I felt sure the note wasn't a blueprint to overthrow our government.

Chalk it up to another happy ending for judo.

81

THE FILM *COMING TO AMERICA*, STARRING EDDIE
Murphy and Arsenio Hall could have been the backdrop for the newest judo player to grace our humble dojo. Lovette was from Nigeria. She actually showed up at our house. When I answered the bell, Lovette was standing there. She didn't speak. She just looked at me and then handed me a note. The note was from a Japanese judo instructor, Mr. Toriyumi, who was teaching in Nigeria at the time. He said that she would be living in the US for a while and asked if I take care of her, judo-wise that is.

Her appearance was striking. She was tall, about five feet, eight inches, strongly built, with a solid 158-pound body. She had an attractive face, except for the three long gashes on both sides of her face that ran from the side of her lip to just under her eyes. They were exactly the same in length as in the distance between them. I couldn't stop staring, as the only time I had seen those types of marks were in the *National Geographic* magazine. I would later learn these were the tribal markings of the Yoruba people, used to identify tribal heritage, and as a cultural symbol of beauty[21].

I welcomed Lovette into the house and we talked about judo. Her English was very broken, but I learned that she had also trained in Japan. I gave her our judo schedule and address and told her I would see her at the club.

When Lovette walked through the door, all the students looked at her and froze. They were not staring at the facial gashes, but at the enormous amount of eye makeup she had on. It sure was a distraction from the scars. For whatever reason, Lovette had worn shiny yellow eyebrow shadow, purple streaks of eye shadow below that and to top it all off, a bluish-green on the eyelids.

I welcomed her, introduced her to the group, and showed her where the changing room was, hoping she would remove her outlandish makeup. She came back to the mat area with her judogi and her black belt on. She also still had all her makeup intact. I didn't want to hurt her feelings, so practice just continued. She was amazingly strong and fast. The guys in the dojo, including a few of our champs, soon forgot about her face, as they were fighting for their lives and their pride. She had them all over the place, into the walls, on the ceiling. I salivated as I watched this lovely, soft-spoken creature—who I knew would be the next champion of the world— working out just three feet from me.

Rusty in her Kyushu dojo gi.

Lovette never missed practice. We got friendlier, went out to lunch, and I got her makeup straightened out. I didn't tell her to refrain from using eye makeup, but taught her a little eye makeup technique, just not during judo practice or competition.

She competed and won in both local and regional tournaments. In the women's divisions she didn't even break a sweat. She *always* won. I could not enter her nationally because she wasn't a citizen; she probably didn't even have a Green Card.

I got her a little part-time job for pocket money while we were trying to figure out what to do with her. She was living with her aunt in Brooklyn, so at least she wasn't homeless. She could have moved in with us otherwise.

I was away at a competition. When I called home to check in, my husband told me what had happened outside our Kyushu club, and then inside it. Everyone was practicing. It was a warm day so the front door was open, when a long stretch limo pulled up in front of the club. A well-attired man with very colorful African garb got out, went around to the passenger side, opened the door, and an exquisitely dressed man with a long satin and gold robe with matching hat got out of the vehicle, bringing his gold staff with him. They approached the door and asked permission to enter. Everyone stood there dumbfounded, but Ryohei answered, "yes."

The driver introduced the prince to my husband. The prince looked over at a sweaty Lovette..

"My dear sister," he said. "I am here to take you home. Mother and Father are very concerned about you."

They seemed embarrassed and started speaking in their language at a very fast pace. The tone seemed somewhat argumentative. The prince thanked everyone, told Ryohei to please watch out for his sister and attempted to give him some money, which he declined.

Dammit! I should have been there.

He then left. By that time the whole neighborhood was around the car and club checking out the scene.

Princess Lovette from Nigeria stayed with us for a long while, teaching some of the men humility. Not too long after the limo incident, she found a boyfriend and went off somewhere. I am sure the princess is fine and one day will come back to my door to say hello again.

82

THE STORY ABOUT OUR STUDENT IS BITTERSWEET in the sense that judo almost saved him. Meeting him for the first time would knock anyone's socks off. He was five-foot-ten, about three hundred pounds, with a huge fifty-eight-inch chest, and the largest biceps in the world according to the *Guinness Book of World Records*. He wore horn-rimmed glasses as he was as near-sighted as he was strong. The top of his head had a thin coating of hair, but he made up for it with his sideburns and beard. I stayed cool and collected and acted as though he was a normal human being.

We were introduced by a guy from our club that I wasn't too fond of. I always had the feeling that what you saw was not what you would get with this guy. As I mentioned earlier, we threw the sleaze out of the Kyushu Judo Club.

Gary's good buddy, Dusty, had a big weight lifter type body, offset by being tall, so his weight was more fairly distributed. These fellows were power lifters and bouncers at clubs in New York. Gary was already a legend for his huge biceps. The sleazes intent in introducing Gary around was just to show off his big prize, not to introduce him to judo. Sleaze had become Gary's manager, as they lived in the same building. Somehow I managed to persuade Gary and Dusty to come to judo practice as my personal guests, meaning no monthly dues. I felt something towards Gary. It was similar to a feeling I had when I was in Luna Park as a kid with the sad but highly unusual people at the freak shows. Gary arm-wrestled for money because there is no real money in powerlifting, just new records and pride.

Gary and Dusty came to practice. I had some old judo uniforms at the club and gave them a gift of the judogi. Gary had some trouble with the flexibility exercises. They learned to fall and began to study judo techniques. The regular class students were kind and accepting of the new, large kids on the block. Why not? The new kids could demolish them with one blow.

Teaching them how to off-balance their partners was a joke, especially with Gary. He would pull on someone's uniform by the sleeve and lapel and either toss them across the room in an awkward power throw, or rip the heavy burlap uniform from their bodies. As a sturdy volunteer, Gary would practice his forms of throwing with me. I knew when to relax and when to tense my stomach to keep me more grounded.

After a few months of training, including the randori free play, where you try to throw each other without cooperation, Gary started to really enjoy judo. Given his extraordinary strength and size, he learned to use skill and not solely depend on brute strength in order to catch and throw a lighter and faster, albeit less strong opponent. He obviously loved the challenge. Dusty was not steady at practice, but Gary was.

His background was Armenian and his family—one brother and a mom and dad—were devoted to him. Our son, Ted, who was about twelve years old at the time found his role model for life. He followed Gary around like a loyal kid brother. Gary was about twenty-two years old when he came to our dojo. Our daughter, Jean, quickly became friends with him She was about sixteen or seventeen at the time. Gary liked her very much as his friend and probably more. He had not been involved with any girls, because he had been too self-absorbed. He hadn't given girls a thought.

Jean and Gary became friends and out of respect for us, Gary was always a gentleman with her. It wasn't difficult to see that it was more than platonic. He was a quiet guy but tough, though he wouldn't start a fight. But just like us, he would finish one.

We didn't want to put Gary into competition prematurely, because just by looking at him, one would expect him to be a winner. These are judo and skill rules!

I received a letter from the German Judo Federation, also known as Deutscher Judo-Bund. They had a young team of high school girls, coach and manager who wanted to visit New York to train with us and go sightseeing. It was a good opportunity, not only for our club, but for all the young women from New York to train with a good foreign team. The Germans were doing real well in international competition.

There were eighteen of them expected on the trip. I contacted my friend Alice Rubin, who was a devout Jew. She had the largest home of all my friends. Her son David was my judo student, plus she was a proactive judo mommy. Alice only asked for how long. I told her ten days to two weeks. She agreed to lighten my load of visitors. I called her back and said I had contacted them and they were so happy and would be here in a week or so. "Oh, and by the way, they're Germans," I threw in.

My friend Alice, at that time an attorney now a judge[22], is a kind and liberal person and said to bring them on. When they arrived, I deposited sixteen at Alice's house and the coach and manager at ours. The manager indicated she was pregnant and needed to be away from the team.

Great.

Oh, well, Alice would manage.

I rented a very large van and recruited my kids, Gary and Dusty, to run around with us. This was at the end of June, 1984. Every day I did the pickup at Alice's place, took them sightseeing, thrilled them at the World Trade Center, Chinatown, and the usual sights.

We didn't have enough room in the van so Gary was in the front with me, the driver, and I should note that I had never driven a commercial van before. The rest of the gang found their own places in the back.

Going through the Brooklyn–Battery Tunnel for some reason encouraged the German team to sing all their traditional songs. We got some stares. Maneuvering the singing team through the narrow streets of Chinatown was a major challenge for me. I drove slow but steady through the city. Every once in a while, some driver behind me would beep and send curse words my way for driving so cautiously, but they changed their tune when Gary got out of the van and told them to knock it off. Gary's typical outfit was a tank top that showed his bulging chest and biceps, which may have encouraged courtesy from the pissed off driver flinging the curses. After a day of touring, each night we went to our dojo where the visiting team and our students had a great exchange of judo techniques.

I wanted publicity for judo and the team from Germany. Alice arranged a meeting at the borough President's office. They had a little reception, gave the team some gifts, and had a photo op. One of the girls lifted Billy Thompson, the Deputy Borough President, up on her shoulders. Billy is now the City Controller and still remembers his lift vividly. The press loved it and it made a good story in the *Daily News* the next day. And that was only the beginning.

Alice had a connection with Nathan's Famous Hot Dogs in Coney Island. She gave me the number to call to get some judo girls invited to the hot dog eating competition coming up on July 4. They agreed after careful discussions. We put a girl from the German team, Birget Felden, and our very own American judoka, Jean Kanokogi, as our competitors.

The big day came. All of us went to Nathan's Coney Island, taking our bodyguards Gary and Dusty, and our mini bodyguard, Ted, just for fun.

Our delegation was about forty or so. I was the hot dog eating competition coach. The girls and six men competitors were given the rules. Birget weighed one hundred and twenty-three pounds, Jean was one hundred and fifty-eight, and the men were humongous. I thought we were dead, but would give a good fight. My strategy for the girls was to keep them steady and not gorging. They only had a three-minute time period. There was press galore, print and TV, as this was the first time females had entered this event—though, for once, it wasn't prohibitively difficult for them to do so.

When the starter shouted "Ready? Get set! Go!" the men began stuffing their faces. I coached methodically shouting, "Chew. Chew. Chew." They did, and when the whistle was blown at the end, our German girl, Birget, had eaten nine hot dogs for the win, and Jean had finished second with eight and a half. The cameras were going like crazy. You would think this was the Olympics. We were ecstatic.

Hooray!

Now for the prize: a yellow beach bag with Nathan's logo and tickets to come back in the future for free hot dogs.

Thrilling.

We received international press. It was a tremendous PR coup for judo. That was the real prize.

Since Ryohei starred as the judo talent in several commercials, I had relationships with entertainment agents who would call me from time to time when they were looking for an unusual body or skill set. A few months later, I would get Gary a part in a movie, *The Last Dragon*. Ted was in it also.

Time was flying. We were all getting worn out. The group from Germany was getting ready to depart for their homeland. After all the thanks, kisses and tears, we took them to the airport and waved and said *auf wiedersehen*.

Now it was time to get back to the regular schedule of training. Jean and I were leaving for a camp at the Olympic Training Center in Colorado Springs and the US Open Tournament. Over the last few months Jean and Gary would see each other at judo. We would all go to lunch together and their relationship blossomed. Gary told her they would date once she was eighteen years old. My husband and I saw they had a special friendship of mutual respect.

Jean and I left for Colorado Springs. We were concerned because Gary had just landed up in the hospital. We said we would call him when we were changing planes in Denver. First, I spoke to him, then Jean. He was diagnosed with pneumonia. We gave him all kinds of advice, wished him well and said we would call again real soon. The camp was starting and as I was one of the coaches, I had to concentrate on my job and Jean on her training. When I called again, the number in his hospital room just rang and rang with no answer.

Oh, good, I thought. *He's better and must have gone home.*

I planned to call him at home later. Later that day I checked in with Ryohei and to say hello to Ted, and received the shocking news that Gary had died during the night. Ted was devastated. I couldn't breathe or believe it. I asked how in this day and age someone could die of pneumonia?

I could not tell Jean. She was competing the next day.

After the tournament, I told her I had to talk to her. She thought it was going to be a judo pep talk, but realized it was something more when I had her walk with me to the base of Pikes Peak that was very close to the training center. We sat down. I told her to look up at the top of the great mountain with all its beauty, strength and splendor, as Gary's spirit was now in the mountain, and in doing so informed her of his death.

We both cried for a long time as we hugged each other. We could not get back in time for his funeral, but we did get to the cemetery with his mom and dad when we returned. We still stay in touch during the holidays and send each other Christmas cards. After all, we could have been related later in life.

The bitter part of this story is that Gary had been on mega doses of anabolic steroids, encouraged by Mr. Sleaze. Gary was seriously falling in love with judo and us and was soon going to stop his power lifting and the steroids that ultimately killed him. Unfortunately, he saw the light too late. We still have him in our hearts.

83

WE HAVE HAD SO MANY MARVELOUS PEOPLE
pass through our doors at the Kyushu Judo Club, some still remaining with us in body and many in spirit. The satisfaction one gets from touching so many lives is extraordinary and certainly makes up for the lack of revenue. Our wealth came from the experiences we had with the development of our students, getting to know them, teaching them a sport and principals we both love, helping to get them on track when they strayed, and keeping them going in the right direction. Judo has done that for both my husband Ryohei and me.

I would have to write another book to cover all our students, both the ones that glittered and the ones that shone brightly. We feel that all who have been involved at the club have made a mutual impact on each other.

The quest for women's judo in the next Olympic Games seemed to be going downhill. The IOC stuck with their idea that we were a new sport, which was, of course, not true; men's judo has been included since 1964. The false claims that women would hurt their reproductive organs by engaging in judo and that participation would encourage lesbianism was sheer rubbish! The IOC mucky mucks could just not get it through their thick heads that it was okay for women to fight. Period.

It was just about a daily job, the constant communication with the ACLU and the IJF, looking under every rock for a solution. We had to make the IOC bend. There were schemes going on in Brooklyn that would soon rock the sports world. Filing a complaint with the Division of Human Rights in the State of New York against the US Olympic Committee and USA Judo for discrimination against women's judo worked. Why couldn't the same thing work against the network that won the bid rights to the 1988 Seoul Olympic Games for between three hundred million and five hundred million dollars. After all, their corporate headquarters was in New York and we had just won out against the United States Olympic Committee, where they conceded. I decided to have an injunction put on any and all revenue to be paid to Korea for the Games as the New York State law stipulates that no New York corporation can go into contract with any entity THAT IS FOUND GUILTY OF DISCRIMINATION AGAINST RACE, RELIGION, COLOR, CREED OR GENDER.

By Jove, I think I have them.

Around the same time, I was making my case all over the place, making sure that everyone knew what the trouble maker was doing, the ACLU in California was preparing to file suit against the IOC with the help of the International Women's Law Association headquartered in Lausanne, Switzerland, for discrimination against women in judo.

Dr. Matsumae had the inclusion of women's judo into the Olympic Games high on his daily agenda. We met at least once a year in Japan or another country. He and I, though in two different parts of the world, had the same obsession and we were relentless. I had the New York and other state politicians lobbying. He had the ears of aristocrats and world politicians.

I had petitions traveling all over the world, being signed by judo athletes and their families. Unfortunately, when I had two friends, Ms. K. Miyagi from Tokai University and Ms. Yoko Mitsuya, a sports marketing person, go to the Kodokan to get the signatures of the Japanese girls and women during a competition, they were asked to leave and not do that type of politicking there[23]. I was very frustrated and my many years of high respect for the Kodokan was now tarnished. I'm sure if Professor Jigoro Kano was alive at the time, he would have helped us because one of the major principles of judo is *jita kyoei*[24], mutual benefit for all.

I managed to get 25,000 signatures on the petitions. I also managed to get the private home address of the president of the IOC in Spain. I made copies of all, then sent them to President Juan Antonio Samaranch. His mailman must still be cursing me for his hernia. The threats were made as the possible negotiation was coming up. Something had to give!

Our team went to the 1987 World Championships in Essen, West Germany. Two of our women placed—Lynn Roethke, at 61 kg, won a silver medal, and Margaret Castro, at plus 72kg, won a bronze. Michael

Swain also won our first gold medal by a male competitor. We were ecstatic and a force to be dealt with.

Finally, after in 1987, the deal was made by the IOC with the IJF—a huge and monumental win for women's judo, and the work I'd dedicated the last twenty years of my life to. They would allow women's judo in the 1988 Seoul Korea Olympic Games, providing the men give up the open division, which is basically redundant anyway because the same heavyweight men that fought in the heaviest weight category usually enter the open weight class. It was just another way to increase the medal count for themselves and their countries. It basically discriminated against the lighter weight guys, so I felt it was no big loss.

After working so long toward this one end, receiving the news was a surreal experience. Jean was still recovering from her knee injury, and the knowledge that we'd finally made it was bittersweet for her, as we both knew she wouldn't be able to compete. Knowing I had finally won after so many years waging fight after fight left me feeling a mix between jubilation and loss; what exactly would I fight for now?

What else is there?

The IOC left it up to the IJF to come up with the formula of how to select the women that would compete at the 1988 Games. A cap of eight women per division was set. The IJF remedy for the selection was to first choose the women that placed in the 1987 World Championship. Other available slots would then be chosen from women who placed first in their union championships, with second placers as the alternates. We had Lynn and Margie for sure. Later that year we were informed that Cuba would not participate in the Seoul games. This opened the 52 kg slot to our student, Eve Aronoff, who had placed second in the Pan Am Games. She was a ferocious and skilled fighter and I was thrilled she made the team. Eve was part of our Kyushu Dojo family and Ryohei and I couldn't be happier. She was now our third competitor.

The men, as usual, were allowed to field an entire team of seven. I was elected by the USA Judo organization to be the Olympic coach, I think not just because of my deeds of helping us get into the Olympic Games, but because of my success rate with the US women's team.

Banzai! Hooray! Nostrovia! La cheim!

We were going to the Olympics!

Oh my God, we were really in the Olympic Games.

It didn't matter to me, or most likely anyone else, the how or why of our dream finally being realized, or which strategy worked. I believe in all of them. The IOC saw the light, or just got sick of hearing from me. Who cares?!

Seoul, here we come.

RUSTY KANOKOGI

The United States Olympic coach for Women's Judo is Rusty Kanokogi. Rusty is bringing to Seoul three strong competitors and two alternates and plans to return home with medals. Rusty is recognized as a trainer of champions and one of the world's top coaches. She herself is a fifth degree blackbelt with 35 years of Judo experience. Women's Judo competition in the 1988 Olympic Games in Seoul is Rusty's "dream of a lifetime", a dream only realized through her own indomitable strength and perserverance.

Dr. S. Matsumae, past president of the International Judo Federation, the world governing body of Judo, credits Rusty with the rise of Women's Judo to Olympic status. According to Rusty, this feat wasn't easy. And wasn't easy is quite an understatement.

Rusty enrolled in her first Judo class in 1955. At that time she was aware that few, if any, women were in Judo. From then on, her love and loyalty to the sport grew as did her desire for Women's exposure on the Judo scene. Until 1974, the only National Level Women's Competition was in Kata. Then in 1974, after more than 15 years of hard work and dedication, Women's Judo competition was allowed entry at the National Level. Following this victory, Rusty pushed ahead and actually gained admittance for Women's Judo competition at the Union Level. It was in 1977 that Rusty, along with two other unions holding their respective Women's Championships at the Union Level, organized the first Pan American Women's Judo Championship. These championships were particulary noteworthy since three unions holding Women's Judo Championships at the Union Level gave Women's Judo competition acceptance at the World Level. In 1980, with help from friends, Rusty not only organized but actually hosted the first Women's World Judo Championship in the prestigious Felt Forum of Madison Square Gardens in New York City. This event, which many said could not happen, did happen and in so doing made history. Rusty, as tenacious as ever, was now gaining in her pursuit of Women's Judo in the Olympic Games.

It is now 1988, 14 years after the first Women's Judo Championship in the United States, and Rusty's dream is being realized. She and her Judo team will be in Seoul, Korea, for the Olympic Games, where Rusty will be coaching the U.S.A. team, where Women's Judo will compete side by side with Men's Judo. This is truly the crowning achievement of a dedicated and courageous athlete and coach. Good luck, Rusty!

Mel Appelbaum, Ph.D.
President, North American
Judo Confederation

84

*T*HE CONSENSUS OF THE US COACHES AND MAN-
agers after a planning meeting was to get the team to Santa Rosa, California to train for several weeks at our manager, Willy Cahill's club. It would help with acclamation for the East Coast athletes. California weather was closer to the heat in Seoul than New York was. Our men's coach, Yoshisada Yonezuka, lived in New Jersey and had the team train with him at his club prior to leaving for the West Coast. He planned to join us in California later.

Both teams trained on a daily basis. The routine would be judo training, getting to the gym for lifting, cardio and general exercise, and somewhere between all that during the day time to develop stamina by running. All fifty-three years and two hundred pounds of me was getting into super shape. Somehow, I felt like I too was competing.

All of the US Olympic teams were to meet in Los Angeles for a big send off at Disneyland. We all received the same outfit to wear on the patriotic floats we were going to be on: white shorts and red or blue golf shirts.

As our spiffy Olympians boarded the floats, the bands played and the famed Disney characters—all dressed in different sports attire—danced around us. It was fun and exciting with the crowds cheering, waving, and filming us. We waved our American flags at all and gave the victory sign. It is amazing how you are treated like a hero without really doing anything yet. I'm sure it was for encouragement. In any case, it was wonderful. Finally, I could relate to the ultimate superstar, Mickey Mouse.

We each received adorable pins and some gifts from the Disney group. The gold medals we were awarded were in the shape of Mickey Mouse and affixed on a red, white and blue ribbon. For some of our competitors, this would be the only medal they would receive on their quest for Olympic gold. Still, the event was a celebration of the American spirit, and it certainly made us all feel like winners.

Rusty with the US women's judo team celebrating their Olympic sendoff at Disneyland, 1988.

The next time we met was when we were boarding our flights to Seoul. The athletic and Olympic superstars and the first-time Olympians sat side-by-side, exchanging war stories, hopes and dreams. As soon as we landed in Seoul, we began going through all the processing points, obtaining our identifications, getting our clothing for the opening ceremony, and receiving gifts and the like from good old corporate America. It felt like Christmas in July.

Rusty with her hero, Mickey Mouse.

85

WE ARRIVED AT THE OLYMPIC VILLAGE AND GOT our assigned rooms in a newly built complex that would serve as housing for the Korean community after the Olympic Games. Actually, our rooms were suites. There was a room with two beds, and two single rooms, one bathroom, a small kitchen and a common room. Obviously, these suites were not built for big Americans.

Margie and I took the small but adequate single rooms and put our smaller companions, Lynn and Eve, in the double. It worked out nicely, but we did have a problem with Margie's bed, which was way too short for her over six-foot body. I went downstairs to speak with a monitor who allegedly spoke English. His pretense was good, but when all was said and done, the new bed he delivered to us for Margie was a child's crib.

After we all got up from the floor, where we had been laid out laughing, we tried to communicate once again. This time—with some pissed-off New Yorker vocabulary—they took the crib back. Margie would have to tough it out by putting the mattress on the floor.

Just as I thought: a conspiracy against us!

We adjusted our physical time clocks and got serious for our daily training schedule. We were bussed to the training site every day, and went through very serious inspection both coming and going from the Olympic Village.

Other national judo teams rode the bus with us. I knew many of the athletes and coaches, so we had a good time on the slow trip to the training site. During training the guys all worked out together and the four of us practiced on our own. Naturally, I had to be Margie's training partner. It wasn't easy for me, not just because of Margie size, but because of how I pushed them to do more and more every minute and be relentless. Continuous psychological input from me was also part of the training. I had to pace it so they didn't turn into raving maniacs prematurely.

I remember during practice when Margie and I were playing randori, we caught each other a few times with different throws. It wasn't a big deal to her, but catching her, our heavyweight Olympian, meant the world to me, as that would have been my division thirty years earlier. And I, the almost senior citizen, was still able to handle myself.

Hmm, should I send twenty-three-year-old Margie home and fight in that division? I got over my hallucination very quickly after, when I incurred some minor injuries during practice. Fortunately, Steve Cohen, the heavyweight competitor for the US men's Olympic team, was kind enough to be Margie's training partner when I was in limp mode. The guys had to concentrate on their training and we understood they could not lend us their bodies too often, as they had a war in front of them also and needed to train their guts out.

I called home and bragged to Ryohei a bit that I had caught Margie a few times during practice.

"So what?" he replied, squashing my buzz. "You are the coach, not the competitor."

It just felt good to know I still had something left.

There were many things to do in the Village. Our favorite was to go to the disco, which was open daytime through early evening. Naturally, there was no booze, just soft drinks. Still, we all liked to hang there. It was a nonstop dance-fest for us that we used as a form of continued conditioning. We had plenty of dance partners, as the African men's team had the same idea. So, we boogied and made new friendships.

It took a few days to get the skinny on the shopping opportunities in a district called Itaewon where there were supposed to be good, cheap clothes. The problem was getting there. We could not get a cab from the Village, but could get one on the way back.

The plan was made: On the return from training, when the bus driver stopped for a red light, we would bail out. Not all, just big Margie and me—I didn't want to put the little ones in jeopardy. Margie and I were like a tag team. It worked. The driver ranted at us in Korean as we ducked out the back door. Everyone on the bus was laughing as the tag team took off down the street.

The shopping was fabulous. You could go into a shop, pick what you wanted and they would have it hand made for you by the next day. With our sizes, this was a God-send. We went to a leather shop and selected what we wanted, got sized, and the shopkeeper and assistants took photos of us.

The next shop was for men, recommended to me by a friend in the IJF. I had my husband's sizes with me and had them make him an exquisite tuxedo that he still uses until this day and that, in my entirely biased opinion, makes him look like James Bond. I also ordered two suits of leather, a red and a black. The prices were ridiculously low—far under a hundred dollars. I couldn't buy a pair of shoes in New York for that price. I especially liked the jacket because of the deep slash pockets. Margie placed her order. They promised to deliver all our outfits to us at the Village in a day or so. When we had shopped to our hearts' content, we got a cab, went back to the Village and caught up with the team.

We received our merchandise a day or two later, as promised, and everything looked good. I tried on my outfit and noticed the slash pockets were missing in the red suit. I swore a little bit and decided to make the trek to Itaewon one more time to bring back the jacket. When I arrived back at the shop the next day, I told the salesman what was wrong, no pockets. His take on English was rapidly deteriorating, getting me more and more pissed off.

"Pockets?" he replied. "What **are** pockets?"

I showed him, and bellowed, "the fucking pockets are missing!" in his direction. He then got on the phone and called his sub-contractor yelling, "the fucking pockets are missing!"

At least we had a common word that helped us communicate. He sent the jacket back. The pockets were put in and sent to me at the Village the next day.

We were getting ready for opening ceremonies the following day. It would be a big mishmash, with some smoke and mirror entertainment.

1988 US Olympic Judo Team autographed picture, including athletes Eve Aronoff-Trivella, Margie Castro, Lynn Roethke, Coach Rusty Kanokogi, and Coach Yoshisada Yonezuka in Seoul, South Korea.

86

THE ROAR OF THE CROWDS WAS DEAFENING AS the United States delegation was approaching the Olympic Stadium in Seoul, South Korea. It was the games of the XXIV Olympiad.

We had been lined up standing for several hours waiting for the signal to enter. The sun smiled on us all day and we were rarin' to go. There were six hundred in our delegation, the largest in attendance. Word had gone to our United States Olympic Committee (USOC)[25] President, Robert Helmick, that our delegation was too large, and he should cut some of us out of the opening ceremony.

"We all march, or none of us march," he said.

I will never forget President Helmick's response. The Korean officials buckled immediately.

Indeed we all marched! We were so very proud of him.

Several days before the event we received our outfits for the big show. The American women's opening ceremony outfits consisted of long flowy white skirts, white blouses with little red crossover ties that went around the neck, white shoes and, to top it all off, powder blue acrylic—or some sort of other uncomfortable blend—sweaters with embroidered red flowers and a squiggly white wave going across it. We all looked like adorable Quakers at a wedding party.

This outfit was a clear violation of the Joan Rivers' Fashion Police.

The US men's outfits were sharp. They were decked out in navy blue blazers sporting an Olympic insignia on the left breast pocket, like a badge, with red ties, crisp blue and white pin-striped shirts and white trousers. Each and every one of these guys looks like Wall Street powerhouses or corporate executives.

We were to be lined up in an area adjacent to the major area several hours prior to opening ceremonies. The countries were lined up in marching order but were allowed to mix and mingle in between marching in time. We were on deck for approximately five hours. I spent the time walking around with my camera, which I had received as a perk from the Canon company talking to and taking photos with many of the US delegation and all the foreign judo players. It was fun, especially with some of the judo teams that had on their national costumes. The Mongolian men's team was almost bare-ass with their scanty but delightful garb. Their powerful bodies were pretty much exposed, and I wasn't complaining. They didn't field a women's team that year. It could have been interesting.

Rusty & Eve Aronoff-Trivella at the 1988 Olympic Games in Seoul, South Korea.

1988 US Olympic Judo Team: Margie Castro, Lynn Roethke, Eve Aronoff-Trivella, and Coach Rusty Kanokogi at the Olympic Village before the opening ceremonies in Seoul, South Korea.

As I made my way around, I inquired about how their judo women were doing. Specifically, I wanted to know if they had a team at the Olympics and, if not, encouraged them to support their women judoka. I knew many of the athletes, coaches and referees. It was also a kind of reunion. They took photos of me, possibly for their post office wanted poster.

Finally, we were ready to march in. Because we were "U" in the alphabetical lineup, we still had a little time before it was our turn. As we approached the final entrance gate, instead of walking in military style, the athletes and officials made their own course. At least we all were going forward in the same direction.

Our flag bearer led us into the stadium, proudly holding our red, white, and blue colors high. The crowd was huge, with over 30,000 attendees packed in the stadium around us. The roar of the spectators almost deafening as we wandered in. You could almost feel the breeze from the massive amount of American flags waving for us.

What a reception!

We waved and smiled, and cried, all at the same time. As the American delegation was the largest at the Games and one of the last to enter for the opening ceremonies, true to our values of individuality, we broke formation and drifted through the arena in semi-organized chaos. Each of us seemed to be marching in our own personal parade. Nearly every American in the delegation wandered off in a different direction, exploring their surroundings and interacting with members of other nearby teams. Our formation—large and floating on an adrenaline high through the spotlight—couldn't be contained.

It was thrilling.

The speeches began. Key buzz words and phrases kept being flung out of the dignitaries' opening remarks—phrases such as *fair play*, *equality*, *perseverance*, and *justice*. There was certainly no equality in the extended endeavor to get women's judo to this level. It had taken monumental perseverance to get any justice for women in judo thus far. I guess because of all the battles and frustration and hard work it took to get us here, I didn't have patience for all the public, and hypocritical grandstanding and back-patting. Where were they for the past twenty years?

It occurred to me that just by being there as the Olympic coach for the women's judo team representing the United States, I had already won the fight— the upcoming roar of the crowd I was anticipating would be my gold medal.

As the festival part of the opening ceremonies were about to begin, I started wondering where we were going to sit, as the stadium was packed to the brim. My question was soon answered, as they marched us out to the buses that would take us back to the Olympic Village, where we could watch the entertainment part of the ceremony on television from our rooms.

In between training we were invited to several receptions honoring the Olympians. The reception one afternoon would have several celebrities including Arnold Schwarzenegger and Maria Shriver. They walked around the large dining room meeting and greeting. When Arnold and Maria came over to our table, he recognized me as a past traveling acquaintance of his. We had a friend in common, Margaret Roach, a writer at *The New York Times*. Margaret did a very good and impactful story for us on our plight to get women's judo recognized. She also did a story on Arnold, who then became friends with her, just like Margaret and I had become friends.

Arnold and I first met in 1977 in Israel at the airport as we were both returning to the United States. He was in Israel as a judge for an international beauty pageant, I was there as the coach of the women's team to the Maccabiah Games. The team stayed after the games concluded, but I was going home, as my husband and young kids were waiting for me. With a three-woman team, we'd won two gold, one bronze, and I walked away with a black eye. Arnold had a crowd around him, even near the critical inspection area. He was popular back then for his world bodybuilding titles.

He noticed my eye, which was very black and blue, and asked me what happened. I explained I was in Israel for an international judo competition, and while I had been working on grip fighting, where you grasp the judogi in a good place to get your best advantage for a throw, one of my teammates accidentally missed the gi and clocked me square in the eye. Arnold was fascinated. I let him know that his country had some of the best women judo players in the world at the time, and that they consistently earned top medals in international competitions. I also let him know about our mutual friend Margaret. We bonded pretty well.

As we boarded our flight, first to London, then to NYC, we separated—he was seated in first class and I was in coach. When we were in Heathrow Airport in London, awaiting our flight to the States, he invited me for tea and crumpets in the cafe. We chatted about sports, and I gave him some friendly advice.

Rusty with Fenglian Goa and Chinese Judo Team at the 1988 Olympic Games in Seoul, South Korea.

"You have a great upper body," I said, "but you need more work on your legs." "Do you think so?" he asked.

Actually, he was winding down his body-building career, so in all fairness, he wasn't working out as he had in the past. I was just trying to be helpful.

When we arrived in NY, Ryohei was there waiting for me. Arnold and I walked down to the pickup area together, and my dear husband did a double take, but being his calm self said only, "isn't that the weightlifting guy?" Then he noticed my colorful eye.

Eleven years had passed, but Arnold still recalled our first meeting. I think he will remember his judo friend, Rusty.

Rusty & Lynn Roethke at the 24th Seoul Olympiad.

87

THE PRESSURE WAS ON. THE COMPETITION WAS in two days. With all the effort and heartaches there was no way I was going home without winning some medals at these 1988 Olympic Games.

We were at the training site. Conveniently, there were large plastic partitions between the mat areas, so several countries could train at the same time without being viewed. My old friend Dick Schaap from the ABC network would come by every day to watch our training and schmooze with me. Dick was a writer, author of thirty-three books, and a terrific sportscaster.

Dick was a super mensch to my way of thinking. I really liked him a lot. He always had time for me and was sympathetic to our lack of TV coverage for women's judo. He would make sure we got some coverage this time.

We were working like crazy. We were doing form practice, which means you just move rapidly and constantly attack with a throwing technique that you do not complete. Margie and I were moving like speed demons towards the end of the mat, where the plastic curtain was. I kept pushing her harder and harder and faster and faster until suddenly, we fell over and down. We landed—her on top of me, both of us laughing hysterically—under the partition into the other country's training area, which just happened to be where the very solemn Japanese team warm up was going on. They looked right at us and never laughed. Fittingly, we couldn't get ourselves up; they didn't think it was funny, and that only made us lose control more.

The next day I took the women's team's judo uniforms to the washing machine in the Village. I wanted them to be fresh and clean for the upcoming competition. The washing machine area had to be the busiest part of the Village, as everyone was sweating during workouts and it was pretty hot in Seoul. All the machines were in use.

The judogi is a heavy cotton burlap-type of uniform and usually would take a few days to dry, let alone wash. I had a big problem. The next person in line heard me mumbling to myself over this dilemma. He kindly offered me his turn at the washing machine. I blessed superstar Greg Louganis for his kindness. This good karma paid off too, as he won two gold medals in his diving events just a few days later.

D day was here—the judo event. Eve didn't fare too well. As outstanding a judoka as she is, she gave it her all, but was outclassed at this time. She showed great fighting spirit. Nevertheless, she is an Olympian and that is something she can keep forever.

Uh, oh. One down.

Lynn was next to compete. I knew her opponents pretty well. Of course, she did also. Her match with the Polish woman in the semifinals was so scrappy the referees even got confused. As her coach, I certainly added my mouth to the confusion. The Polish competitor threw Lynn with an inner leg reap, and received a fair score from it—a *yuko*, which is similar to a quarter of a point. A full point would have ended the match immediately.

Lynn was attacking like crazy to catch up, plus get a full point. Then, her opponent made a mistake. She stepped out of the safety area that gave her a penalty. The referee gave her a chui, which is the equivalent of a *yuko*, so now the score was even. Every time Lynn made any kind of move, futile or not, I yelled "Good job!" "Way to go!" "You're looking good!"

Lynn didn't stop her barrage of attacks. Time was up and the buzzer sounded.

It was going to be a decision. Usually, it would go to the person who actually scored with a technique, but there was no score here. Hopefully my mouth would have convinced them to see it our way. The center referee holds two flags, one white one red, then calls out, "*hantai.*" The two corner judges on either side of the mat simultaneously raised the flag of who they thought should win. The competitors were standing facing one another, one to the right of the central referee, and one to the left. The tape on the right is red and the opposite side tape is white. That's how the communication is done, with the flags. The several seconds it took for the referee to call hantai seemed like an eternity. The flags went up and they voted two for Lynn and one for her opponent. Majority ruled.

Now Lynn would be going into the finals with her nemesis, Diane Bell from Great Britain. For months prior to the games, Lynn had Bell's photo hanging over her bed and every day she would say, "I'm going to get you" to it. Lynn had lost to Diane in a few international competitions already. It was a grueling battle. In the end, Lynn had to settle for the Silver medal, but we were happy she had placed. Bell was a superb competitor too.

Margie's division was coming up. I considered myself an expert in the heavyweights, as that would have been my division a few years back, plus New York had some of judo's finest heavyweights, including my daughter Jean. Geez, I miss her and wished her knee injury never happened so she could be here.

Anyway, Margie was doing well until she decided not to follow the game plan. I had warned her about the excellent counter technique the Dutch opponent, Angelique Seriese, had against Margie's best throw. Out of habit, Margie attacked with her favorite throw and was countered. Nevertheless, she managed to win. However, because she had lost one match in the preliminaries, the bronze was as high as she could go.

Not too bad.

Three US women, two medals. Seriese went on to take home the gold that year, and later became world champion in the 1995 World Judo Championships in Chiba, Japan.

For the women's division it was over. We were cheering for our men. Kevin Asano from Hawaii won a Silver medal and Mike Swain from California was moved into third place from fifth as the bronze medalist did not pass the drug test. In my opinion, Kevin should have taken the gold. He had received a penalty, but his Korean opponent who committed the same infraction never received a penalty. Kevin should have won the decision. The hometown crowd of 6,000 screaming Korean nationals certainly helped to sway the referee's opinion.

It was over.

I needed a break big time. Going home through Hawaii, I would take a few days off for R and R.

What a year!

Women's judo in the Olympics and two medals!

88

THE TWISTS AND TURNS THAT I WOULD EXPERI-
ence over the next decade would bring me to the highest and lowest levels of my life. It would be Hollywood calling me into fame and fortune, and the nightmare of almost losing a child through a shot in the dark.

While judo has long been recognized as the most popular combat sport in the world with millions of international practitioners, and the second most popular sport in general after only soccer, like soccer, it's popularity in the US doesn't reflect the fanfare it receives everywhere else. After years of contacting *Sports Illustrated* in an attempt to get them to report judo competition results or do a story on a great athlete in women's judo, I finally received a call from them. I could not believe it; they wanted to do a story on me.

Barbara La Fontaine, writer, editor and an admirer within the ranks of the *Sports Illustrated* staff must have instigated the whole thing—she, like me, was a persistent tree-shaker that made things happen. Super writer Gary Smith was assigned the story, so I got really lucky.

This guy is as good as they get.

Gary and I had worked together before on Mr. Yasuhiro Yamashita's story. He decided to be with me from morning to night, twenty-four seven. The photographer followed me around for another week.

Rusty & Parnel Legros practicing at the Kyushu dojo.

I wanted to keep up the tough Brooklyn exterior. Gary had the ability to see right through my answers.

It is part of my image. It took me so many years to build that identity, I can't let it down or I will get hurt again and again.

In short, it was no whining, get to it, and suck it in.

Gary was not fooled by my outward appearance. He was able to read me straight and put what I said in the *Sports Illustrated* story. "Rumbling with Rusty"[26] came out on March 24, 1986. It was at least a dozen pages with many photos.

The story and Gary won some literary prize for the feature. It may have been the longest story on a female athlete at the time—it certainly seemed that way at the time. I loved the story, photos, and quotes. Sometimes, when I spin my own wheels, I'm really not aware of what's coming out of my mouth. When I finally read it, it made me laugh.

The story also made me cry.

It was so good for judo; it was the biggest story we ever got. An athlete making *Sports Illustrated* is like winning the Heisman, or a movie star winning an Academy Award! I received letters and telephone calls from all over the place. One letter still makes me laugh. It was from a woman.

"You were my judo instructor," she wrote. "You threw me. I hated you then and I still hate you."

What did she expect me to do, breast-feed her?

Oh well, you can't win them all.

The story from *Sports Illustrated* was picked up by the famous Japanese sport magazine *Number*. It was amusing to see the American version of the story in kanji letters. Soon after the story was on the newsstand, I received a call from Don Ohlemeyer, a big shot producer from NBC. He said that they were developing a TV movie called *Fast Copy*. It was to be a one-hour show that would highlight a few magazine stories of special interest and they had picked up the *Sports Illustrated* piece and wanted to feature me. Yes. *Yes, I will do it.*

This was getting to be really fun. Judo was getting lots of coverage. The kids in our dojo on Flatbush Avenue were along with me in everything I was involved in, plus my family. Was I making money? No, of course not. Was judo in the limelight? You bet.

The show aired in 1985 on the Oxygen Network and it was a big hit. My segment, combined with the larger judo piece, became the star of the show. People loved it. It was funny, interesting, certainly different, and continued to open doors for me and for women's judo.

89

IT IS INTERESTING HOW MANY MAGAZINES DID stories on me after *Sports Illustrated* and *Fast Copy*. They were all good, as each one had a different twist to it. *Fast Copy* gave me great visibility as it aired on prime time on NBC and was rerun several more. I remember being in Tijuana, Mexico with my family just doing some sightseeing, when some US Marines came over wanting my autograph.

How did the judo world react?

Well, it was a mixed bag. I received several calls and letters of congratulations. However, for the most part, there was animosity that I will never understand until the day I die. I heard that instructors would bring the *Sports Illustrated* magazine to their clubs, show it and say things like, "This is terrible!" "Rusty's promoting herself again."

They didn't have a clue, which was unfortunate. However, the fact remains even today, judo needs all the publicity it can get!

Interestingly enough, the right people had seen *Fast Copy* and thought it was a good story—more than just some wild woman pushing her sport at every level.

One of the first telephone calls I received was from Jerry Weintraub. The conversation went something like this.

"Hello Rusty, I am Jerry Weintraub, do you know about me?"

"Are you in judo?" I answered.

There was a slight pause, then: "I do movies and I would like to do a movie about you."

Oh sure, another pervert who wants to be strong-armed by a powerful woman!

He mentioned some films he produced: *Diner*, *The Karate Kid*, and so on. He asked who my agent was and would I come out to see him in Los Angeles or should he come to New York for our meeting and discussions?

I took his number and told him I would get back to him. I called Ted, my son, and told him to get over here fast. My husband looked at me, figuring Ted was in trouble again. I told Ted, "Run to the video store and look up this guy's name, Jerry Weintraub, and see if he is legit! Is he, in fact, the producer of all those films?"

"By the way, look when you cross the street so a car doesn't hit you," I added before he ran off. "Now move!"

Ryohei was getting used to my craziness. He didn't pay too much attention to what was going on. Ted was back shortly with a videotape of one of the films, and sure as hell, there was Jerry's name. It sunk in.

I got excited and told Ryohei, "I'm going to Hollywood and become a star!" "OK," he said, then went back to reading his judo magazine.

I called Jerry back, trying to control my voice, and said it would be better if he came to New York for our meeting.

My imagination went wild about this new direction that my life could take. Boy, there would be no limits to where I could bring judo.

I decided I had better get an agent, as I didn't know what the hell I was doing.

90

A WEEK LATER, I RECEIVED ANOTHER TELEPHONE call from Jerry. He told me he was in town, gave me the address and we agreed on the date and time. Jerry and Hollywood were coming into my life.

When the meeting day arrived, I got all spruced up and boarded the subway from Brooklyn to Manhattan. I entered this fancy doorman building on the Upper East Side, gave my name and was quickly escorted to the elevator with directions to the apartment.

I rang the bell and this gorgeous hunk opened the door. I put out my hand for the greeting as I said, "Pleased to meet you, Mr. Weintraub." He immediately informed me that he was not Jerry, but the butler. I then followed the butler into the massive living room, where the real Jerry was waiting to greet me.

My first impression was that he did look familiar and was a rather attractive guy. I also noticed he had something of an East Coast accent, possibly Brooklyn, even though he'd been living in Beverly Hills for a long time. He indicated his wife, Jane Morgan, would be joining us for lunch.

Jane Morgan, the famous singer?!
Oh my God, this was too much.

Jane came in from another room and greeted me. I told her how much I loved her music. She had on huge sunglasses that covered up much of her face, but from what was peeking out, she still looked pretty.

Lunch was served. I was trying to act casual like I have lunch with Hollywood moguls every day. Jerry liked my story. He felt something happen when he saw the *Fast Copy* piece and he thought it would make a great love story.

When he said that, it kind of knocked me for a loop—I thought of our marriage as a sports story. Of course, we loved each other, but that seemed to be a natural thing. I couldn't see a romantic thing, dancing around like Fred Astaire and Ginger Rogers.

Oh well, he's the pro, so if it's a love story, so what?

He then said we would also do a sitcom.

Well, hell, that's more like it!

I felt like my life was family, judo, and a comedy, sometimes even a tragic comedy.

A gentleman joined us whose name I can't remember. He was very famous. Jerry said he would be doing the musical score for the film, obviously already forming in Jerry's head. Before we parted he told me to have my attorney get in touch with his attorney to work out the contract, also known in Hollywood circles as "the deal!" We all shook hands and indicated we would be in touch. I gave a big "ta-ta" to the butler as well.

I floated into the elevator and couldn't believe what had just transpired.

This big shot producer wants to buy the rights to my life story and make a movie and television show about me?!

He had not even read the story in *Sports Illustrated* yet.

My thoughts were moving so fast when I got to the street I called Ryohei and babbled my good news, which he only partly understood. I then realized I was hungry; I'd forgotten to eat at lunch with all the excitement going through me. I went into some shop on Broadway and had a bagel and a cup of coffee. While sitting on the subway for the ride back to Brooklyn, I began to think.

If and when all this happens, how very famous judo will be...

It was an overwhelming thought.

Reality raised its cold little head and I realized I didn't have an attorney to get in touch with Jerry's lawyers. All I knew were criminal lawyers.

Just like everything else, it would come to me, and it wouldn't be normal.

91

GO FIGURE. I WAS THINKING, WHAT DOES
Howard the Duck and *The Texas Chainsaw Massacre* have to do with me? Lots, as I soon discovered. Now I will unravel the story regarding my entertainment attorney.

I attended the first national Women's Sports Foundation conference in Washington, D.C., in the mid '70s. The impact from that first conference was the beginning of an ongoing campaign for the betterment of girls and women in sports in every arena—opportunity, equality, recognition, and justice.

I was all in. Even though I believe in being involved with helping others in sports, my main priority at the time was to make inroads for women's judo. The speeches were touching and invigorating, to say the least. The room was filled with like-minded energy. Now I knew I wasn't alone anymore.

It was like the hand of fate that put us all together. We just seemed to attract one another and turn into a small group of rabble-rousers for the evening's festivities. The group consisted of Kimberly Butler, the event's official photographer and a lunatic in the best sense of the word; Larry King, Billie Jean's ex-husband; Peggy Fleming, the darling of the ice-skating world—quiet, but like a firecracker ready to go off; and Henry Holmes, an attorney and active member of the Women's Sports Foundation executive board. There were a few more people with us, but not for long.

After the serious meetings, the group decided to go have a few drinks and dinner. Earlier that day there had been a luncheon in the hotel and George H.

W. Bush, who was the Vice President of the United States at that time, came to the luncheon. He spoke and was interesting and encouraging. The US Secret Service hung out all day and evening. During the day prior to the luncheon, they followed bomb-sniffing dogs around the venue. I checked out the dogs, as they were scoping out the bread on the table.

The drinks were first on the agenda, so we went to a local club that was also a celebrity disco. That was right up my alley, as I loved to dance. Larry King and I chatted about judo, and that I should do the same thing as Billie Jean did—beat a man. I told him I had, several times, but nobody had cared. He replied that it had to be done in formal competition. I told him I had already been thrown out of formal competition. Plus, the powers that be wouldn't let it happen.

Besides, there is a big difference between a racquet and a body.

As a street fighter before judo, I was used to getting dumped on occasion. I could handle that, including on the judo mat with the boys, but I thought it might not be good for some of the women; physiologically speaking, not all women could handle a formal competition with a man, and doing so may ultimately be counter productive to the acceptance and support of women in judo, or even set us back.

We had a beer and a dance, boogied and got down. Our whole group was wild in their dancing and drinking. I was feeling good and was egged on by Henry and Kimberly and ended up picking up the very large, tall bouncer over my head and dancing around. Of course, he cooperated. He was a TV double for Mr. T. My next partner was one of the Secret Service guys who was off duty and decided to come and play with us. He asked me how often I went to Cuba. I asked how he knew.

Duuuuh?

I let him know that I went only to referee at a competition.

We were having such a good time we forgot about dinner. We floated back to the hotel to have a snack instead. In the hotel we heard some unusual music and followed the sound. We landed up in a recreation hall where there was a Thai wedding going on. Of course, we crashed it. The bride and groom seemed relieved as they were bored with the stiff family members in attendance.

I left for New York by train the next morning. The group would be joining me that evening to continue the party. Kimberly invited her friend, a big-name NYC clothing designer. We met at Rusty Staub's restaurant, had a great dinner and then continued on to the famous Red Parrot nightclub and disco. Eddie Murphy and his entourage walked in. We invited him to join us. He did and the fun just kept flowing.

Meanwhile, back to the subject of lawyers! I needed an entertainment attorney, and definitely not the criminal lawyers I was more accustomed to. I thought I would ask Eva, the executive director of the Women's Sports Foundation. She referred me to Henry, who she indicated was very good and did some business for Billie Jean and Martina Navratilova. The Women's Sports Foundation dinner was coming up real soon and I was told he would attend.

Good timing!

I decided to meet the gentleman and see if he wanted to represent me.

I was officially introduced to Holmes at the pre-dinner cocktail party. We looked at each other and couldn't believe we were set up to meet to speak about business, as we never hooked up the names of one other before entertaining this possible client-attorney relationship—we just knew each other as two fun loving party people.

"You may be my lawyer?" I said.

"You are the one they want to make movies about?" he replied.

It was a mutual shock. Henry calmed down very quickly when I told him the deal was with Jerry Weintraub. We agreed that he was going to represent me and he was very happy and pleased with his new client. There would be lots of paperwork going from California to Brooklyn just for this one agreement. It was the beginning of a wonderful relationship. I contacted Jerry, gave him my new lawyer's name and said he would be in touch with his lawyer.

Oh yeah, Henry was the Executive Producer of *Howard the Duck* and *The Texas Chainsaw Massacre*—all in all, a pretty famous guy. Somehow, I felt my new venture would be a cross between those two movies—comical, dark, inevitably combative. Sound familiar?

92

WE FINALIZED ALL THE CONTRACTS BETWEEN Jerry Weintraub and me. Henry actually went to the Weintraub estate for some of the dealings and told me that Jerry and Jane's home was absolutely incredible. I guess that was part of being a Hollywood mogul. The contract was more than fifty pages when all was signed, sealed and delivered. My lawyer was good. He even put in a clause that if my movie and/or sitcom was shown on any other planet in the universe, I would get residuals.

When all the signing was done, Jerry sent us plane tickets to go to California and have some meetings. As you can always depend on Murphy's law, the unexpected happened. Jean, the US women's judo team, and I were recently back from the 1987 Pan American Championships in Havana, Cuba. Jean had a pretty bad knee injury, as she refused to stop competing when her kneecap dislocated and almost went around to the back of her knee. After some pushing and duct tape, and in the short time from about one minute to complete the task, she managed to pop it back in place but significant damage was done. She didn't want to forfeit her chance for a medal, and in fact, did take the bronze even with her busted knee. She needed surgery to repair everything that was ripped around her knee while it took a ride around her leg. The front of the leg had to be opened for about fourteen inches to secure the patella. The scar would be huge, both physically and emotionally; this injury was significant enough to squish her chances to compete in the Olympics.

After her release from the hospital, we were to leave for California. *Oy, What a mess!*

I couldn't change the trip as other important people possibly involved with the upcoming projects would be there. It's not easy to get heavy-duty producers and directors together unless it was for a post-production meeting or the Oscars. I let Jerry's secretary know I could not leave Ted in Brooklyn without one of us being around to keep an eye on him, so we needed another plane ticket. We couldn't take Jean, as she was incapacitated. When we picked up Jean at the hospital, she had on a complete leg cast. They gave her crutches, which were relatively useless in snow and ice.

We arrived home. It was a snowy day and lots of powder was on the ground. Jean hobbled out of the car and tried to make it up the front steps. She wasn't used to the crutches in the snow and ice. We could not hold her, as she insisted, she could go it alone. She then proceeded to fall down the steps. I began yelling at her while Ryohei was picking her up. It was like the old saying, "Don't get hit by a car, or I will kill you." So, we dragged her through the snow into the house.

I had friends look in on Jean, as we were going to be gone just a few days. We boarded our flight to Los Angeles. Teddy and I were in constant conflict; we had too much of the same personality, and the war began immediately. I cannot tolerate the perfume Giorgio. It reminds me of Raid, the bug stuff. The woman next to me must have used the whole damn bottle on herself. Ted was sitting several rows in front of me, so I asked to change seats. I don't remember where Ryohei was sitting. He wasn't a complainer and would not make waves. When Ted refused to change seats I threw some pillows at him, not jokingly, as I wished they were rocks. To get even with me, when the movie began, he stood up and held as many pillows as he could to block the screen so I could not see it, nor could anyone behind him. I swore at him. The stewardess intervened and we both behaved.

What a joyful flight.

We were told to pick up a rental car of our choice, and proceed to The Beverly Hills Hotel where we would receive instructions for the upcoming meetings. When we checked in to this magnificent historic hotel we were taken aback by the look of the place. They had so many portraits of the big time Hollywood stars that had stayed there over the years, I thought I might even land up in Boris Karloff's bed, as he was one of my favorites. We went up to our lovely room and, to our surprise, there was a very large basket of goodies all wrapped up with pretty paper and bows. The card read, "Welcome to Hollywood, Rusty Baby. Lots of Love, Jerry."

Oh boy. Am I going to like this kind of lifestyle?

After getting squared away, we had a little free time and decided to get to the Beverly Hills shops—I would have to get used to this type of shopping. Goodbye Macy's and John's Bargain Basement. We parked the car and walked around. When Teddy saw all the top-of-the-line vehicles parked along the curb, all he could say was, "check out those hubcaps!"

He was informed with the iron fist: hands off!

Rusty & Ed Harris, during Rusty's Hollywood days. The two met while Ed was researching for his role in the 2000 film, *Pollock*, in which he played the famed painter (and husband of Rusty's aunt, Lee Krasner).

93

WE WALKED INTO A SLEEK, SHINY BLACK building. You could almost swear it was made of solid onyx. As we were going up the elevator to our meeting with Jerry and company, I gave Ted final instructions: "Don't talk, curse, or touch anything." We both laughed.

Aubrey, the butler, greeted us. I think by his physique he must also have been Jerry's bodyguard. All the introductions were made. Colin Higgins, who is well known in the Hollywood director circles (*The Best Little Whorehouse in Texas* and *9 to 5*) was there. A gentleman from Columbia Studios—I forgot his name but I know he was a big shot—was Jerry's assistant. A nice woman who would be looking after us for dinner that evening and any shows that we wanted to see.

The hunk served us soft drinks while the plans were being discussed for the movie and the sitcom. Much of it was technical stuff that was going over Ryohei's and my heads; however, Ted joined in when they were discussing the sitcom and voiced his opinion on where the third camera should be when they begin shooting the show. My heart stopped. I thought they would think, "who the hell asked this fifteen-year-old anything?" It was quite to the contrary; Colin Higgins actually turned towards Ted and they bounced ideas off each other regarding the filming process. Jerry didn't seem surprised. Ryohei and I were dumbfounded. Ted rarely attended classes. He did go to school, but mostly conducted court outside of it. Where did he get this seemingly knowing insight for filmmaking? It must have been the millions of hours he spent watching TV or innate intellect.

The meeting lasted for several hours. Jerry was in the process of setting up the next meeting, which would take place in New York as both Jerry and Collin had some films in progress on the East Coast. We left with handshakes and hugs and looked forward to our next meeting. Jerry's assistant would stay with us the rest of the day. We went to dinner at a famous Hollywood restaurant, and ordered Chinese food, of all things, which is much better in New York. She asked us what show we wanted to see, and Ted answered immediately: Universal Studios. She would get us VIP passes and we could go before our trip home, where Jean was hobbling around and waiting for us.

Later that evening in a side lobby of the hotel I noticed a little art show. I went over and viewed the small but colorful works, especially the sweetness in the eyes of the portraits. I asked who the artist was.

"I am the artist," a small voice from a near-by wheelchair said.

I looked over and noticed a frail woman, her body distorted, her head twisted to the side, with lovely pepper and salt hair and kind but sharp, penetrating eyes. I became aware when I walked over to shake her hand, that every digit on her hand was totally twisted. She, with the help of her medical assistant, introduced herself as Christina Savalas.

Hmm, Savalas?

We gave her our names.

"Are you..." I started to ask, but before I could finish, she answered. "Yes, I am indeed Kojak's mother."

She lived in the hotel, loved to paint, and was really quite good at it. As I was now on the Hollywood route, I could afford to buy a work of art, especially from this brave woman with Lou Gehrig's disease. I spotted the one I wanted and bought it. It looked like a more rounded Picasso piece. I would find a nice place for it next to my abstract works and Disney pieces.

We spoke for a long time. I told her why we were in California and that we were judo people. She was fascinated with our story and wanted us to meet her sons, but they were on location filming. We promised to stay in touch, which we did, until she passed away in 1989.

As coincidence would have it, it turned out that my brother's wife had a cousin who was Christina Savalas's cousin through marriage, or something like that. I could not figure out how Christina painted those lovely heartwarming pictures, which is another mystery of life.

In the end, Jerry Weintraub did buy the rights for my life story a year, with some options but somewhere along the line the deal went sideways—I hear that can happen in Tinseltown now and again—and the projects never materialized. I became a Hollywood almost-hit. The whole experience was not for nothing, though; every now and again I still get a check in the mail for thirty-four cents or some other miniscule amount for my small, showstopping part in 1995's *Blue in the Face*[27].

94

BEFORE THE FINALIZATION OF THE DEAL WITH Jerry, for whatever reason, I received other offers through the mail and by telephone. Henry had already advised me not to accept anything nor speak in length to anyone or give any information on what was pending.

One call that I thought was quite interesting was from Mrs. Marilyn Hall, wife of Monty Hall of *Let's Make a Deal*. She wanted to come to New York and sign up with her company.

Wow! It's great to be wanted.

I understood I was a commercial piece of property with good potential. As with all the stories in this world, I knew mine was unique.

The initial contract between Jerry and me was for a year, with the option of renewal. He opted to renew several times as he was trying to pull everything together, plus he was in the process of opening a corporation—the Weintraub Entertainment Group. Jerry had been with Columbia Studios all along, but the contract was just between Jerry and me. Now he would have to sell me to the Weintraub Entertainment Group. More money, more paperwork, but at least it was fun.

With all the negatives going on, after a few years the Weintraub Entertainment Group went belly up. I felt bad for Jerry and the group, as they were good people making bad choices. I had a great run with them, and the fact they kept me with them through the whole ride told me I had a worthwhile story or two. Every Christmas, like clockwork, Jerry and Jane would make a generous donation to a Catholic charity in our name, and then the sisters would send me a thank you note for my generosity. I like that, as not being a religious person myself, that when the time comes for me to leave this earth, at least I will have some brownie points for whoever's in charge.

We said our goodbyes and "good lucks!" and went our own ways. It wasn't long before word got out that I wasn't on contract with Jerry any longer, and soon some more offers came in. An interesting one was from John Bloomgarden, a producer and the son of Kermit Bloomgarden, the well-known Broadway producer behind Pulitzer and Tony-winning hit *The Diary of Anne Frank*.

We made an appointment.

Here I go again...

95

JOHN BLOOMGARDEN WAS QUITE DIFFERENT from Jerry Weintraub in terms of personality. John was soft spoken, humble and fairly new at being a producer. He had a modest office in Manhattan near the Garment District. His wife, like Jerry's, was a classical singer. We met, we spoke, then we signed.

It was a simple agreement with simple financial impact.

What the hell? I figured. *It's nice to receive money for doing nothing.*

At this point, because this deal was kind of small, my attorney suggested that I meet and speak to his friend, Miriam Altshuler, who worked for Russell & Volkening, a well-respected literary agency in New York. She would be my agent for this deal and become an overseer and advisor for me. Miriam was experienced in dealing with Hollywood and local television, as she represented books that would turn into movies.

Hey, you never know.

John pitched me around to several of his connections. One was a fellow at the major ad agency, J. Walter Thompson, who represented a major personality, including Roseanne Barr, who liked my story; her people wanted to talk to my people.

It was a great opportunity, but something kept eating at me. After all was said and done, I declined to meet Ms. Barr—not so much because her singing of the national anthem at the Padres game with a voice worse than mine[28] was a turnoff, but because I just couldn't see the crotch-grabbing before millions of viewers as appealing in any way. I thought that would bring my story and judo down. There are certain principles that are much more important than money or fame.

I floated along with Bloomgarden for about a year until we both decided to part ways, not for anything negative, but after learning about the ways that your life story, once completely sold, makes you virtually powerless on what happens next. If they decide to shelf your story, it's their prerogative. I couldn't let this be a possibility. I wanted to write a book so that no matter what, the real story would be told by me, in my own words.

The next decade would take me through a half dozen writers. I would read their work in magazine or newspaper articles they wrote, like it, and one at a time recruit them to help me pen my story. I made a different agreement with each one. Miriam was cranking out the agreements as I requested them, then had them write about me, would read what they wrote, and then ultimately reject each one. As a non-professional writer I didn't get it. I thought their work was good.

What the hell did I know? I even had my judo friend, Nicolas Soames, come from England to work with me. At the time he was writing for *Matside Magazine*, British Judo's quarterly publication and co-authoring judo books with several superstars of the sport. He was a wonderful, intelligent guy. It looked good to me.

I arranged for his flight and he stayed with us for a week or so. He began work on my story when he returned home. I knew we were in trouble when I received the first round of pages and Nick asked, "What does *schmuck* mean?" There was going to be a language barrier. Miriam received all the writings of everyone involved, and it was, "No! No! No!"

Her reason was simple.

"Rusty, it is not your voice," she said. "It took me a long time to figure it out." Dick Schaap and I almost had an agreement. God knows that man could write,

plus, we really liked each other. The problem was the lawyers; they could not get it right. The contract would have been very intricate and included movies, TV rights, and even Rusty dolls. He wrote a foreword for this book's earlier iteration, and though the project never went anywhere, we remained good friends until his early demise in 2001. For ten years friends and acquaintances alike heard the same old story. It went something like, "I'm working on my book, which means it sounds like *War and Peace* will be coming out in the future again."

96

THERE WAS A CONSTANT UPHEAVAL GOING ON in my life. One part of me was happy running around the world for judo. Sometimes there were speaking engagements, sometimes demonstrations, but always I always found myself mentoring and promoting judo in every which way I could.

I became a member of several sports organizations outside of the judo world, and anything I learned I kept on a back burner until it might become helpful for the judo community. As a member of the Women's Sports Foundation for over thirty years, I was thrilled when someone proposed that I sit on the board as a trustee. Not only did I believe in the mission of equality for girls and women in sports, but as a pioneer and major troublemaker for women's judo, I was part of the evolution of judo as a sport and a calling. I enjoyed participating, working on projects and adding new ideas to the crew at the WSF. I was a trustee from 1996 to 2001.

Near the end of my time on the board, I began to feel something was missing within the foundation. It is amazing how something so simple can elude you when it's right in your face. We always had an outstanding group of women and men on the board. They were intelligent and high class, many of them world-class athletes, so what was missing?

Our founder Billie Jean King was missing. Yes, she would attend the Women's Sports Foundation dinner and some major events, but her ideas and opinions seemed not to be sought out anymore. I knew she had a busy schedule, so I just chalked it up to that. It appeared that she was used only on the occasions that the organization would benefit from her appearance.

As time went on, it disturbed me more and more. Finally, after several discussions with members of the board and the executive committee, they saw the light. I personally wanted to see our founder, Billie Jean—one of the most visible icons in the world at that time—get recognition for the fantastic job she had done. Not only had Billie Jean founded the WSF, she had helped support the organization for years with her personal contributions and by creating relationships with sponsors on behalf of the foundation.

Throughout that time, she would receive some credit, however certainly not what she deserved. I was pleased to see that after we pushed hard to make the others on the board see the light, it was done. Not a shred of stationary or a word would go out from the foundation unless it had the acknowledgment, "Women's Sports Foundation, founded by Billie Jean King." I finally felt justice had been served.

Who knows what's in my genetic makeup that seems to push me to want to fight when I believe there is any type of discrimination, intentional or not.

It's what happens to you as you are growing up that really has an impact, and you can handle it in a few different ways: just let them dump on you, or fight, regardless of the consequences.

Whether a blessing or not, one of my personality traits has always been to focus only upon the results and that there has to be a change, and not the ultimate consequences.

It is almost like a constant battle of wills.

You may achieve some good results but within the family structure with your kids, the battle can easily turn to a war.

I was already estranged from my son Chris from my first marriage, because his problems were self-inflicted through substances and I would not go down that road again. I did everything possible to help him, but after many, many years, I finally recognized that it wasn't working.

Finally, because he was an adult, I had to resort to my survival technique: cut your losses and move on. Even a fighter has to know when to quit. The anger I felt neutralized the guilt. I felt his genes from the other side of the family were tainted, and he would have to fight very hard for normalization. And that was his problem, not mine.

It would be nice to think of myself as a strong-willed person, perfect in every way, with the character of a saint, but I cannot lie to myself. And no matter how hard you might try to push it down, the realization of the truth will always shine its ugly little head up. The trials and tribulations with my other two children would almost do me in. My husband Ryohei, a kind and respectable person, was so helpful during the early years of raising the kids. He was a true partner in the basics of rearing the children and taking care of the home. He really tried considering how difficult I probably made things by always being absent and off fighting for equality for women's judo.

The overwhelming differences in our ideology, and race, constantly came into play. It became a game, or production of sorts; I was always cast as the bad cop, and Ryohei was always cast as my good counterpart. I spoke to him about it on many occasions, but he just didn't get it.

The kids, especially Teddy, knew how to play their roles. In Japanese culture parents always give in to their children, as they are only children and are expected to grow out of any little mishaps. But this was Brooklyn, where my home became a battlefield.

I felt very alone, as I was out-numbered three to one. As typical family spats and disagreements grew more frequent, the problems became more significant, I threw myself into volunteering more of my time outside of the house.

Who could I turn to? My image is so important to me. How could I ask for help for myself, or even indicate there were serious problems with my family?

I could blame Chris's problems on his genes, but what about now? These two kids have good genes.

Well, maybe some of Ryohei's are flawed too.

The next few years were total chaos and almost became the end of my marriage and my relationships with Jean and Ted.

My world was crashing down on my head. I could not think clearly.

Where could I run to?

This was misery, with no end in sight.

97

IT WAS THE LATE '80S AND THE STRUGGLE WAS in full force. Our teenage daughter, Jean, was training very seriously in judo. It was difficult for her, as she had the notoriety of being Ryohei Kanokogi's daughter. He was a super technician and that same high level of performance was also expected from her. The other stigma she faced was being my daughter, the child of Rusty Kanokogi, a tough judo fighter with a kamikaze attitude. My irreverent, never-give-up-or-die-trying demeanor was expected from her also, so more and more pressure was heaped onto her shoulders just because of who we, her parents, were.

Of course, Jean was more than a good athlete in her own right, and also excelled as a softball player. Her skills not only got her on the team at Sheepshead Bay High, but on its Wall of Fame recruited for semi-pro teams and eventually college scholarships.

My husband and I both worked with Jean on her judo training. She so much wanted to please us and would never complain about being tired or sore. As a coach I was relentless in what I expected from any athlete under my guidance. The tough always won out. In my teaching there were no excuses and very little compassion. How Jean survived is amazing. My sense of humor probably helped. As Jean got older, there was more friction between us. She was starting to take my coach-yelling-at-her moments personally, and I was beginning to resent her if she took off from judo to go to a ball game instead. I would scold her for being overweight on the one hand, and tell her to finish her cake after dinner on the other. She was doing really well in competition. Of course, she was. She probably put my face on every one of her competitors. Not only was she throwing them, but in some cases, she was knocking some of her opponents out cold, like at the 1986 National

Collegiate championships where she competed and won in both the heavyweight and the open class divisions.

Jean Kanokogi practicing her throwing skills at the Kyushu dojo in 1983.

It was difficult for me to tell the kids how much I loved them when they got older, and if I did, they most likely didn't believe me. My always pushy ways— interrogating them and being suspicious— was inflammatory to them. I was always sure that they were up to something dubious, but that was really just me projecting my childhood onto them. I thought I was being protective, maybe even more so because Ryohei believed everything they told him and joined them in the excuse department. Perhaps I was overcompensating.

This went on for many years, and though I tried to talk it out, East was just not meeting West. Jean and I moved further and further apart. I hated it and did not know where to turn.

It must be all my fault. Damn my pushing!

All I had accomplished was successfully pushing her further away from me.

Jean excelled as an athlete despite our relationship, won medals in international competition in judo, and moved out of the house as soon as she was of age—and we drifted further apart. She worked and was capable of supporting herself, and was a likable young woman.

Well, at least she was going to survive.

After a few years of small, casual talk between us, we began to come back together again. She went on to college and graduated with honors. Her field was law enforcement, and she became a special agent for the US government. We love each other dearly, and have had some good laughs about the past over the years.

I am so very proud of her. So is her dad.

Jean at the Kyushu dojo, 1983.

98

IT IS SO NICE TO BE ABLE TO SKIM OVER YOUR life and condense the unhappiness.

I guess this is part of survival, or we would all go nuts.

Mental scarring makes us act out in different ways because we do not have much of a choice. How can your family feel that you are the enemy? I always tried to right a wrong with the kids, and would protect them with my life. I wished that when a chance accident sent a bullet into Ted's stomach, ripping through his guts, that it was me instead. It ripped me to the core seeing my son in so much pain and so close to death.

Teenage tragedy, I could relate to—but this? Not so much.

Ted had a tough guy image—physically strong, macho, and invincible.

What the hell did I do to these kids?

Ryohei and I sometimes were on two different planets. It was frustrating that we could not have a conversation regarding the kids, as it always turned into a fight. His claim was, "I don't understand," while my claim was that he was too soft with them.

And didn't know how to say no!

Ted was in the wrong place at the wrong time and as a result in the line of fire. He almost died twice—once from the shot and once from the infection—and in the hospital after surgery he got a staph infection and needed another two major surgeries and tons of antibiotics. No one wants to outlive their children.

This horrible tragedy helped Ted see the light, big time. He became a super human being, always helping others and even more so helping the United States of America as one of the best military men that they now have.

Now that Ted and Jean are both adults, there is so much love and compassion in our family that I almost worry about it being codependent though, I don't really think so. Ryohei and I realize that the responsibility falls on both of our heads. We all made grave mistakes, but the good news is that we survived and thrived into the future, of course with lots of scar tissue.

Rusty, running a judo demonstration in 1990.

99

WHEN I REMINISCE ABOUT THE LAST FIFTY YEARS; I remember the major events alongside the smaller things. Some might think the smaller events were insignificant, but the survivor in me remembers everything, large and small, so that when challenged, I can bring out one of my greatest weapons: my memory.

A great deal of the high points of my life and judo career were attributed to being able to go all over the world and not be a sightseer. I could tell you more about the judo players and officials of most of the countries I visited than of their interesting sights. I may have been abroad as a coach, but we were engaged in very serious business; we went to win and indeed we did.

If I was in a country as a referee at a judo competition, it was more relaxing than coaching. During my judo adventures, I made friends with many competitors, coaches and officials. It was a great feeling to get along with and even like the people that had the same passion and so much in common through our mutual love of judo. When it wasn't yet appropriate to have friends in East Germany, the Soviet Union, or other countries that our government did not have friendly relationships with—and in my opinion, justifiably so—I did not care, as I looked at the person and not their country's politics. My relationships with many judo athletes are still going on to this very day. Although the world has changed since then, our friendships have endured.

Meeting the average person and athlete in other countries gave me more of an advantage than just being a tourist would have. The people I met let me in their hearts and minds; basically, we all wanted the same things—to enjoy our sport, stay healthy and be successful in our future. We really only wanted to fight on the mat.

I was probably more aggressive off the mat than most of my international friends. It got to the point that on my second trip to any given country, I knew enough players and their families that I could bring practical gifts to everyone, wives and children included. I gave them nothing elaborate, often just some used clothes or T-shirts—gifts of necessity rather than extravagance. I made an exception for the kids by bringing them little toys from the USA, and music for the teenagers. One of my good friends from France, Paulette Fouillet, called me Santa Claus. I think I was closer to being the Red Cross.

I received gifts from people all over the world, typically homespun, traditional stuff representative of the culture of their homeland. It really made me feel good to be liked and well-respected—not just for my interaction with them, but by the accomplishment of opening all the doors we did for women's judo. The people of the judo world know how difficult it is to put on a world-class event in our sport. Especially when there was not any help from your country's judo hierarchy. It was wonderful to have an open invitation to visit and stay with my judo friends worldwide.

One of the highlights that I will always remember was in Great Britain, during a break at the British Open. Charles Palmer, president of the IJF at the time, along with the British Sports Council under the auspices of the Queen of England, made a speech and called me up to the award area, presenting me with the Dame Enid Russell award—named for one of the first British women to achieve *shodan*, earning her the level of black belt[29]—for the mothering of women's judo.

I still have and cherish the award. Ironically, in the US at that time, most of the male dominated judo organizations would not even associate with me, let alone reward me with anything, except maybe a one-way ticket to the moon.

When you do something because you absolutely believe in it, you will sacrifice whatever you have to and not expect anything in return. If you are lucky and there are some smart people around, you may get a little recognition. If you don't, you should never be discouraged or disheartened. I always think back and ask myself why did I do it and what were the results? If you got good results, then that my friend, is the best recognition in the world.

My dear departed friend, Dr. Shigeyoshi Matsumae did the ultimate regarding my achievement for women's judo. Every year as part of the Tokai University graduation commencement, he would tell my story. The point was to convey the message that you could accomplish what seemed like the impossible if you believed whole-heartedly and never gave up.

When I heard about this flattering presentation that he made at every graduation, it made me feel good—until my Japanese friend at Tokai told me that now that he had heard the same story for ten years in a row, he thought he could repeat it verbatim.

In other words, "I'm tired of hearing your story."

I meant no harm, just the truth. But I chuckled about it, still.

Dr. Matsumae wrote several books about his incredible life story. One of my favorite of these stories about him was when he opposed the war against the US in the '40s. He believed in peace, but because he was from a famous family and basically an aristocrat, as well as the inventor of the underwater cable, Tojo didn't know what to do with him. When it was Dr. Matsumae's time to serve in the Japanese military, they placed him on an ammunition ship, probably waiting for the good ole USA to blow it up. When I heard that story, I could easily relate.

It was a very sad day in my life when, in 1991, I received the telephone call from Japan that Dr. Matsumae had passed away. I was informed that the service would take place four days later at Tokai University. I immediately booked flights for Ryohei and I and we were on our way to Tokyo. It felt like the most loved and respected elder of my family had died.

The service was incredible. They had set out a one-hundred-by-one-hundred-foot photo of Dr. Matsumae with thousands of white chrysanthemums laid beneath it. I was invited to sit with the family and the judo leaders. We were invited after the speeches, which included representatives of the emperor, to go up to the urn and place a flower and say a prayer. I would have given some of my life to have this great human being and humanitarian live longer. He passed away in his 80s. The world still needed him, and I needed him more.

I never forgot the kind words he wrote about me in one of his books: "There are three women in this world I have the greatest respect for: Mrs. Gandhi, Madame Berlioux, and Rusty Kanokogi."

When you are respected by the best, who can hurt you?

100

I DIDN'T HAVE TO LOOK VERY HARD TO FIGURE out what cause I would take up next; it quickly seemed to find me.

Some of my personal thoughts and the commitments I have made almost contradict one another. Yes, I believe in women's rights, but I do not believe in giving anyone a job because of their gender or race. If they have the qualifications to compete for a job, they should be given an equal chance. However, if all qualifications are equal and it turned out that gender was the characteristic that tipped the scales, it was time to act. My philosophy has always been simple; it's called fairness. This is an important word that seems to have lost meaning over the years. When I teach judo, I try to communicate the meaning of these words, not only by word of mouth, but by example.

In the practice of judo, your partner is just as important to your growth as you are. Your partner must cooperate when you are trying to do form practice to improve your entry into a throw, or your timing. If your partner is afraid of being thrown, or is too stiff or too loose, nobody will be able to benefit from the practice. All students must learn cooperation; not only is it vital during form practice, but it helps one's coordination both physically and mentally.

Selfishness is one of the most devastating traits a person can have. It may be beneficial in the short term, but in the long term, you become a miserable, lonely individual. Quite often, after a student receives large amounts of attention, such as being asked to demonstrate regularly, or compete successfully during practice or a high level of competition, they tend not to pay attention to the performance of their teammates. This is selfish, and is something that will spill over into their adult life if it is not addressed when they are young.

Being a teacher is an enormous responsibility. The development of a youngster lies in the hands of its parents, and its teachers. I have found that when you are teaching kids, you have a tremendous impact on their lives, especially if your field is sports. An academic education is without a doubt a critical part of a child's education, but its domain is the improvement of the mind; it does not directly address the general personality and character of a person the way sports do. In judo, a child usually views their teacher as some sort of black belt superhero. When you teach, your personality comes out immediately in a way that cannot fool the students. I usually teach kids starting as young as six years old. Children should not have to deal with learning something like judo—which is both dangerous and requires much discipline—before that age.

My philosophies about working with children exist to set boundaries, let them know that I want them to enjoy themselves, but ultimately to be serious and ready to learn when it is necessary. In other words, I try to guide them through the beginning of self-discipline. Their love of learning judo makes them try to discipline themselves the best they can. The problem with many teachers is that they do not recognize that children can adapt fairly quickly. The secret to teaching is extremely simple: make the teaching understandable—challenging, but attainable—and make them use self-discipline with no excuses. The children will then step up to the plate, and get as much out of judo as they put in.

Many teachers and coaches seem to live vicariously through their students. For some reason, in the United States, there is an incredible pressure on young athletes to win in competition. I recommend competition only when I feel that the student is ready for the experience, and I deplore the pressure that is commonly put on children, both by coaches and parents, to win at any cost. They seem not to understand that under that kind of pressure, if the child loses, much of the self-esteem that they have built up through judo training can disappear in mere seconds, and they risk burning out before they reach their thirteenth birthday.

This is what life is like. Sometimes we win and sometimes we lose; but losing doesn't make you a failure or a bad person. Judo should be a great experience for kids, and should be one of the building blocks for success in their character, as well as for other sports they might participate in. Over my years of coaching, I have seen that the children that participated in judo were some of the first to be recruited to join the junior varsity or varsity teams, and they seem to excel because of the discipline that they learned and practiced in judo first. The "let's win now and to hell with later" mentality is the same as a quick fix, and it is unfortunate that it is so widespread. Hopefully, more coaches and parents will understand how awful that is for a child and will change their ways.

Do I like to win? Of course I do!

I am one of the toughest coaches on the face of the planet, as many athletes who won medals for the United States will attest. The simplest and most beneficial way to coach is to promote a mentality that supports learning, enjoyment, and winning *when you can*; fixing the mistakes that become obvious when you don't win; not gloating when you do win; and above all, respecting your opponent and yourself. Many other countries that win countless medals at the World Championships and the Olympic Games use similar philosophies to mine. I sincerely hope that folks in the United States will catch on.

I have been called the "mother goose of judo," since my relationship with the students is firm, and definitely not patronizing. I hate that, and so do children, since they are actually very smart and can tell when adults are talking down to them.

However, being a loud no-nonsense sensei does not mean that I don't have a sense of humor, because we definitely have had our laughs. Since I feel that I have an obligation to my students, when I find that from time to time my students seek me out to talk to me about things that may be a big problem for them, I always try to help them work it out.

Anyone in their right mind knows that children are our future and will be our legacy, so I am adamant about their protection, whether they are in judo or not. There is a group of sick and dangerous individuals that look for children to exploit. I am talking about pedophiles.

Pedophiles exist in the judo community, just as they exist in the church, and just as they exist in the rest of society, to the horror of everyone else. Somehow, they manage to find their way into positions of power, and start to prey on the children.

For the protection of our children, parents should not just turn their kids over to anyone. They should know who they are dealing with, avoid being lazy, and check them out first. This is one of the toughest causes that I have ever attempted to take on. It is a subject that constantly eats away at me inside. So many people go into denial or do not want to get involved as they are so concerned about the almighty lawsuit that may be used against them, but that too is one of the tools of the predator. You must have courage, face the truth, and protect the children. When something happens to a child you're working with—if you see that they are out of line, smoking pot, or doing pills—call their parent. Be a responsible person and instill that attitude in your own children. Forget about the old bull that you would be a tattletale or, more bluntly, a rat. Do your share to give our youth a chance to live, thrive, excel and succeed.

Finally, teach your children what responsibility is—*No Excuses!*

Another thing I wonder about is how a five-year-old qualifies for a black belt? There is a sucker born every day, and so many of the alleged martial arts schools know the weak points of suckers.

Here's an example: You want your child to be behaved, strong, happy, well- disciplined and have a ranking of a ninja turtle of some kind, so you pay the money, your child gets the unearned rank, and you saddle the teacher with the task of being the disciplinarian because you don't have the guts to do your job yourself. You just want to be loved by the child and love the child back. The child gets bored, even though they have the rank—which, it turns out, does not mean much when it isn't earned—and the poor kids have been patronized up the kazoo and can't fight their way out of a paper bag.

Here are some hints. Check out the teachers. How often they falsely promote the student and why? Do you have to pay for these promotions? If so, why? If your child is getting a false sense of security, false praises or prizes that are downright silly, aren't you doing more harm than good?

Do they really care about your kid or just your gelt?

101

FOR A LONG TIME I HAD ON ROSE-COLORED glasses when it came to the judo world. I had my own perception of how things should be. I held myself accountable and would work to finish the tasks no matter what, without excuses, making sure to have high moral standards, as I always felt like an ambassador for judo and did not have much tolerance for people that didn't meet up to that standard.

Boy, oh boy, that sure did not put me up on anyone's popularity list.

It was a frustrating way to live. I always accomplished a lot, but at what price?

One of the worst things you can do is make your accomplishments in the line of sight of everyone, as it makes people aware of their own inadequacies, and resentful of you for it. This is the way to alienate people. You can't have it both ways. You can either act phony and be adored, or get it done with no bullshit, and tell it the way it is.

You know the road I chose and stayed on.

Granted there is a time and place where you have to have the sense of when to pull back and reign it in, but for the most part, it is always best to practice seeing yourself realistically, knowing your personality defects, occasionally working on them and trying to be a good example for the folks—especially the kids—around you. I found by keeping the standards high, letting kids know what you expect from them will, in fact, help them much more than a phony "atta girl" or "atta boy."

One of the very basic practices in judo that disturbed me the most was awarding a permanent ranking. I always believed that you had to earn your promotion. It is a simple event that happens when you are diligent and improve within your skill level, in most cases your competitive level and, of course, your knowledge level.

Not all, but so much of the judo ranking in the United States of America is a huge joke on judo and our innovator of the sport of judo, Professor Kano. Had he not been cremated, he would have been turning in his grave.

One of my biggest gripes regarding having rankings in judo is the way it has been used as a reward mechanism for people that give certain amounts of money to judo organizations, and as common as "you wash my back, I'll wash yours." The way I see it, the ranking systems and promotion, for the most part, have been prostituted. I am aware of judo athletes and officials from all over the world, their contributions, and/or competitive records in judo, and it makes me shudder when I compare them to the rankings of black belts that have been awarded in the United States. We, by far, have the highest rankings in the world—and the most abundance of them—and yet we cannot win a gold medal in the Olympic Games in judo[30]. Something is wrong with this picture, and the sorry part of it is that most believe in their own greatness because they are legends in their own minds.

The black belt that goes around your waist is not only to hold your judogi closed; the rank is supposed to signify your growth in judo, technically, and your character development. How can people live with themselves or look in a mirror and really believe they are entitled to wear a high-ranking black belt in judo? I am so ashamed of what has become of our ranking system; it used to comply with the highest standards set in Japan. Even in other countries they have not lowered the bar as much as the US standard.

It is a farce.

Many times, an individual will go from one organization to another just to get promoted. They apparently have no pride and no shame. What have they received from judo? Certainly none of the philosophical teachings of Professor Kano. The world of martial arts has deteriorated.

There is an abuse of rank that has resulted in a diluting of rank value in nearly every judo organization active today. Your first black belt is supposed to simply mean you will now be on the road to understanding judo. The belts that follow all must signify your competitive achievement, your skill level, and your contribution, and this does not mean financial contribution. We have so many phony, high-ranking black belts in this country. Can you imagine following a phony general into war, or having a phony doctor give you heart surgery. We all need some form of accomplishment and approval, but at what price? To demean a way of life and sport such as judo is inconceivable. I would like to ask the judo community if you have achieved a black belt ranking and have to face Professor Jigoro Kano one day, will you be able to look him in the eyes and thank him for our great sport and your personal accomplishment?

102

WHAT DO YOU WANT TO KEEP AS YOU HEAD towards your seventh decade on Earth? I can tell you from personal experience, that your health leads the list, and is easier said than done.

In my case, as a type A personality with a love for my coffee beans, it is amazing that blood pressure medicine works for me. I know some of the ailments that we get come through genetics, and I am definitely predisposed for something big. My father died of hardening of the arteries when I was a kid, my mother died of a stroke that took her life in 1966, just before my own daughter was born, and my brother has already had a quadruple bypass—and in my opinion, can still kick ass[31].

I am always fighting the battle of the bulge; most times I lose the fight, not the weight. Still, I will never give up. Thank goodness I do work out on the treadmill, with the weights, and run in the pool. I do not do the training necessarily for good health. On the contrary, I just want to stay in shape to defend myself in case of an attempted mugging or confrontation.

Hey, you never know.

I decided a long time ago that I don't want to die weak.

When Aunt Lee died in 1984, there was a memorial at the Metropolitan Museum of Art in New York City, but it was the eulogy, strangely enough, that left me feeling unsettled. In my opinion, the praises about her were beautiful and sincere, but they came far too late. Her work will live on forever, not as Mrs. Jackson Pollock, but as Lee Krasner, brilliant artist and extraordinary woman. I found strength in her diligence and try to remember her no-excuse bottom line.

When I do go, I want to be remembered for the life that I led and the good work that I did.

I am Ryohei's medical watchdog, I make sure he eats the right food, take him for his annual checkup, and don't give him too much stress. We women seem to live longer than men, and I want to keep this guy around as long as I am around. He is my husband and my very best friend. East did meet West after all, and we have a love that is not a mushy kind, but instead, a sincerely deep, respectful and extremely caring one.

I think I have been very lucky, being passionate about a sport, although frustrated with injustice and being able to do something significant about it. I have met and got to know so many people that have an impact on the world by their generosity, intellect, art, and compassion.

Every group or organization that I had the privilege to interact with was a learning experience, and many of them resulted in continued good relationships. We all can't expect to click with everyone we meet, but it does happen occasionally. Even if the chemistry isn't there and we do not seek each other out, we can still find and support each other. How fortunate I have been to have found so many friends and companions in this lifelong judo journey.

Teaching, coaching, and staying with children keeps you grounded, as you continue to be part of their evolution and they touch upon yours.

It never ceases to amaze me how things work out. The more I seem to promote my sport and several of the amazing athletes in it, the more it seems to come back to me. It proves that it doesn't pay to be selfish or jealous. I like the way my husband says it, "if those traits are present in someone that we are dealing with, they have a small heart."

In May of 2004, I received a telephone call from the great Peter Diamond of NBC, who wanted to know if I would like to go to Athens and do the color commentary for the Olympic judo event. Without missing a heartbeat, my answer was an immediate YES!

This was the ultimate, a new hat to wear at the Olympic Games.

What an honor, to say the least.

I knew Peter well and he certainly knew me, as for several years I had bugged him to get judo on the tube. Just like the rest of the judo community I was annoyed that we never had our share of the pie.

I did the best job I could for NBC and got one of the best learning experiences that one could possibly get from the inside world of broadcasting. The experience also revealed my next mission: to pass on to the International Judo Federation all the gems of knowledge from my recent career in broadcasting to help improve the understanding of the sport of judo as it is packaged for the public. Up until this point, it seemed to be that judo was interesting just for the judoka themselves.

For many years there were important people within the US judo community that were estranged and disenfranchised from me. For some reason they believed everything I did would be self-serving. What they didn't know or want to know was that all the publicity I ever received was a result of my constant promoting of the sport, coupled with the fact that I came through the ranks in the men's division of judo. In other sports you would be making mega bucks for that, while in my sport both men and women would shun me.

It was as Gary Smith wrote in the *Sports Illustrated* feature about me; I was "a ship with no port to land at."

After many years of continuing on my track and being able to accomplish quite a bit—not only for my sport, but many individuals in it—the people that count finally opened their eyes and gave me the respect that was due a long time ago. Maybe their hearts got bigger.

Memories are a wonderful thing to dwell on occasionally, but they are only good for a short time, especially if you have much more work ahead of you.

As when you have a child, you want to show the world and sing their praises, and that is how I still feel about judo, a sport that has given me so much—my life, family, good friends and thousands upon thousands of students that will continue to carry with me, always remembering that time of their life that we shared.

Ryohei, Rusty, Ted & Jean dressed in their gi, circa the mid-1990s.

103

AS A YOUNG MAN IN JAPAN, RYOHEI WAS totally entrenched in his judo career. He left his hometown of Yatsushiro Prefecture in Kumamoto Ken, on the island of Kyushu, when he was eighteen years old. As one of the very best high school judo champions in that area, he was scouted by Nihon University, a judo powerhouse in Tokyo, where he received a full scholarship. He majored in economics and, of course, judo. It was similar to our great college football players in the sense of support and admiration.

As in high school, there wasn't much time to explore his family's roots, although Ryohei had heard many stories from his father and grandfather. As a child he read about his great, great, great grandfather in the school history book during his lessons.

It would have been totally unacceptable for him to ponder the samurai aspect of his family at school, as it was part of history and not for bragging about or personal gain. The name in itself, Kanokogi, always brought an inquisitive look or question from a Japanese person that had studied or read the name in their history book.

It did not get my curiosity going until our son was born. Prior to the big event, just like any parents, we were trying to figure out the best name for the soon to arrive bundle of joy. Our daughter Jean's middle name is Sumiko; that was easy pickings, Sumiko meaning "quiet beautiful brook."

Well, the beautiful was there but the brook should have been a tsunami.

Ryohei suggested the name Chikakazu, the name of his very important relative, the samurai. It was pronounced "sha-cock-is". I did not think that name would go over too well in a Brooklyn public school and put the kibosh on it. I wanted our son's middle name to be after Ryohei's father, Toraki, however that was not possible as my father-in-law was still alive and kicking at the time.

Finally, we agreed on Ryoichi, which means "Ryohei's first son," which I thought would be very appropriate. The baby's first name would be easy, as I loved Teddy Roosevelt's stories and character, so the baby boy came into this world known as Ted Ryoichi Kanokogi. And he would turn out to be a warrior just like his great, great, great grandfather.

Over the years, when Ryohei and I visited his mother and family in Japan, after his dad had passed away, the visits went by too quickly. We spent the time with family and friends and had little time to research or go back to the samurai scene. Several years ago, Ted decided he wanted to know more about both our families.

My own family's entry into the United States is similar to countless others. In 1904, my grandfather, Joseph Krasner, came to the United States from a part of Russia that is now in the Ukraine. He worked morning, noon and night to save money to bring the rest of his family to the promised land. My mother, Ides— in English, Edith—was fourteen years old, my grandmother, Chane—in English, Anna—was thirty-three years old. My Uncle Isak—in English, Irving—Aunt Rosie, Aunt Esther and my mother all came over in January of 1908 on the Rijndam Rotterdam via Holland. My mother, being the oldest child, carried their money and papers. Their finances consisted of exactly forty dollars.

They all stood in awe at the site of the Statue of Liberty as they approached Ellis Island. It was a dream come true.

L'chaim!

Two additional siblings would be born in Brooklyn, New York—my aunts Lee and Ruth. There was nothing outstanding in their arrivals, just hard work to survive.

At Ted's urging, Ryohei and I decided that on our next trip to Japan, we would take time out from the normal visit and begin to research his family's history. When that time finally came, we got much more than we bargained for. In fact, we were stunned by the magnitude of his family's history.

The Kanokogi Samurai burial site in Kumamoto, Japan, where Rusty's ashes are interred.

THE WOMEN'S AND MEN'S CHAMPIONSHIPS

were held on alternating years until the 1987 World Judo Championships in Essen, West Germany, when the events were merged. The combined championships have been held biannually ever since then. In September of 2003 the event was held in Osaka, Japan, I was invited to sit on a blue-ribbon panel with several other women that had made their marks in judo history by being world champions, Olympic champions, or international referees.

The meeting was held in conjunction with the IJF meetings prior to the upcoming World Championships. The theme was, "what does a former female world-class competitor do after retirement?" In essence, it was designed to educate the male-dominated sport that these women got to the top because of their intelligence, determination and fortitude—and that we would like them to get to the top as coaches and administrators for their respective countries and future world leaders in judo.

There were one hundred and three countries present for the IJF meetings. During the IJF Congress in Japan, awards were presented by then President Yong Sung Park, who is also a member of the IOC. I was a recipient of a medal for the World Pioneer of Women's Judo. Needless to say, I was thrilled, as I knew in the future it meant that more women that contributed and had a significant impact on women's judo in the future would get recognized.

But I was the first!

While President Park was presenting me with this great honor on stage, he also called Ryohei up. I thought it was a wonderful gesture, as without Ryohei supporting me all the way, I could not have done it.

After the World Championships, we continued our trip to Kumamoto to visit the family, see old friends, Ryohei's classmates, and begin our family root finding journey, as we promised Ted we would do.

During our visit to Kumamoto, we had a reception with the mayor and other state officials, as I am on the International Advisory Board for the upcoming World Conference on Women's Sport scheduled to take place there in May 2006. One hundred countries are expected to participate.

The charming and handsome mayor was curious about the name Kanokogi; he remembered the name from his school history books about a famous samurai from Kumamoto. Ryohei let him know he was related and a direct descendent of Kanokogi Samurai. As luck would have it, there were several month-long celebrations going on in Kumamoto on the notorious Musashi Miyamoto Samurai, who spent many of his days in the Kumamoto area where he took time to reflect on his life after killing hundreds of adversaries—and to write his famous, *The Book of Five Rings*. There was a weekly television series made on Musashi's life airing on national television produced by Nippon Hōsō Kyōkai, , the prestigious network in Japan known in the US as Japan Broadcasting Corporation. We had a chance to see a few of the shows.

The mayor gave us a lovely book on Kumamoto history and sent us in the right direction for our family history research. We met with a gentleman who was in charge of international affairs. Not a moment was wasted. He immediately recommended that we go to a famous cave in a nearby mountain. He wanted us to see an extraordinary sight that related to the Kanokogi family.

He provided the car and driver and escorted us on the journey. After leaving the city and heading up the mountains, the terrain was unpaved with jagged and winding roads and I felt like my life was passing before me. Occasionally a car would come towards us on the other side, except there really wasn't another side. It was just enough room for one vehicle at a time with the wheels on the very edge of this treacherous road.

We finally arrived at a place where we had to leave the car, as the road completely disappeared. For one of the first times in my life I really wasn't dressed for this trip—I had on a skirt, dress jacket and shoes. For the next part of this adventure, you needed mountain boots, ropes and a few donkeys.

As we continued our way on foot, we started to see a hundred or so concrete shrines of what appeared to me as the same holy creature. There were some small tree branches that appeared to have been in the area for a very long time that were on the ground and acted as steps. At this point my yellow silk jacket was dusty and the kick pleat of my skirt was riding close to my rear end. It didn't matter, as the excitement was mounting.

This better be good!

It was more than good. It was amazing!

We had climbed into the cave where Musashi Miyamoto wrote *The Book of Five Rings*[32]. Musashi was a renowned sword master of the early Edo period who fought over sixty battles during his lifetime, losing none. His book *Gorin no sho*, translated as *The Book of Five Rings*, is widely considered one of the greatest works on swordsmanship ever written.

Musashi had traveled to the cave to reflect and meditate prior to writing his book. Entrenched with the demons of his kills, he had needed to clear his head. The large rock where he sat to meditate and write the book stood about six feet high and five feet wide and actually resembled a large skull. It was eerie and exciting at the same time.

The Kanokogi family owned the cave and gave their permission for Miyamoto to settle in for as long as he liked. There was a mutual respect between these samurai. Inside the cave there is a large marker with the name Kanokogi etched in it as part of the history of Japan's feudal times and ownership. I could see by the expression on Ryohei's face that this revelation was overdue. This was our first step of discovery. Next day we would be going to the castle that once belonged to the Samurai Kanokogi and his clan.

We didn't have much time left in our visit to Japan so Ryohei, his mother Akiko and I discussed the best plan of action to see and study more of the Kanokogi family history in a short amount of time. It was decided that after we should go to the site where the original Kanokogi Castle was built and where most of it was destroyed by fire. The town honored the site several centuries ago by planting a splendid cedar tree.

105

KUMAMOTO CASTLE WAS ORIGINALLY BUILT IN another part of the city and was owned by the Kanokogi family. After many bloody wars with other prefectures and neighboring towns, the Kanokogi Castle was almost burned down to the ground. A very small area survived the destruction.

In future years a special memorial would be built in that exact place—it's original home—as a legacy to Kanokogi Samurai. Out of the ashes arose the new Kumamoto Castle, however it was moved to the center of that prefecture.

All we could find out regarding the first Kanokogi in Japanese samurai legend is the year of his existence of power. It was 1349 in Kumamoto, and the beginning of the Kanokogi family line.

Forty-five years later Samurai Jacshin Kanokogi rebuilt the Kanokogi Castle. Jacshin was his first name until he retired from the active samurai order. After that his first name went back to Chikakazu, as he was born. One had to take a special first name with some historical and religious significance upon becoming a samurai. The head of the Imperial Service had given him the name.

Jacshin Chikakazu was approximately thirty-five years old when he designed and built the Kumamoto Castle. Although he was married, we have not found any information regarding his wife as of yet. In those days, and for many years to come, women were there, yet treated as entirely insignificant.

The castle that was built was different from the original, as it not only had to be strong and aesthetically beautiful, but it also had to be the main fortress of the clan Kanokogi. Chikakazu had the castle built on a hill for good observance of the enemy. It was a revelation in the trade. He made sure it had a great yagharami, or look out point, which was the most crucial part of the castle. Rather than having a direct road up to the huge wooden entrance, he designed it with sections turning in different directions in order to trap any intruders. His warriors were then able to bombard them with stones, arrows and the like, preventing them from reaching the main entrance.

As with samurais, you have to be born into the bloodline of a samurai, family to family. There are exceptions, as in the case of Musashi Miyamoto, who proved himself a great warrior who maintained his status and respect, despite not coming from a family line of samurai. We tend to think of warriors as ruthless fighting machines. After learning more about Samurai Kanokogi and how it was in the Japanese feudal years, however, you start to rethink your views. In the case of my husband's family there was a good explanation as to why the towns needed great leadership and why some Samurai are in the history books not only for their incredible fighting skills, but also for their leadership in saving their communities and its people, as in the story of Kanokogi.

Great, great, great Grandfather was as intelligent as he was strong. He had to use his sword many times in battle and was a noted sword fighter. However, he probably saved more people than he killed. The reason for the bloody feuds was simple—politics and greed. Someone always wanted to take over your town and absorb its wealth.

Kanokogi's reputation was unusual in the sense that he was as much a conciliator as he was a fighter. If there were a way to negotiate, it would happen. Kanokogi and his clan saved so many of the townspeople after a tsunami, and his constituents loved him for it. The samurai ordered all of his troops to save the people and helped them quiet the drowning land so the farmers could once again plant their rice and live, as that was their staff of life.

He reigned for fifty-five years, until his son took over the protection of Kumamoto. Almost a century later, in 1603, a castle was built in Edo—now Tokyo—as almost the exact replica of the Kumamoto Castle designed by Kanokogi. Much of this information is from the book, *Kumamoto-no-Sakigake* ("The Birth of Kumamoto"), republished in 1998.

It was time to visit the castle. I got winded from the hike up the steep hill, but also, from the vision of the beauty and strength of this monument, which was overwhelming. To know that your family founded it and were the protectors of the castle was mind-boggling.

Fortunately, it was not a holiday or weekend so there weren't huge crowds at. We wanted to take our time and reflect on every stone and artifact in this wonderful structure. As we walked into the castle the ambiance immediately brought us into another world. The very first large drawing we saw was my husband's ancestor Jacshin Kanokogi, regally sitting on his legs adorned with his colorful kimono and his samurai long and short swords displayed. He had a long, thin mustache. I kept looking at the large colorful sketch and then back at Ryohei, looking for a family resemblance. When Ryohei sported a mustache years ago, he looked like Emiliano Zapata. Whereas, grandfather looked like Fu Manchu.

We viewed many of the artifacts, then went back to see grandfather's sketch again before we left.

Several times we bumped into American tourists. Can you imagine how nutty they thought I was when I told them that this was my castle.

From the streets of Coney Island to the Kanokogi Castle, what a trip it has been.

The castle is now owned by the Japanese government and has been for many years. Though the thought of asking them to give us back the castle did go through my mind.

The same day we would go to the cemetery where Ryohei's ancestors' ashes were kept, including his father's, Toraki. Only the Kanokogi samurai family and designated relatives would be privileged to be laid to rest in this sacred place. We would also visit one of the Kanokogi temples later in the day.

Ryohei's good friend of fifty years, Take-san, was our driver and Mom was going to accompany us on this trip. She looks fantastic for an 80-year-old woman and not a day passes that she doesn't say a prayer and serve a bowl of rice to her husband Toraki's shrine in her home. It is very traditional, in fact; when someone visits the home they first go over to the shrine in the living room, bow from the kneeling position and give respect and greetings.

We drove to the town of Tanaka Kitamachi in Kumamoto to visit the tree. Although we had seen a photo of the tree, we were not prepared for what we were going to encounter. As we approached the park on the walking path, a large bronze plaque praising and giving great accolades to Samurai Jacshin Kanokogi greeted us. The same portrait that I had seen in Kumamoto Castle was beautifully etched on the plaque.

Continuing on the path brought us to the old cedar tree. Kusunoki, or camphor tree, is a humble word for the spectacular, magnificent white cedar tree to honor and thank Kanokogi for his great deeds for that town. This was the town that he and his troops saved after the tsunami. It almost sounds like an exaggeration when trying to describe this monumental tree. It is mystical how the tree reached such a great size. The diameter is more than one hundred feet wide and one hundred fifty feet tall. Stanchions had to be used to hold up the eight-to-ten- foot circumference branches that sprung out at about a hundred feet in every direction. There was no way to fully realize this view from a photo in a book. Legend has it that white snakes, which symbolize good luck in Japan, live in the tree.

Once a year there is a special holiday when the town people come together at the tree to pay homage to Samurai Kanokogi for his good deeds. There is a little box near the tree where visitors can leave notes to be read aloud during the next celebration[33]. Because of Kanokogi's love of horses, the last horse he rode in his last battle was buried near the tree to stay forever with his spirit.

A highway was built in the area; however it was constructed around this sacred ground where the original Kanokogi Castle was built and the imperial cedar tree still stands.

Kumamoto Japan is one of the warmest places on earth. It was a sunny day with a slight breeze, which was a gift to us. As we were going to the Kanokogi temple and cemetery, I knew I could not wear my shorts and T-shirt. Respect in Japan is everything.

Once again Ryohei's friend Take-san, along with Mother and the two of us, proceeded on the day's journey. We got lost on the way to the cemetary. It was located in a very rural area and not many people were around to get directions from. We spotted a barbershop with the old fashioned red and white color pole in front of the place. Ryohei got out of the car to ask for directions to the famous Kanokogi samurai cemetery. He was in the shop for several minutes and on his way out, the men inside, including the proprietor, followed him very bowed over, repeating the bow many times as Ryohei walked backwards exiting the shop. Some of the men had shaving cream on their face with a large white cloth cover draped over them.

When Ryohei returned to the car he explained the whole ritual to us. When he had asked for directions, the shop owner gave them to him and curiously asked why he was going there. He informed them of his name and that he was from the United States visiting his family and ancestors. Once they heard the name Kanokogi, they immediately went into the major respect routine. In the old days you were not allowed to look into the face of a samurai or his relatives, as it could cost you your head.

We arrived at the cemetery. It was amazing for me. In the US you have people all around you once you're in the ground, but things were different in Japan. The Kanokogi have their own cemetery, which means only family can enter. There are small, interesting monuments in the family's samurai area where the ashes were kept.

When we went to Ryohei's father's site, we stayed a while and all said a prayer. I did as well and let my father-in-law know that all was well with his family and that I would always look out for the Kanokogis, for the rest of my life. I was so grateful that I got to know my husband's family over the years. We had love and mutual respect. I know that my family in Japan is proud of all of us. As we walked these sacred grounds, Ryohei and Mom told me that I had a place in the special cemetery. Although extremely flattered, I told them how much I appreciate it, but that I did not want to take them up on the offer too soon.

The next place we went was the Kanokogi temple. This was not the largest one, as it was awarded to the family and was basically a smaller version of the larger one elsewhere in Kumamoto. Once again, the family names were inscribed on bronze plaques. The temple was solemn and very old. The shrubbery was tangled and seemed to surround the area like a small brigade of protectors.

We would be returning to the USA the next day. There was still so much to see and discover about Ryohei's heritage. There is the town of Ryohei Kanokogi, as that was his great grandfather, who he is directly named for. There are areas and streets, train stops and the like, with the name on it. All that will have to wait until next time, along with the Shimada Museum of Arts, which houses exhibits on Kumamoto's samurai warrior culture.

We sure had enough for Ted. The stories and photos would bring him up to date for now about his warrior ancestors.

106

HOW FORTUNATE I HAVE BEEN TO SEEM TO LIVE in the middle of hopes, dreams and progress. Just like most people, I wish for this or that, but more importantly I become part of the wish and work as hard as I can to make it happen.

As a board member of the New York 2012 Olympic Bid Team, I share the hopes and dreams of our city winning the bid for the Games. Not only do we deserve it, but also, we will have the best Olympic Games ever. We have so much to offer to the world and the world has so much to offer us.

I have worn many hats at the Olympic Games since the 1980 Games in Moscow. The boycott really messed up so many athletes' lives in 1980. I am still pissed off at Jimmy Carter. What did the boycott really accomplish? For many years I wore my "pissed off" hat.

In the 1984 Los Angeles Olympic Games I was totally committed to challenging the IOC, as they were still discriminating against women's judo and would still not allow us to compete or participate. My hat at this time was "total trouble maker."

In the 1988 Seoul Olympic Games we made it and were finally there! My hat said "US Olympic Coach for Women's Judo—wearing my "coach's hat".

In the 1992 Barcelona Olympic Games, with the accomplishment of bringing women's judo to the Games, I could finally take a step back and finally be a spectator. However, that didn't happen. My student, Parnel Legros— "the Haitian Creation" with dual citizenship, had made the team for Haiti and I was selected as his coach. My hat was "Coach of Parnel."

In the 1996 Atlanta Olympic Games, I was selected as an official and wore "my official's hat." For the 2000 Australia Olympic Games, I took a break. In the 2004 Athens Olympic Games, I was selected as the sports expert by NBC, a.k.a. my old gig as the color commentator, where I wore "my broadcasting hat." What a trip it had been to have these tremendous experiences, meet these fantastic people and the great athletes, and have the chance to contribute.

For the 2008 Beijing Olympics, your guess will be as good as mine. I don't think about where or why; just as in my past, if I am needed, the opportunity will knock on my door. I know where I want to be for the 2012 Olympic Games: right here in New York City and any hat will do.

Life promises many things, and we have to give and most times not receive. The trick of it is not to expect too much, but truly appreciate when life's promises do come to you.

It's now 2005 and I have had seventy years on Earth so far and I am only looking forward. I want peace and understanding between the nations of the world. It can only happen through communication and education.

Sports has done that for me.

As I continue through the maze of life, I am looking towards the day that the Women's Sports Foundation can use their energies only on programs and grants for athletes and not have to go to battle for women's rights in sports any longer. I hope that the lawmakers see the light. So much time is being wasted, so much talent underrepresented, so much potential untapped.

My wish for judo in the world is for some fame and fortune, as it is one of the truest amateur athletic sports in the Olympic Games, as we do not have professional judo competition. My wish for United States judo is a gold medal at the Olympic Games.

There is still so much to accomplish!

—Rena "Rusty" Kanokogi, from
Coney Island, May 2005

EPILOGUE

THIS BOOK HAS TWO AUTHORS. FIRST IS MY mom—Brooklyn's own Rena "Rusty" Glickman Kanokogi—known as the mother of women's judo for her pioneering work as a lifetime international advocate of women's judo. After having to disguise herself as a man to compete in 1959, which was then only for men, Rusty spent the next two decades fighting for women's rights to participate in judo, creating the first Women's World Judo Championships in 1980 in New York City and. Eight years later, she proudly marched for the United States as the head coach of the first US Women's Olympic Judo Team to compete at the Games in the 24th Olympiad held in Seoul, South Korea in 1988.

Mom achieved a seventh-degree black belt, which was no easy feat for a man or woman. Fifty years after being stripped of her first-place medal for not being a man in a YMCA judo competition, the New York State YMCA presented her with a gold medal for her lifetime achievements. She was also honored by the Emperor of Japan with the Emperor's Award of the Rising Sun, Gold Rays with Rosette, on foreigners who have had a positive influence on Japanese society. She returned to the Olympics in 2004 as a commentator for NBC. Mom left a detailed chronological memoir/paper trail of the important times and moments in her life and her career before she passed away on November 21, 2009. This memoir was never published.

The second author of this book is my mom's daughter—which is me—Jean Kanokogi. I was taught judo by both my mom and my dad, Ryohei Kanokogi. My dad is a ninth-degree black belt judo champion and judo sensei— a teacher/coach/mento and what many deem as, "the quiet Father of Women's Judo". He could have been a champion sensei anywhere in the world when he chose to be in New York with mom and a key part of her support system. With both mom's and dad's help I became a member of the US Judo Team, traveled to judo tournaments all over the world, an experience in which I achieved the rank of sixth-degree black belt. I am a retired special agent for the US government, hold a PhD in psychology and have been a consultant for television and movies. I am an instructor in behavioral science, defensive tactics, use of force, firearms, and judo; an editorial board member and the Director for Mental Health and Peer Support Services for the Federal Law Enforcement Officers Association, a national organization with over 35,000 members; and an author of articles for various police journals. I also used my, 'Get Up & Fight" to endure two brain surgeries to prevail over a 9/11 related brain tumor.

I grew up in the orbit of Mom and her accomplishments in women's judo. I know many of her contacts in the field and participated in a number of the stories she describes in her unpublished memoir, including, of course a significant part of my dad's life with Mom.

Mom was larger than life, a ferocious advocate of women and women's judo who threw her entire heart and soul into elevating the sport to the highest levels. And yet, despite all she accomplished in her fifty years in the sport, the immense impact she had—like so many of the truly greats—wasn't fully seen by those outside the judo world until after she was gone.

In the years since Rusty and I completed the first draft of her memoir, her story continued on. In these pages, I share the rest of that story, not in Rusty's words, but in my own—from her diagnosis of multiple myeloma, to the YMCA medal award ceremony that came fifty years too late, the co-naming of "Rena 'Rusty' Kanokogi Way," and finally, seeing this promise through and her book in print, at long last.

Mom's legacy lives on, and continues her work. Her miraculous story needs to be told. This is more than a story about judo, although those accomplishments were monumental. This is more than just an underdog tale; more than the hundreds of sports stories that populate both the big and small screens. This is more than the "You go, girl!" tropes you come across when you happen across the rare adaptation actually about a female athlete.

This is a story about what one tough woman can accomplish when she refuses to be dislodged from her dreams against all odds—poverty, physical weakness, the women's weaker sex mythology, false pride, macho men, bureaucratic foot dragging, aging, fierce competitors, broken bones, naysayers, what has never been done before, disappointment, and the kitchen sink. You name it, she did it. Rusty's story goes beyond breaking the mold (and the glass ceiling)—just as she always did, she eviscerated them both.

She was one in a billion.

2006 | Rusty and I spoke nearly every day while processing this manuscript. I would call her most of the time on my way home from work just to check in and she would tell me about her day, the classes that she taught and of course all the happenings of the judo world. Sometimes she would call me during the day and anytime she called I would always pick up the phone; it didn't matter what I was doing. At times, she called while I was on surveillance and, being the typical mother, she would tell me to make sure I was wearing my vest and make sure my shirt was buttoned up because it was cold outside.

She told me she wanted to get this story out since we had completed the manuscript. She planned to work with some writers to see if they could help edit it to best capture her voice the way it was written, but her frustration level was high—or maybe her patience was limited—because every time she tried working with a different writer, they could never do it; they just couldn't get her Rusty-isms, capture her words or express her sentiments in exactly the way she wanted. "They're just too damn fluffy," she'd told me, more than once. "I wasn't fluffy. I have a story to tell and this story will give others the guts to follow their dreams." She would then exclaim that she was driven by a force deep within and she had not yet finished fighting for equality. There was still a lot of inequality, especially in women's judo, and she would make sure that women's judo would be supported enough to produce a champion who would win us a gold medal in the Olympics.

Rusty's energy, true to form, could not be contained, so my father simply supported whatever mission she was on without debate. Rusty's other passion, discussed somewhat in the book, was ferreting out pedophiles and making sure justice was served, including weeding them out of the sport.

"There's no room for these degenerates in a sport where we're constantly fighting uphill battles already," she'd said.

We had some amazing conversations, and sometimes we just giggled like schoolgirls. Although we did have some rough patches through the years as I was emerging from adolescence into adulthood, all was sorted and she really was my mentor, coach and best friend, even after I had retired from competition.

She and my father would regularly play handball at Coney Island early on Sunday mornings and at times I would meet them, and we would walk on the boardwalk and grab some hot dogs. These times she wouldn't get me to go on the Cyclone.

At this point life was pretty good for Rusty; she had her judo battles, she won tons of wars for equality, and she had plans to visit Vermont with my father and have a few vacations visiting friends all over the world, all while staying sturdy and strong in the judo world, as well as continuing to teach.

When teaching judo, of course, some bumps and bruises are common—and even more so with age—but for quite some time, her ribs had been ailing her a bit. Rusty didn't complain. pain was part of the game she loved. She attributed the aches to the typical post-judo soreness and figured she'd be feeling better in a few days. Then her ribs began to continuously hurt, but she ignored it until after the holidays, and then promised to get it checked out.

2007 | She kept her promise and went to her orthopedist to check out her ribs. At this point she had some bruising on her abdominal area and again chalked it up to judo injuries acquired while teaching. Her orthopedist told her that her ribs in the area that hurt were broken. Rusty was perplexed and couldn't imagine how that had happened. He ordered some blood tests and then the darkest day soon followed, when she was told she had multiple myeloma, a rare cancer that forms in the white blood cells and accumulates in bone marrow. Rusty had no idea what this was, but she knew she was in for another battle.

I was away at some tactical training when she got the news, and when I called her, I could tell she sounded a little different. She told me that she'd just been very busy doing a few things and that when I returned home, I should come over. I assumed that we would go out to eat someplace, or that she just wanted to see my face, because this was common.

We sat in the living room and she said she needed to talk to me, looking very serious. The last time I saw that serious look on her face when she said she had to talk to me was when she'd broken the news that Gary, our close friend, had passed away. Right away my mind went there and I asked her who had died. I knew it wasn't my father because he had opened the door for me when I'd arrived at the house. She looked at me and she told me she had cancer.

Mom assured me she was getting the best oncologist in town and then proceeded to tell me, in true Rusty fashion, who some of his other patients were— all high society people, so I knew she would be in the best of hands. I asked her what came next.

"I'm in for the fight of my life," she said, "but I will fight, and I will fight with all of my guts, because I'm not ready to "slip away" just yet."

We hugged, and then cried. I told her that I would be with her every step of the way. That same week, an opportunity that I had been waiting for, to transfer out of New York, was dropped into my lap, but I immediately passed it up because there was no way I was leaving her side.

At first, I didn't think the cancer was so serious, because Rusty began her chemo treatments and carried on with her everyday life; she was strong as ever. My father took her from Brooklyn to Manhattan for each treatment, and would sit outside in the car and wait, and then transport her home. In our circles, my father had always been considered a saint, but this was when I saw his full-blown sainthood first-hand; this is where his dedication and devotion was epitomized.

Rusty assured me that she would get better and beat this cancer. She said she would go to the Olympics in Beijing, although she wasn't quite sure in which capacity, coach, referee or spectator, or who knows what, knowing her—but she was adamant. She even considered that maybe we should all go as a family, beaming with pride at the thought every time it came up in conversation. I thought she was going to be okay; she looked strong, her attitude never changed, never wavered— she had this!

2008 | Things started to change for the worse. The chemo was starting to take, but she was told she also needed to undergo radiation. Soon she was undergoing chemo and radiation treatments three times a week. Rain, snow, or anything could not stop my father from bringing her to each and every one of her appointments. My father asked me to please purchase a bright colored rain jacket for him so people could see him as he's helping her out of the vehicle to get her treatment. He waited for hours just so he could retrieve her and bring her home to make her comfortable. "The hell with comfort," she would say, "I've still got things to do!" and would go up to her office and email away. I don't know where she got all of her strength, but I know that strength was used during each chemo and radiation treatment. I took her to some of her appointments and waited to give my father a break, though it was difficult to convince him to let me take her, because he did not want to leave her side.

On the day I took her for her cataract eye appointment, she got some damning news from her oncologist. He told her that her kidneys were failing, and she needed to start dialysis. He recommended one of the top nephrologists and we did not hesitate; we made an appointment that same day.

In between appointments for chemo and radiation and dialysis, Rusty still insisted that we go see some Broadway shows. I took her to see *Young Frankenstein*, and as they were raising Frankenstein into the lightning to revive him, she laughed hysterically, smacking me and pointing at the stage, telling me it was her in her radiation pod and should something ever happen, I was to do exactly that. I loved her amazing humor. I told her, in jest of course, that I would book our flights to Transylvania now to ensure she could get the proper lightning. After that, we went out to eat and she maintained her appetite. We brought tons of food home to my dad, who was ready to eat like a king.

Another show she insisted we go to was *God of Carnage*, starring our friend, Marcia Gay Harden. We went backstage to say hello after the curtain and Marsha introduced us to the rest of her cast and crew. My mother told Marcia how proud she was of her. Marcia had already won her Oscar for her role, playing Aunt Lee Krasner Pollock in the movie *Pollock*. In preparation for the role, Marcia had come to the house to study Lee, immerse herself in her things, and learn about her through Mom's memories; the three of us became instant and lasting friends. Driving home from this show, my mother and I chatted about how she was doing. She said she was in pain—but she was used to pain—and then joked about how she had survived the Kodokan and the streets of Coney Island. This pain was different, she said; it was a deep pain, but she would still fight like hell, because she could take it. She was not ready to go anywhere, she said, because she still had a lot of work to do. She paused just then before adding, "Plus, your father needs me and I'm not ready to leave him."

When I was away for work, I flew home early because Rusty called me to tell me she slipped in the shower and hit her head. She was in the hospital and had a slight brain bleed. Because of her condition, they kept her overnight for observation. By the time I got back into town, she had already returned home, so I went to the house and just spent time with her. That evening, she said she wrote an email to herself saying exactly how she felt because she couldn't really get herself to tell my brothers, father, or me what she felt inside. She didn't want us to worry, but she thought we should know what was really happening inside.

She let me read the letter so I could have a peek. She was still full of piss and vinegar, even then, but for the very first time she admitted she was scared. Rusty had never been scared of anything, but she was scared of where the road ahead was leading; she was physically weak, but her mind was strong. She was adamant that she didn't want to leave my father or us, but she feared she may not have a choice in the matter, for the very first time. Despite her fears, she forged ahead in each day with as much vigor as she could muster.

About a month later Rusty was not doing very well, but was still fighting each and every day to stay with us. She told me she'd the strangest dream: she was warm and felt no pain. She wasn't alone either. She had a meeting and her companion, whomever it was, presented her with two possible roads.

"You have a choice," they said. "You can stay and continue fighting this and feel all of this pain, or you can come with me and be free."

She said she decided she was staying. To me, this was the most selfless decision she ever made in her entire life. Multiple myeloma weakens your bones to the point that they break continuously, and at this point, she already had a broken arm, broken collarbone, a few broken ribs, and several other dislocations.

During this fight, Rusty had to forgo any plans to go to the Olympics in Beijing. Not long after that sad decision, she received a call from the Japanese Embassy informing her that she had been selected to be awarded the Order of the Rising Sun, 4th Class (Gold Rays with Rosette), one of Japan's highest civilian honors bestowed on foreigners who have had a positive influence on Japanese society. She got the call in June and was absolutely thrilled and excited to receive this honor in front of her friends and respected colleagues, including Billie Jean King, who attended the ceremony at the Ambassador's residence in November of that same year.

When Rusty told me the news, she reminded me about how all amazing things seemed to happen to her in the month of November: this award, the first Woman's World Judo Championships, marrying my father, and the birth of her first child. She rambled on, stopping only to remind me, again, that November was always her month.

Later that year, the Rusty Kanokogi Fund for the Advancement of US Women's Judo was established from a generous donation by Richard and Pamela Ader. Richard was a Trustees Emeriti of the Women's Sports Foundation, who has remained committed to the cause of supporting women's judo. The award is maintained by the Women's Sports Foundation, and provides $5,000 annually to support coaching, specialized training, equipment, attire and travel for a female judoka in training for national or international competition. This legacy fund was one of her dreams, ensuring that women in judo had the opportunity to obtain some additional funding for travel and training purposes. Rusty asked that I be on the selection committee, but for this first year, 2009, she would make the selection herself. Rusty selected Kayla Harrison as the inaugural recipient of the fund.

"Who is Kayla Harrison?" I asked her. "You'll see!" she replied.

2009 | Rusty was inducted into the International Jewish Sports Hall of Fame in April.

Rusty's dear friend, retired Judge Alice Ruben, myself and a few others started a letter writing campaign to the YMCA. There was another wrong that needed to be righted; Rusty's gold medal that had been stripped from her in 1959 because she was a woman, was long overdue to be returned and we were determined to ensure that happened.

In August, the YMCA threw a gigantic party and ceremoniously returned her medal to her, fifty years after she'd won it. Of course, Rusty didn't miss an opportunity to say her piece after a half-century of waiting. She accepted the return of her long-lost award gratefully, then exclaimed, "it should have never been taken away from me!"

In November, Rusty took another fall, which landed her in the hospital. On my way to visit her I called my brother Chris and told him to come to the hospital too. By this point she and Chris had made amends and they had a good relationship. I also called my brother Ted and told him I would let him know her condition when I got to the hospital. She was intubated, but fully awake and aware of her surroundings. When I arrived at the hospital my father was sitting by her bedside, blood all over his shirt—they had both taken the fall. He needed stitches in his head but refused to leave her side, so the nurses had to treat him at Rusty's bedside.

On the evening of November 20th, as my father and I were leaving the hospital and mom was resting, I saw an older nurse standing next to my mother, comforting her and being gingerly affectionate. The next morning, I was heading in to pick up my father and go to the hospital when I received a call from the doctor who told me they could not get my mother's blood pressure to rise and that she passed away. I called my father to tell him; this was the hardest call of my life. The next call I had to make was to Billie Jean and Ilana Kloss, who were planning to visit my mom in the hospital that day.

Earlier this year—in preparation for this moment, I now see—my mother told my father her wishes. She wanted to be cremated and scattered in the ocean so she could travel the world and continue seeing her friends, with some of her ashes laid to rest in the Kanokogi samurai gravesite in Kumamoto, Japan. She reminded him that they had accepted her in her youth and took her in with open arms—the Kanokogis were her family and she wanted to rest with them forever. Her love and respect for the Kanokogi family ran deep.

2010 | In January, we had Rusty's celebration of life, in complete Rusty style. A production team, the Chelsea Pier, and an RSVP by reservation only was how Rusty would want it done. She dreamt of having her fiftieth anniversary with my father at Chelsea Pier, so the next best thing would be to have her celebration of life there. Billie Jean King and Richard Ader along with the Woman Sports Foundation produced an amazing tribute. We had video from Marcia Gay Harden, sports icons and fellow trail blazers from around the world, contingent from Tokai

University with messages from Mr. Yamashita. Her urn was placed under the 1988 Olympic flag that was flown in for her event.

While going through old family photographs, I found a photo that stopped me in my tracks. It was Rusty in her wedding gown with the nurse from the hospital. How could that have been? I never met my grandmother, she had passed away a few months before I was born, but when I showed it to my father, he told me that it was my grandmother in that photo. That wasn't a nurse by her bedside the night before she passed away, it was her mother getting ready to take her home.

As we began to heal, we flew to Japan to honor Rusty's final wishes. When in Tokyo, we met with Dr. T. Matsumae, Mr. Yamashita, Keiko Mitsumoto, Mr. Yamaguchi and more for dinner. While speaking about Rusty, Dr. Matsumae said that his father's wishes too were to have his ashes scattered in the ocean so he could travel the world. It was a moment they both took pause and, in their hearts, they knew that once again the lifelong friends would be spiritually together.

We left Tokyo and flew to Kumamoto, where Rusty's ashes would be placed in the Kanokogi samurai grave. Approval was easily obtained from the elders. She was the first American woman to be interred in this hallowed gravesite. The stone is etched with the words, "Rusty Kanokogi, American Samurai."

2012 | I was glued to the television set as I watched Kayla Harrison fight in the Olympics in London. She won a gold medal and I cried and cried tears of joy. The first gold medal won for US judo at those Games was won by a woman—the first recipient of Rusty's fund.

Mom, I see!!!

This medal was, of course, Kayla's because she earned it, won it, trained for it. It was more than just her gold medal too—it was another of Rusty's dreams to come true.

2013 | Mr. Ogura's book about Rusty was released in Japanese only and won many awards. We returned to Japan and visited the Matsumae Judo Juku.

2016 | I was again glued to the television set as I watched Kayla Harrison fight in the Olympics in Rio de Janeiro, where she won the gold again! Thank you, Kayla, you are a champion—on and off that mat.

2018 | I kept my promise and obtained my PhD. Dad was bestowed his 9th degree black belt, at the age of eighty.

On September 18, 2018, Rusty was the first American woman to be inducted in the International Judo Federation Hall of Fame, one of the highest honors a judoka can receive.

2019 | Thanks to the efforts of Kings County Supreme Court, Civil Term Judge, Devin Cohen, on October 27, 2019, a street in Coney Island was co-named "Rena 'Rusty' Kanokogi Way" and Rusty finally got her way, literally! This street is located in Brooklyn on the corner of Surf Avenue and West 17th Street, in the heart of Rusty's old neighborhood.

2020 | Sadly, in the months leading up to the publication of Rusty's memoirs, her first son, my brother Chris, passed away and returned to his mother.

At the time that Rusty's memoirs finally went to press, in autumn of 2020, we were spending energy preparing to celebrate the 40th anniversary of the first Women's World Judo Championships around the world, releasing her book in her voice at long last, and working with the IJF, USA Judo and the US Olympic and Paralympic Museum to continue celebrating and fighting for equality for women in judo and in life.

2023 | Carrie and I retraced the exact steps my parents once walked when we visited the cave (Reigandō Cave, Kumamoto, Kyushu) where

Miyamoto Musashi wrote *The Book of Five Rings* Just as Rusty described, we navigated the narrow bamboo paths and reached the sacred cave, where we found the very rock he sat on to write. We saw the stone where the Kanokogi name was edged. That was very surreal. The atmosphere was deeply spiritual. We prayed, meditated, and Carrie felt a powerful connection to her late grandfather, a World War II hero. I'm sure there were many spirits around us and watching over us.

Later, my father, Carrie, and I visited the samurai resting place where Rusty's ashes, my grandfather's ashes, and those of our samurai ancestors are interred. A beautiful praying mantis sat atop the stone and refused to move as we approached to clean. The moment was filled with meaning. Rusty's spirit is everywhere.

2025 | Rusty's Impact Lives On

Even years after her passing, Rena "Rusty" Kanokogi's legacy continues to inspire, empower, and ignite change around the world. Her influence is seen in the growing number of women stepping boldly onto judo mats, into leadership roles, and into arenas where they once felt unwelcome. Athletes, advocates, and everyday fighters still draw strength from her story - her grit, her relentless drive, and her unapologetic voice.

Rusty's life was never just about medals, it was about breaking barriers, lifting others up, and demanding fairness when the world said "not yet." In 2025, her name is still spoken with reverence, her teachings shared with pride, and her mission carried forward by those who refuse to stay silent or sit still.

Rusty may no longer be with us in person, but her spirit fights on, in every person who dares to rise, challenge the status quo, and refuse to give up.

– Jean Kanokogi, PhD, a.k.a.
"The Daughter of Women's Judo"
July, 2025, New Jersey, USA

Jean & Rusty at Nathan's, one of their all-time favorites, in 1986.

ACKNOWLEDGMENTS

I WOULD LIKE TO THANK THE FOLLOWING people—most on behalf of my mother and myself, but the first one, just from me: Rusty Kanokogi, a.k.a. Mom, world of thank yous for everything you did in your life's path, for being our mother and the mother of women's judo. Thank you for showing me through love, guidance and grit, the road to follow, in your footsteps but on my own path.

Ryohei Kanokogi, a.k.a. Dad, you truly are a saint. Your incredible support, and devotion to our family. You are the unsung hero here because without your pure heart and support, Mommy could not have accomplished all that she did.

Ted Kanokogi, forever my little brother and the only person I know who can give me an accurate historical quote and a cartoon laugh in the same breath. It was fun growing up with you and feeding you M&M pancakes while women's judo history was taking place.

Chris Stewart, for always jogging my memory when needed, for the laughs while reminiscing about Rusty's family elders and always showing up. Rest in Peace, dear moose.

Carrie Lloyd, for totally getting it from the beginning. You saw Rusty's message and as an accomplished athlete, you knew how important it was to get her message out to all athletes and all people. Your support and love throughout this process has been invaluable and immeasurable. I am truly grateful for the incredible value you add to each day.

Billie Jean King and Ilana Kloss, for your relentless fight for equality on and off the court and your deep-rooted friendship with Rusty and our family.

The Women's Sports Foundation, for your unwavering support for Rusty and for equality.

Richard & Pamela Ader, for your lifelong friendship to Rusty and our family. Thank you for giving Rusty one of her dreams, the Rusty Kanokogi Fund for the Advancement of US Judo. Rest in Power, Richard.

The International Judo Federation, for your support and clarity in the 1970's that carries through today. Your influence continues to open doors for judoka worldwide and your current support and involvement helped when the judo world needed healing. We are "Stronger Together."

USA Judo, for growing into a beacon of change; you stepped up, took responsibility for an existing injustice, and eventually made the often-difficult changes toward inclusivity. You've grown into an organization that not just supports, but advocates for women's judo today and in the future. Evolution doesn't happen overnight, but with slow, steady, conscious change, and Rusty and I are forever grateful for your capacity to do just that.

Devin Cohen, Michael Poster, Hermes Torres and Eve Aronoff-Trivella, for always being part of the Kyushu dojo/Kanokogi family and truly giving your time, dedication and energy to support all endeavors.

Thank you to all the men and women from our dojo and judo community around the world that helped Rusty along her crusade. Your support made her stronger and fueled her determination.

Tokai University and its many great judo leaders and legends—Dr.'s Matsumae, Yamashita Sensei, Hashimoto Sensei, Keiko Mitsumoto, Mitsumoto Sensei, Yamaguchi Sensei and the rest of the Tokai family. You have become our family. Your deep connection and support of Rusty during her most crucial time will always be cherished.

The Federal Law Enforcement Officers Association (FLEOA) and FLECA Foundation. Thank you for the work that you do and for supporting my efforts to continue my mom's legacy by helping people.

My dojo mates and lifelong friends that made this story possible, you are the story and will continue to be. You are part of this legacy.

Chris Beresford-Hill and Robyn Makinson for jumping in head first and celebrating Rusty through your incredible creative talents.

My lifelong friends that had to put up with me talking about judo, my academic research and this book, all the time!

To the men and women that sacrifice so much to protect our country and keep us safe and healthy. Thank you for your continued service.

To all of Rusty's allies and advocates throughout her life—in judo and outside of it—she may not have had the chance to thank you herself, but your support was instrumental to everything she accomplished. If she were still with us, she'd be the first to say she couldn't have done it without you. From the bottom of her heart, and mind, thank you.

You have all walked with me along this path and are a huge part of my mother's and my story.

NOTES

1. **"shoot-the-chutes"** Bitzer, G. W., Camera, American Mutoscope And Biograph Company, Paper Print Collection, and Niver. Shooting the Chutes, Luna Park, Coney Island. United States: American Mutoscope & Biograph Company, 1903. Video. https://www.loc.gov/item/00563608/.

2. **"scare children into behaving"** McGuire, Peter, "Do Roma 'Gypsies' Really Abduct Children?," Huffpost, October 24, 2013, https://www.huffingtonpost.co.uk/ peter-mcguire/roma-gypsies-children_b_4152869.html.

3. **"burned down to the ground"** Maeder, Jay, "The blaze that brought down Coney Island's Luna Park," NY Daily News, August 14, 2017, https://www.nydailynews.com/ new-york/blaze-brought-coney-island-luna-park- article-1.789001.

4. **"my protector and smilin' Jack"** "The Adventures of Smilin' Jack" was an aviation comic strip created by cartoonist Zach Mosley, which first appeared in the Chicago Tribune on October 1, 1933 and ran until April 1, 1973, making it the longest- running aviation comic strip in history.

5. **"The Blow-Hole Theater"** "Steeplechase, The Blow Hole," AuthenticHistory, last modified August 29, 2011, https://youtu.be/eFaQdPZ0Inc.

6. **"Brooklyn High school for Homemaking"** "Brooklyn High School for Homemaking," Brooklyn Visual Heritage Project Chart, photo

taken on June 18, 1940," http://www.brooklynvisualheritage.org/home/brooklyn-high-school-homemaking.html.

7. **"what nice mess have you gotten us into now, ollie?"** A nod to the catchphrase, "Well, here's another nice mess you've gotten me into!" popularized by the comedy duo Laurel and Hardy in their 1930 movie *The Laurel-Hardy Murder Case*.

8. **"harai-goshi"** Ohlenkamp, Neil, "Harai-goshi: Sweeping Hip Throw," JudoInfo. com, last modified January 12, 2005, https://judoinfo.com/haraigo/.

9. **"hane-goshi"** Ohlenkamp, Neil, "Hane-goshi: Spring Hip Throw," JudoInfo.com, last modified January 12, 2005, https://judoinfo.com/hanegoshi/.

10. **"*Sports Illustrated*"** SI Staff, "Rumbling with Rusty," *Sports Illustrated*, March 24, 1986, https://vault.si.com/vault/1986/03/24/rumbling-rusty.

11. **"for decades to come"** Hogan, Jan, "Call her sensei: Martial arts a saving grace for 69-year-old," *Las Vegas Review-Journal*, August 11, 2015, https://www.reviewjournal.com/life/call-her-sensei-martial-arts-a-saving-grace-for-69-year-old/.

12. **"Franklin school"** The Franklin School merged with the Dwight School in the early 1990s.

13. **"climbing the judo ladder"** Dr. Ann Maria's daughter, Ronda Rousey, won a bronze medal in judo at the 2008 Olympic Games becoming the first American woman to win an Olympic medal in the sport, and later became one of the biggest names in mixed martial arts.

14. **"amateur sports act"** Amateur Sports Act of 1978, S. 2036, 95th Congress (1977-1978), https://www.congress.gov/bill/95th-congress/senate-bill/2036.

15. **"Us Olympic Committee"** The US Olympic Committee changed its name to include the Paralympic movement in 2019, https://olympics.nbcsports.com/2019/06/20/us-olympic-committee-name-change/.

16. **"historic apollo Theater"** "Apollo Theater History," Apollo Theater, 2020, https://www.apollotheater.org/about/history/.

17. **"new york state has a law"** New York State Human Rights Law (NYHRL), article 15 of the Executive Law (chapter 18 of the Consolidated Laws of New York), https://dhr.ny.gov/law, originally passed in 1945 as the Law Against Discrimination, and expanded with the passing of Executive Order 177 by Governor Andrew Cuomo in 2018, https:// www.governor.ny.gov/sites/governor.ny.gov/files/atoms/files/EO177.pdf.

18. **"spirit of Bushidō"** Pletcher, Kenneth, "Bushidō," *Encyclopedia Britannica*, last modified September 9, 2019, https://www.britannica.com/topic/Bushido.

19. **"Pan american Judo Union"** Name was changed to PJC in 2009: https:// en.wikipedia.org/wiki/Pan_American_Judo_Confederation.

20. **"against Usa Judo and the Usoc"** See associated documentation of the complaints made by both Jean and Rusty in Chapter 81 (pages 323-327).

21. **"cultural symbol of beauty"** Onyeakagbu, Adaobi, "Tribal marks of Nigerian people and what they mean," *Pulse NG*, September 16, 2020, https://www.pulse. ng/lifestyle/food-travel/tribal-marks-of-nigerian-people-and-what-they-mean/.

22. **"now a judge"** In the time between writing and publication, Alice has since retired.

23. **"that type of politicking here"** Eventually the Kodokan did come around and put their support behind Rusty's initiative, despite

having been very careful not to involve themselves in any controversies in the past.

24. **"jita kyoei"** "What is "Jita-Kyoei"?" Kodokan Judo Institute, accessed November 1, 2020, http://kodokanjudoinstitute.org/en/doctrine/word/jita-kyoei/.

25. **"United states olympic committee (Usoc)"** In 2019 the United States Olympic Committee formally changed its name to the United States Olympic & Paralympic Committee, but at the time of the writing of this book it was known by its former name and is referenced as such throughout its pages.

26. **"rumbling with rusty""** "SI Staff, "Rumbling with Rusty," Sports Illustrated, March 24, 1986, https://vault.si.com/vault/1986/03/24/rumbling-rusty.

27. **"Blue in the Face"** "The Brooklyn attitude as far as Rusty is concerned is to 'follow through on what you believe in'." Facebook, posted April 6, 2020, https://m.facebook.com/watch/?v=308636196768941&_rdr.

28. **"voice worse than mine"** Geoff Edgers, "Roseanne on the day she shrieked 'The Star-Spangled Banner,' grabbed her crotch and earned a rebuke from President Bush," The Washington Post, July 23, 2015, https://www.washingtonpost.com/news/arts-and- entertainment/wp/2015/07/23/roseanne-on-the-day-she-shrieked-the-star- spangled-bannergrabbed-her-crotch-and-earned-a-rebuke-from-president-bush/.

29. **"level of black belt"** Svinth, Joseph R. 2001. "The Evolution of Women's Judo," InYo: The Journal of Alternative Perspectives, http://ejmas.com/jalt/jaltart_ svinth_0201.htm.

30. **"in the Olympic Games in judo"** Since the writing of this passage, Kayla Harrison won Olympic gold for the USA in judo at the 2012 Olympics in London— the first American in history to do so. She defended her title and took home the gold again in the 2016 Olympic Games in Rio de Janeiro.

31. **"can still kick ass"** In the time between the writing and publication of this book, Rusty's brother Seymore "Charlie" Glickman passed away (on June 25, 2006).

32. ***"The Book of Five Rings"*** Evangelista, Nick Forrest, "Miyamoto Musashi," Encyclopedia Britannica, last modified June 9, 2020, https://www.britannica.com/biography/Miyamoto-Musashi-Japanese-soldier-artist.

33. **"during the next celebration"** In 2010, Ryohei and Jean left a note in this box on their next pilgrimage to Japan in 2010, so the townspeople would know a Kanokogi was there.

ABOUT RUSTY

RUSTY WAS A FIGHTER—FOR WOMEN, JUDO, and equality. Her career in the sport spanned more than fifty years, as a competitor, pioneer, national and international coach and referee, advocate, commentator and promoter.

Early in her career, Rusty defied the rules of gender by competing with—and winning against—men. Too aggressive for the "women's groups" at the Y, Rusty was considered an exception to the male-dominated judo community; her boisterous energy and passion were tolerated, until she began to win. When she was swiftly banned from the competition arena based solely on her gender, she vowed to do all she could to ensure this would never happen to a female competitor again.

In her quest for women's inclusion in the sport, Rusty founded, organized and financed the first Women's World Judo Championships, held at Madison Square Garden in New York City on November 29 and 30, 1980, putting women's judo on the map and earning the United States the international women's level competition status required to qualify for inclusion in the Olympic Games.

Rusty served as the USA Women's Judo Coach from 1974 to 1996, bringing women's judo to the 1988 Olympics in Seoul, South Korea for the very first time. Rusty, along with her husband, Ryohei Kanokogi, founded the Kyushu Judo Club in Brooklyn, New York, teaching students from all over the world, many of which went on to place in the Pan American Games, World Championships, British Open, Maccabiah Games, Pacific Rim Games and the Olympics.

Rusty served as the President of New York State Judo, from 1991 to 2009, was a member of the NY2012 Olympic Bid Committee, was a delegate to the International Olympic Committee meeting in Singapore, 2005, and served as Trustee and Vice President for twelve years with the Women's Sports Foundation. She also served as a consultant with Tokai University, in Japan, the Japanese Association of Women's Sports, and was the Vice President, Legal Lives, of the Brooklyn District Attorney's Office, and a judo commentator for NBC at the 2004 Olympics in Athens, Greece, and a media panelist for the International Judo Federation in Cairo, Egypt in 2005. In her fifty-year career, Rusty taught at least 100,000 people at colleges including the Pratt Institute, John Jay College of Criminal Justice, Brooklyn College, as well as countless elementary and high schools. All the while, Rusty continued to be an advocate for all athletes in judo and Title IX, the 1972 civil rights law for gender equality in education, campaigning and litigating for women's judo inclusion in the Olympic Games and every level of competition. She has been recognized as "the mother of women's judo" for her inarguable contribution to the sport.

In her life, Rusty rose to the rank of seventh-degree black belt—the first woman ever to do so. In 2008 she was awarded the Order of the Rising Sun, Gold Rays with Rosette from the Emperor's Order of Japan for her lifelong contribution to the promotion of judo. Her ashes are interred in the Kanokogi Samurai family grave site in Kumamoto, Japan, marked with the epitaph "American Samurai."

PHOTO CREDIT PETER PERAZIO

ABOUT JEAN

DR. JEAN KANOKOGI, PHD, IS A RETIRED SENIOR Special Agent for the U.S. Government with over 25 years of distinguished service. A 9/11 first responder and lead investigator on high-profile cases, she played a critical role in both national security and public health protection efforts. Jean holds a B.S. and M.S. in Criminal Justice and a Ph.D. in Psychology, blending tactical experience with academic rigor.

She currently serves as the volunteer Director of Mental Health and Peer Support Services for the Federal Law Enforcement Officers Association, where she spearheads initiatives to address the mental wellness crisis in law enforcement. Jean helped author and advocate for groundbreaking legislation, including mental health language in two bipartisan bills that became public law (2021/2022), as well as contributing to a Presidential Executive Order.

A respected speaker and writer, she has published extensively on law enforcement wellness, peer support, and trauma recovery. She is the co-author of the award-winning bestseller *She Wears the Badge – A Women's Guide to Empowerment*, a book to help women in law enforcement navigate their challenging careers. One of her treasured experiences includes consulting on the television program *Law and Order, Special victim's Unit*.

Dr. ean is a 6th-degree black belt in judo and former U.S. National Team member; Jean has medaled internationally and remains dedicated to empowering others. One of her treasured experiences includes consulting on the television program *Law and Order, Special victim's Unit.* Her legacy is one of resilience, service, and advocacy—from Ground Zero to Capitol Hill.

www.rustykanokogi.com
www.drjean007.com

Thank you!
ありがとうございました
¡Gracias!
Merci!
Grazie!

www.ingramcontent.com/pod-product-compliance
Lightning Source LLC
Chambersburg PA
CBHW052203090526
44583CB00015BA/1112